METAPHYSICAL ANALYSIS

METAPHYSICAL ANALYSIS

JOHN W. YOLTON

University of Toronto Press

82442

For
Professor J. Loewenberg

Preface

A NUMBER OF FALSE MOVES has infected recent philosophy. It has been said that philosophical problems are not genuine, that they have been generated by a careless attention to language. Meaning has been closely associated with use and rules for use on specific occasions; reference has been treated as one function which an utterance can have under particular conditions, but no proper part of meaning. Human action has been analyzed in terms of what we do in specific circumstances; terms like "intention," "motive," "understanding" have been discussed without being grounded in a philosophical psychology. Metaphysics has been identified with *descriptive metaphysics*, the revealing of conceptual necessities and impossibilities in our thought and talk about the world.

My concern in this book is not with attacking all of these false moves in detail, although most of them come in for their share of censure. The main burden of my argument is that philosophical talk occurs in various conceptual systems, that an analysis of any of the issues which have worried philosophers which fails to recognize the plurality of what Oakeshott has termed the "voices in the conversation of mankind"[1] can result in little more than a debilitating distortion of issue and solution. In particular, I have tried to illustrate the proper way to analyze and understand philosophical problems, by placing them in the context of their conceptual system, seeking for the rules which govern each system, discovering what can be said within the system. At the same time, I am contending that analysis of this sort requires an external perspective as well, that philosophical understanding demands both internal and external points of view. The philosopher engaged upon the analysis of any system of thought must not, as analyst,

[1]Michael Oakeshott. *The Voice of Poetry in the Conversation of Mankind.* (All books which are listed in the Bibliography, pp. 208–11, are identified in the text by author and title only.)

have allegiances to any system himself. The neutrality of the meta-philosophical perspective is threatened with philosophical sterility; intellectual progeny can only be the product of bias. But the false moves in the contemporary scene make it imperative that we assume the meta-philosophical position long enough for us to re-learn how philosophical systems are structured.

For these purposes I have concentrated attention upon two onto-logical positions which have figured in the debates of the first half of the twentieth century, phenomenalism and dualism. I have taken phenomenalism in its generic sense, as including idealism and sensory phenomenalism, Hegel and Berkeley. The new dualism in this century has been the issue of sense-datum theory. The chapters that follow attempt to get inside phenomenalism and sense-datum dualism, to deal with the detailed problems of each ontology, showing where each is closed to the other. My remarks on the particular versions of the ontologies considered here are not, however, tied down to these specific examples. What I say about phenomenalism and dualism ought to be true, in general, of any form of these ontologies. My purpose is not to revive Berkelian phenomenalism or sense-datum dualism, although in each case I have tried to state the ontology as sympathetically as possible. I am much more concerned to take these two recent examples as a text from which we can learn how to read any conceptual system. I hope to show how philosophical problems—primarily those of onto-logy—can still be discussed meaningfully. Many of the false moves in recent analysis have arisen from an inadequate theory of meaning. My conclusion attempts to defend the belief in conceptual pluralism, in a variety of philosophical languages.

ACKNOWLEDGMENTS

Some of my comments in this study first appeared as book reviews in the journals indicated: *Perception and the Physical World*, D. M. Armstrong, in *The Journal of Philosophy*, LIX, 14 (1962); *David Hume*, A. H. Basson, in *The Journal of Philosophy*, LVI, 12 (1959); *Perceiving: A Philosophical Study*, R. M. Chisholm, in *Philosophy of Science*, 25, 4 (1958).

Most of "Seeming and Being," *The Philosophical Quarterly*, 11, 43 (April 1961) is reprinted in chapter 4. Chapter 5 contains part of "Sense-Data and Cartesian Doubt," *Philosophical Studies*, XI (Jan.-

Feb. 1960) and portions of "A Defence of Sense-Data," *Mind*, 57, (Jan. 1948). "Linguistic and Epistemological Dualism," *Mind*, 62, (Jan. 1953) re-appears in chapter 5 and chapter 7. (This article was also reprinted, with changes and omissions, in my *The Philosophy of Science of A. S. Eddington*, The Hague: Martinus Nijhoff, 1960.) Chapter 6 is a reprinting of "The Ontological Status of Sense-Data in Plato's Theory of Perception," *The Review of Metaphysics*, III, 9 (1949). Chapter 8 is, after some introductory pages, my contribution to the C. D. Broad volume in the series, *The Library of Living Philosophers*, edited by P. A. Schilpp, New York: Tudor Publishing Co., 1959, "Broad's Views on the Nature and Existence of External Objects." Portions of the Conclusion are taken from "Criticism and Histrionic Understanding," *Ethics*, LXV, 3 (1955).

Professor H. D. Lewis, King's College, University of London, and Professor C. A. Campbell, University of Glasgow, read an earlier, shortened version of this study. The interest and advice of the former and the careful comments of the latter were helpful in enabling me to see some major defects of that version.

J.W.Y.

Contents

III. MEANING AND TRUTH

Introduction

THREE DIFFERENT THEORIES of reality are possible. *Phenomenalism* is the view which says that reality is mind-dependent and hence is as it appears in experience. Examples of this position are to be found in such a traditional figure as Berkeley as well as in the more contemporary attempts of the empirically minded to escape sense-datum dualism. These latter differ from Berkeley in that they try to ignore ontological concerns altogether, claiming only that they wish to show that physical-object statements can be transformed into sense-datum statements. The linguistic form of this sensory phenomenalist position is a mark of its contemporary birth. *Phenomenalist-realism,* or naïve (direct) realism, asserts that reality is independent of mind but revealed through perception. This has been the professed view from which the sense-datum men have begun their analyses. It is also supposed to be the view held by the ordinary, non-philosophical individual. Most recent discussions of phenomenalism and sense-datum theory are made from the implicit point of view of this ontology. This ontology is essentially monistic in that it claims reality is as it is known, a claim which phenomenalism accepts only by making reality dependent upon mind. It is this monism which the sense-datum philosophers have believed necessary to modify in the direction of a dualism. *Dualist-realism* accordingly claims that reality is mind-independent but can never be known directly through perception. The dualism of phenomenal-real predominates in this ontology and the problem becomes one of uniting the two worlds; hence arises the task of making physical-object statements derivative from sense-datum statements, of passing, in knowledge, from sense-data to physical objects.

To the philosopher searching for the ontological presuppositions and implications of methodological or epistemological positions, phenomenalism emerges from the empiricist tradition. Hume frequently speaks of hidden or unknown causes, of the unknown essence of objects, even of the relative idea of external existence. But he so constructs or selects his epistemological principles as to exclude all such factors from his analysis. His philosophizing occurs in a realist context, but what we can know about the world is restricted to our impressions and their correspondent ideas. It would only be conjecture to suggest which came first in Hume's thinking: the epistemological principles or the ontological rejection of Lockean substance. But what is obvious is that these two are intimately related in Hume and in every subsequent version of empiricism. Phenomenalism follows immediately from the empiricist epistemological principles and the empiricist epistemological principles emerge from the phenomenalist ontology. The elimination of substance is achieved by simply pointing out that the idea of substance lacks any sensory base. Similarly, there is no alternative to the Humean analysis of causation once we begin to philosophize with his principles. If we look for a sensory antecedent for all our ideas, many ideas will be found empty. All that Hume has shown with respect to his predecessors' belief in a necessary connection between cause and effect is that their attempts to explain nature in terms of other concepts are inconsistent with Hume's epistemological principles.

Basson objects to reading Hume as a phenomenalist because Hume's epistemic phenomenalism is set in a context of realism. This fact makes his ontology some sort of dualist-realism, except that he disclaims the possibility of dualist knowledge. Basson summarizes Hume's position as follows:

That is to say, everyone is bound to believe in a physical world, which exists independently of his awareness of it, but the truth of his belief can be neither proved nor disproved. Perceptions are the only things whose existence is accessible to the human understanding, and we cannot even imagine the existence of anything else. (*David Hume*, p. 125)

But Basson readily admits that when Hume tries to show how "perceptions are bound together in a single mind," he comes perilously close to solipsism: "Hume must either reject empiricism or accept solipsism." (p. 139, cf. p. 133) Basson's reasoning for this conclusion needs to be read carefully by all who favour empiricism as a mode of explanation or description. For any philosopher who attempts, as Hume and the sceptics do, to show that "we can know only what seems to be so and never what is really so" (p. 145), the *terminus ad quem* is solipsism, where seeming *is* being. Hume was disturbed by this implication of his philosophy; he could not resolve it by reference to his principles.

The phenomenalist cannot operate without a distinction between knowledge and that which is known, between ideas and things; but whereas the phenomenalist must find this distinction within experience, the dualist-realist claims that things—that which is known—transcend experience. Cognition must have something to cognize, but it is one thing to say that the cognitive relations involve present and future bits of experience, another to say that they involve experience and independent objects. Verification—an empiricist operation—is possible only within experience, so that if we insist upon our cognitive claims being verified we commit ourselves to a phenomenalist analysis of that which is known. The stress upon verification, even upon certainty, in point of departure has combined with the principle of parsimony to reduce the number of inferred entities and to annul all entities deemed non-empirical (non-phenomenal) by the empiricist criterion of meaning. The ontology most congenial to these demands is that of phenomenalism, although it is difficult to find in the contemporary empiricist literature any detailed analysis of this position. Most contemporary empiricists shun the ontological commitments implicit in their orientation.

In an important book, Chisholm shows an appreciation for the ontology of empiricism. A defender of direct realism himself, Chisholm formulates empiricism in the language of appearing, recognizing that few who call themselves empiricists would accept this extreme formulation.[1] For empiricism as thus considered is restricted to that which sensibly appears. Chisholm discerns several uses for "appear" words. There is the *epistemic* use, where the locution "X apears to S to be so-and-so" implies, or is accompanied by a belief, that X is as it appears (pp. 43–44). This use of appear words ascribes the appearances to some object. In the *comparative* use (p. 45), the subject is not concerned with *ascribing* but only with *describing* the appearances. To do so may involve references to objects as comparisons, as when we say "X looks red," meaning "looks the way red things look under . . . conditions" (p. 50). The locution, "X appears so-and-so" in its comparative use compares X "with things that *are* so-and-so." The *non-comparative* use of appear words (p. 51) resembles the comparative use in not ascribing anything to objects; it differs in that it cuts itself loose from all references to things: it is concerned solely with appearances as appearances. It is this latter sense of "appear" which Chisholm uses for formulating empiricism (pp. 49–50).

Chisholm observes that some may doubt whether there can be any such use of appear words. "It is sometimes supposed that every

[1]*Perceiving*, p. 69. Cf. his discussion in *Theory of Knowledge*, pp. 29–37.

predicate is essentially comparative; that when we say something is *red*, for example, our intention is to compare that thing with some standard (possibly with what we remember as being red) . . ." (p. 61). If this contention were true, "then what is expressed by 'X is similar to the standard f' would be even more adequately expressed by 'X bears to the standard f a relation which is similar to the standard (first-order) similarity'; and so on" (p. 61). The spectre of an infinite regress leads Chisholm to reject this contention. But he should be reminded of Price's analysis of recognition where recognition of characteristics precedes the recognition of things.[2] Before any appearance can be a content of awareness, we have to recognize it as a member of a class, as being similar to previous bits of experience. Chisholm sees no reason for saying we "first apply our predicates to appearances and later apply them to the things which present appearances. From the first we apply our predicates to the things" (p. 136). If he means to use "first" genetically, there is a certain amount of psychological data which speaks against him. The infant learns how to apply his predicates to the world of things, but he would seem to be aware first of a field of appearances out of which thing-predicates emerge.[3]

Even if there is a non-comparative use of appear words, Chisholm may be correct in suggesting that such a use is inadequate to support more than a solipsism of the present moment. Empiricists have always thought of themselves as avoiding solipsism, as being realists. In general, empiricists have traditionally opposed all forms of idealism; but the impetus of the empiricist tradition has led most empirical philosophers into some version of phenomenalism, or else they have, like Hume, found no satisfactory means of avoiding such an ontology. Some empiricists have been aware that "pure empiricism" demands a reduction to the presentations of the moment; but few have been willing to construct their philosophies with such meagre material. Some have gone a long way before adding, to their theories, entities (for example, physical occupants, scientific objects) not appearing in the sensory data. Others have admitted that empiricism can escape scepticism only by the addition of non-empirical principles. The dualism which results from these amendments to pure empiricism has been realist—the physical world exists independently of the observer—but that dualism has made it impossible to obtain any empirical knowledge of the realist world. We can know that world only if we place our faith in principles of isomorphism, of causal correlation, or other dicta de-

[2]*Thinking and Experience*, chapter II.
[3]*Vide* my *Thinking and Perceiving*, chapter 1.

signed to meet the problem of ontological transcendence demanded by dualism. Dualism has accordingly not always been in good repute among empiricists.

Naïve realism has been proclaimed the genuine empirical ontology: the world is independent of us but is as it appears. The only grounds for asserting this bold claim for the realist-existence of appearances are arguments from other principles not immediately derivable from the appearances; realism is invoked as a necessary means for explaining the appearances. The cognitive requirements of a distinction between ideas and things, knower and known, can be satisfied by any one of the three possible ontologies. That distinction acquires different ontological status in each of these ontologies but it is satisfied in them all. Phenomenalism and phenomenalist-realism differ very little—only in the latter's assertion of the independence of that which appears. The belief in the independent existence of the appearances may be instinctive or a natural concomitant of certain kinds of sensory experience. It is not a belief which can be justified by reference to sensory experience alone. In all instances of the defence of realism (dualist or naïve), some principles in addition to the data of experience are invoked. Realism is not implicit in the appearances but is a predication to appearance: it asserts that the appearances exist. Hume's titanic struggles to read realism from sense impressions resulted in his candid conclusion that belief in realism could not be defended: only carelessness and inattention can leave realism intact. Humean scepticism may terminate only with solipsism of the present moment. Even this stand in the rout of scepticism may crumble under a critical analysis of memory. Scepticism can be a malady without a remedy, especially if we demand a bastion of certainty impregnable to doubt. But empiricism has always been a positive attitude springing from the experiential fact of awareness. Recognition may be illusory but there is substance enough within the illusion to float the solipsist world at least. The empiricist is faced with the alternative of stultifying scepticism or with putting aside the sceptical stance in order to construct knowledge and a world out of the contents of his awareness. This construction is raised upon the epistemological quagmires of doubt. The world thus constructed is a phenomenalist one which can be given realist status only by a further act of faith. Realism can, in other words, only be established on non-empirical grounds, either by assuming that the phenomenalist world of appearance exists independently or by positing a world distinct from the phenomenal contents of awareness.

Realism thus stands in opposition to idealism and phenomenalism, as the non-empirical to the empirical. It is idealism and phenomenalism which go together to constitute the empirical ontology. There are different sorts of phenomenalism. An idealism such as Berkeley defended differs from that of Hegel in the way in which experience is organized. Berkeley strove to organize it in terms of sensible qualities only, while Hegel preferred to organize experience in non-sensible or conceptual terms. But in both cases it is experience which is the subject-matter of ontology. Both these men are opposed to the organizing structure of dualism which employs non-experiential terms, for example, a thing in itself, matter, or physical occupant. The difference between Hegel and Berkeley is not one of ontology but rather of epistemology: they seek to understand the world in different ways by means of diverse epistemic but similar ontological concepts. The Berkelian and Humean formulation of phenomenalism is closer to ordinary experience and more in harmony with the traditional empiricist concerns than is Hegel's formulation of the same ontology. But the difference between Hume and Hegel is only one of formulation or conceptualization, not one of radically opposed ontologies. Kant is the mediator between them. The formulation given to this generic empirical ontology by Hegel can be called *conceptual*, to stress the contrasts with the Humean *sensory* formulation; but it is important to see that the ontology of phenomenalism underlying Hume as well as Hegel stands in sharp contrast, in all its variants, to the ontology of dualism.

There are dilemmas and difficulties in dualism, not the least of which is the problem of the linguistic and conceptual tools required for dealing with a world lying beyond sensible experience. This particular problem is of central concern in later chapters of this study (Part II). But because of its importance for the empirical position, and because of its integral function in dualistic ontologies, it is necessary to explore the ontology of phenomenalism first, taking it in all its variants (solipsism, Berkelian idealism, families of sense-data, Kantianism, Hegelian absolutism) in order to see what we can learn about its generic properties and possibilities.

Part I
PHENOMENALISM

The intent of this part is to develop the ontology of phenomenalism as a single position, as if the form presented here were the ideal type accepted by all who have taken the phenomenalist way. What follows is a reconstruction from a number of different philosophical positions. The criticisms of phenomenalism in this part are based, it is hoped, upon a careful internal understanding of that ontology, not upon the usual quick but external grounds. It is important to appreciate just what phenomenalism can and does claim. The movement in this part is from a statement of phenomenalism in its generic form to sensory phenomenalism. Sensory phenomenalism, and the mis-interpretations of that form by contemporary writers, provides the transition to Part II.

1

Ideas and Things

PHENOMENALISM MUST BEGIN from the point of ultimate scepticism, the datum for consciousness. It would be inappropriate to begin analysis with the *cogito* alone since thinking, whatever its ontological status, cannot, even in Cartesian doubt, be separated from thoughts. Husserl's insistence on this point, in opposition to Descartes, is valid. The datum is a datum for some cognizing or experiencing organism. The minimal point of departure is the awareness of a datum. For the person performing the phenomenalist reflection, no further reduction can be made, unless it be to simplify the datum. The required reduction is not controlled by psychological principles but by logical or epistemic rules. Even so, the reduction and its final product have an element of arbitrariness about them: what we can take as the ultimate point of scepticism is not entirely fixed or closed to alternative claims. But it is sufficient to work from sensible qualities as the point of departure, including all those qualities discernible by our sensory-motor and somatic perceptions.

But the point of view of the self performing the phenomenalist reflection is inadequate for philosophical analysis, for a full exploration of phenomenalism. Two perspectives must constantly be allowed to guide the analysis: the internal one of the reflecting self and the external one of the philosophic self. Every philosophical position entails two orientations, the one under consideration and the one from which the consideration is made. Philosophical understanding, and perhaps other forms of understanding (for example, anthropological or historical), can be characterized by the double play of internal and external perspectives. But the two must be kept distinct, it must be clear from which point of view any given question or answer is offered. Internally, the point of departure for phenomenalism is that of awareness and its data; but for us, reflecting on the phenomenalist perspective, we can further reduce the minimal datum. We can push analysis to a

pre-conscious level. Our questions then become: "How does consciousness of qualities arise?" and "How do we come to discriminate ideas
from things within the phenomenalist perspective?"

The first of these external questions can be answered in the following
manner. We can talk in terms of an organism and its environment,
where conscious discrimination of features of the environment by the
organism is preceded by automatic, physiological reactions. The emergence of objects into consciousness can then be explained progressively
as the collection of qualities into unities which gradually come to
acquire objective properties. Awareness of objects and awareness of
self proceed and emerge from this learning process. The differentiation
of self from object, of *cogito* from *cogitatum* is made in terms of the
different predicates grouped under each of these headings, but those
of objects are characterized primarily in terms of the operations of the
body upon its surrounding environment. The first emergence of
qualities into awareness raises more difficulties. This initial awareness
can be interpreted as an act *sui generis* and without explicit explanation: it is prepared for in the previous physiological stage of behaviour
but is itself an emergent phenomenon. Or the initial awareness can be
explained as the result of a pre-cogito, an infra-consciousness controlled by a pure sensation.[1] Whichever of these alternatives one
follows, a doctrine of recognition and objective specification must be
elaborated after the initial awareness.

In the doctrine of recognition the second of our two external questions, "How do we come to distinguish ideas from things?" finds one
of its answers. Although recognition marks the first stage of conscious
discrimination, it has its immediate origins in unconscious stimulus-
response behaviour; the conscious discrimination is controlled by
irrational forces discerning that which has value for the organism. But
the valuational control of the pleasure-pain mechanism of the organism
takes two forms; the immediate continuum of experience can be
mapped in two different ways.[2] The secondary method consists of
associating, by contiguity, collections of sensations which fill the same
area of space and calling this collection by one name. The object takes
the Berkelian form of groups of qualities, families of sense-data, con-
cretions in existence. The primary method of mapping the continuum
of experience consists in discerning the qualitative identity of various

[1]*Vide* Albert Burloud, *De la psychologie à la philosophie.* My *Thinking and
Perceiving* also sets out the answers to these two external questions in somewhat
different terms than I here discuss them.
[2]*Vide* Santayana, *Reason in Common Sense,* chapters I–VI.

single perceptions: this particular sound now is recognized as a repetition of a previous sound. Without the primary method, no recognition of objects could arise. The collection of numerous qualities must be preceded by the collection of identical qualities under one type or kind. Essences precede existence, the universal precedes the particular, ideas are logically and temporally prior to things.

The discrimination of universals or characteristics precedes and is the foundation for the apprehension of particulars. Things differ from ideas also in their complexity, in their appropriation of many characteristics. Things, the product of secondary recognition, are tied to sensation, while ideas, the product of primary recognition, are free.[3] The recognition of an essence, a universal, even its incorporation into a linguistic form, is an isolated process in need of no further connections, while the recognition of things demands a close attention to the occurrences of sensations, their order and progression. Things do not differ in kind from ideas since both ideas and things are derived from the same source (experience) and are characterized by the same category (quality). But the similarities between their origin and their nature does not prevent a basic difference, even disparity, from arising when this distinction is viewed in its cognitive function. For, since knowledge operates with ideas as somehow representative or informative of things, an object—which is a particular—cannot be adequately rendered by ideas—which are universals. Such a rendering would always fail to catch the particularity of things. I am aware of this particular red book because I perceive it as an instance of redness, squareness, hardness, etc.; it enters my consciousness only because I am able, both physiologically and cognitively, to classify it according to its properties. But to know, to apprehend this book in terms of the universals it embodies, yields no knowledge of the particular and unique aspects of the book. Knowledge by its very nature can never be empirical, if we mean a knowledge of particular existences in their particularity. Only essences can be known; particulars are experienced. The very nature of our cognitive structures and materials precludes, as Hegel argued, our saying what we mean or meaning what we say. Essences alone can be known immediately. Our knowledge of things is always mediated by essences.

The idea-thing distinction, based on the universal-particular relation, raises the question not only of the difference but of the relations, specifically the meaning-relation, between ideas and things. Ideas and things are inseparable but distinguishable; the task for phenomenalist

[3]Price, *Thinking and Experience*, chapter II.

logic is to examine the relations between them, remembering that ontologically they are the same. The distinction is a cognitive one, necessary for thought and judgment, but because of the peculiar ontological relation between them (their ontological identity), the cognitive relations involved in judgment will differ fundamentally from those discussed by a realist logic. Ontologically, the categories pertaining to ideas belong also to things, but epistemologically there are differences of function between ideas and things. There are functional categories of things which do not pertain to ideas. The area where this kind of difference between ontological and functional categories is most evident is in the more complex cognitive processes. But even in relatively simple perceptual judgments the difference obtains. What, for example, is the situation when our phenomenalist logician asserts not only that "there is an X," but also "that X is red"? All objectivity is for him an externalization of felt experiences. The existential judgment indicates the cognizer's recognition of the idea-thing distinction, which is only a functional difference. The predicative judgment seeks to characterize and to describe the thing as opposed to the idea. Since there can be no predicative category which does not belong to ideas as well as to things, every predicative judgment is reflexive: to say "X is red" is the same as saying "I am red"; that is, it is the same when we go from the epistemic to the ontological mode of speech. Existentially, for the phenomenalist, only the self and its ideas exist, but epistemologically the existential judgment finds many discriminations not initially contained in this ontology of self and idea. If in the predicative judgment we find complexities which seem far removed from the simple reflexive, self-possessive assertion, such complexities, like the existential distinctions, arise only for cognition within the phenomenalist context. Ontologically, the phenomenalist context is simple. Epistemologically, it has complexities indigenous to the knowledge claims of the particular phenomenalist. The self which makes the judgment always expresses its point of view in the judgment.[4]

All divisions within phenomenalist logic are logical divisions, divisions within that which is not ontologically divided. All distinctions are posterior to reality; thus, the elaborate and complex ontology of Hegel's logic cannot be taken as giving ontological distinctions. His analysis of the categories of being is not itself a phenomenalist analysis: it is external to the phenomenalist position, since these categorial dis-

[4]Cf. "The Significance of Solipsism," Thomas Kremer, *Proceedings of the Aristotelian Society*, LX (1960).

tinctions are cognitive discriminations only for the external awareness. Phenomenalist logic is confronted with the task of elucidating the meaning of self thinking itself as the whole of reality. That it is the whole of reality follows from the definition of phenomenalism: only the self and its ideas and processes are real. Thus, in knowing or thinking, the self knows itself, and its self exhausts that which is real. But this knowing self functions in two ways, as the object of knowledge and as the subject which knows. Full self-knowledge would consist of the self knowing itself as subject and as object. Unless the self has some sort of independent status, it cannot be known: there must be an epistemic difference and distance. Can the phenomenalist self know itself both as subject and as object, can it know itself as it is *in* itself as well as it is *for* itself? To achieve this sort of knowledge, the self must get outside itself, but such action is impossible for the phenomenalist. Hence, the phenomenalist self must find some way of discovering what its self is *in* itself. This discovery may come about only when the self realizes that the *in itself* self is the same as the *for itself* self. Hegel's modification of Kant, in this respect, was the merging of the transcendental ego with the empirical ego; not that there were two ontological entities, but rather that one and the same self plays two roles. The phenomenalist self is real only as it is object for itself. That which is *in itself* is real only as it is also *for* self. This condition is fulfilled for the self that is known: its reality depends upon awareness. Is the reality of the cognizing self also dependent upon awareness? Both the *in itself* and the *for itself* selves appear to us, the observers of this self, as existing independently but as a unit. The self that composes this unit has to discover the fact of its unity. That discovery will never lead to independence. What it will discover is the reality of itself for itself: the self that is in itself *is* the self that is for itself. Self-knowledge is knowledge of that which *is*. From this point of view, reality—which is the totality of the self and its contents—is reflexive. Phenomenalist logic must explicate the nature of such a reflexive situation.

The ontological identity between self and reality, or between ideas and things, not only renders necessary the distinction between ontological and epistemic (functional) categories; it requires also a recognition that whatever categorial distinctions can be elicited from the phenomenalist situation are at one and the same time epistemic and ontological. But the distinction between logic and ontology—which for the realist can be a crucial and sharp division—is retained by the idea-thing distinction: this distinction can only ultimately yield further ontological categories by the use of external as well as internal perspectives. Internally, all distinctions are epistemological, while externally we can appreciate the ontological nature of these complex internal divisions. These internal divisions are necessary for the phenomenalist self, since it is by these epistemic distinctions that that self is able to cognize its ideas and to form and discriminate things from ideas. The reflexive relations of the *in itself* and the *for itself* self are relations within experience.

But how is it that one bit of experience or one idea can mean another? The environment becomes meaningful to the organism (in a psychological and not just a neurophysiological way) when the normal patterns of response are disturbed by a problem, a tension, a shock which is relevant to the pleasure-pain mechanism of the organism. The exact operation of the transition from physiological to psychological states is obscure, but experience becomes meaningful to the extent that the environment (the group of stimuli) assumes an intelligible pattern for the cognizing organism. The process of objectification is a process of refinement upon this initial point of psychological orientation by the organism, so that the distinction between subject and object, between ideas and things, moves from the first ambiguous and vague situation to the sharply delineated stages of science. For the dualistic self, this objectification process goes so far as to spill over the phenomenalist boundaries of self and object by splitting the object in two. Then the problem of meaning runs into new and special difficulties: how can an idea mean more than idea, more even than what is given or can be given to experience? But for the phenomenalist self, the meaning question is restricted to the interrelations between ideas or between experiences. Since awareness itself is generically awareness of characteristics, the epistemic relation between ideas cannot escape the universal-particular relation. Not only is awareness a classification in terms of types; cognition and meaning involve the reference of universals to other given, not yet given, or already given experiences. Meaning and that which is meant must always be distinguishable. Cognitively, that which is known must transcend that by means of which it is known.

But there are two kinds of transcendence: the phenomenalist sort in which things transcend ideas because of the universal-particular relation or because things are always more than can be given at any one moment (a temporal transcendence), and the dualist sort of transcendence in which objects can never be experienced in any but their sensible aspects. That our ideas and concepts can have this second sort of transcendence is evidenced by the dualist ontologies which play upon this appearance-reality distinction. But a transcendence of this kind must be excluded from the phenomenalist perspective. The idea-thing distinction can involve no more than a temporal duality. The doctrine of substitution replaces the dualistic doctrine of representation. Instead of knowledge referring to an existentially independent object lying outside experience, as it does for the dualist, knowledge consists in the relation of substitution between concept and percept, between intention and fulfillment of intention: a substitution of one aspect of experience for another, either virtual or actual. Experience is its own object, or rather, experience becomes shattered into subject and object, idea and thing. Viewed abstractly and externally, the world of the phenomenalist is constituted by experience, but experience has two modes: an intention and a fulfillment of intention. Fulfillment is not marked by the apprehension of an object external to the experience in which the intention or original meaning was generated. It is the relation between two acts of the same experience. Besides the temporal relation between intention and fulfillment, which functions to hold experience together, to organize and unite it within the experience of the self, the intention-fulfillment relation involves comparison and a recognition of essences, universals, or meanings as exemplified in the fulfillment. All cognitive experience is meaningful, significant, or intelligible. Awareness and intelligibility are co-terminous functions which must operate conjunctively. But from the initial stages of conscious life, when the environment first becomes meaningful, to the later stages of sophisticated awareness and language using, there is a difference in the structure of intelligibility, of meaning. The awareness of a simple sense quality is controlled by recognition processes which may not be wholly on the conscious level. The explicit and deliberate comparison between one sense-awareness and another brings these unconscious processes to consciousness. Both the single act and the relational act are structured around the universal-particular relation; but the processes of awareness become more complex in passing from the one to the other. The structure of the self grows as its world grows. It is precisely this double growth of perceptive techniques and objectification which threatens to disrupt the phenomenalism of the simpler and earlier levels of awareness. The mode of intention is not constituted in exactly the same fashion as the mode of fulfillment nor does it function similarly. Concepts differ from perceptions, thinking from perceiving, the apprehension and intention of meaning from the fulfillment of meaning. Perception and intuition, the cognitive tools for apprehending the relation between intention and fulfillment, tend to appear as processes capable of breaking out of the phenomenalist sphere by confronting the object directly.

In part, such is what the phenomenalist wants to say. For him there is a legitimate difference between perceiving and thinking, a difference expressed by saying that thinking operates in terms of universals while perception confronts the particular. The dualist claim that the object can never be fully experienced finds its phenomenalist counterpart in the universal-particular, thinking-perceiving distinction. But how can this distinction be drawn without violating the essential phenomenalist dictum: ideas and things are distinctions within experience? It will not do to say that one is outer perception, the other inner, the task being to reduce outer to inner; for the inner-outer distinction merely reformulates the idea-thing, concept-perception distinction. The difference can only be drawn and formulated by reference to the self. Viewed externally, the distinctions of subject and object, of ideas and things, of appearance and reality which appear for the dualist as categorial differences, can arise within phenomenalism only in terms of different cognitive processes; different modes of awareness structure differing kinds of reality or objectivity. The idea-things of the phenomenalist world do manifest essential differences of function and cognitive use. Many of the realist distinctions between scientific, metaphysical, and artistic reality can be preserved by reference to the processes of knowledge of the cognizing self, although it would be wrong to test phenomenalism by determining how much of realism or dualism can be retained in its formulations. Phenomenalism is not just another variant formulation for the same distinctions drawn by the realist or dualist. If we treat ontologies as differing languages, we must recognize the autonomy of each language game. Comparisons from one to another are inevitable, however, since each language must be explored from the outside as well as from the inside. But one of the dangers of the external analysis of phenomenalism is the difficulty of casting aside one's own basic reality-distinctions and definitions. (Chapter 4 discusses a number of such external readings of phenomenalism.)

For the phenomenalist, seeming *is* being, but there are different values assigned to different modes of seeming. A careful phenomenological description of all the modes of experience is required. Even here, some good phenomenalists have tended to take one mode as paradigmatic and fundamental; Kant and Husserl tried to introduce necessity as the basic feature of all valid modes of experience, for example, Kant's analysis of the perception of a boat moving down stream or, in general, any veridical perception. Perceptions of the boat sort are irreversible in their order. There are other experiences which are also not under our control. Recognition of this fact should be no embarrassment for the phenomenalist. Cognition for him is generically the same throughout its diverse functions and occasions. Different functions circumscribe a diversity of objects. Kant was inclined to define "object" in terms of the boat example. All object-perception was explained by reference to *a priori* and necessary structures of the self. Objectivity is a function of necessary structural laws of awareness. Whatever distinctions can be drawn between different sorts of contents of awareness must be made in terms of features of the self. The contingent-necessary distinction invoked by Kant and Husserl may be misleading, may only partially characterize phenomenalist objects; but it is to the self and its cognitive structures that the phenomenalist must turn in order to explicate the different kinds of objects which comprise his world.

2

Experience and the Self

IMPLICIT IN THE IDEA-THING distinction is the subject-object contrast. The phenomenalist dictum for the ontological status of objects decrees that objects exist only for an awareness, for a subject. The minimal datum for phenomenalist reflection is the datum for consciousness. To be fully and consistently phenomenalist, one must find a similar relational definition for the subject. But how can the subject of the cognitive process be defined in terms of reference to awareness, since it is the subject which is the awareness? Would it not have to be defined in terms of itself? But if it is defined reflexively, we seem to have a reality *en-soi* in a world where all that is real should be *pour-soi*; nothing can be defined in terms of itself but only with reference to something else in this world. Berkeley did not push his idealism this far but retained an essential dualism within his ontology, a dualism between self and ideas. For him, there are two fundamentally different kinds of reality. The reality of mind is *percipere*, that of ideas *percipi*. The self is not on a par with its objects, since it is the self which generates and preserves the reality of things. Berkeley's analysis can be extended so as to bring one aspect of the self within the phenomenalist definition; we can distinguish between the self as cognizer, as creator of its world of objects, and the self as object of itself. This latter aspect clearly assumes a phenomenalist character since self as object of my reflections exists for and only in so far as it is object of awareness. The self accordingly is split in two. The pervasive self, the self behind awareness of self, the self which is awareness, escapes the phenomenalist definition, and the dualist separation between subject and object reappears within phenomenalism. Kant's distinction between noumenal and phenomenal self completes the subjective dualism while violating the essential phenomenalist rule.

Hegel attempted to objectify the self while avoiding division of it. Self-awareness takes two forms: *a*, awareness of the process of awareness, of the fact that I am cognizing, and b, awareness of the content of awareness. What the realist knows as "nature" is, for the phenomenalist, awareness in sense b; but both forms of awareness confront ideas, mental contents. The Hegelian logic seeks a level of awareness at which the phenomenalist self can assume the role of external observer of itself, knowing itself as both awareness a and b, without in reality being external. To assume this role, awareness a must be divided into awareness$_1$ and awareness$_2$. The absolute perspective is awareness$_1$, the level of objective reflexion where the *in-itself* and *for-itself* selves, *en-soi* and *pour-soi*, are seen as one. But it is not at all clear how the phenomenalist self can achieve this level of awareness without looking at itself from an external point of view. The phenomenalist self which is permitted to assume the critical philosophical perspective—thereby stepping outside its phenomenalism—can view its former position in this light. But Hegel himself showed vividly that every attempt to know ourselves involves a temporal and epistemic distance, the systematic elusiveness of *I*. I can only know myself as I was a moment ago by taking the position of awareness$_1$. It was Hegel's claim that the self is not, however, involved in an infinite regress where awareness$_1$ is replaced by another state of awareness and that by another without end. It is not certain that Hegel meant to say that the absolute perspective takes place within the same knowing self. The more likely interpretation is that awareness$_1$ *is* an external awareness, related to the other forms of awareness but absorbing awareness$_2$ and awareness b into a wider—perhaps a divine—point of view.

Such a move into divinity may render the phenomenalist self real in the phenomenalist way, but we are not yet ready for this sort of exploration. On the level of the single self, there seems no way in which that self can be given a phenomenalist reality. It will not do to seek a way of escape from this problem by pleading that the original category, the basic ground for all other categories, is a consciousness transcendent of the empirical or awareness self only in a methodological way. If the transcendental consciousness is taken as the ultimate presupposition for a phenomenalist ontology, it cannot, as a presupposition or methodological tool, serve as the foundation for phenomenalist reality. To achieve this function, it must have an ontological status in the system. The primordial ego of Husserl's *Cartesian Meditations* (#5) stands a better chance of providing the egological ground for later awareness. But if its status is that of the most fundamental aspect of reality, the generator of all subsequent objects, then the dualism of self and object remains, unless some sense can be given to saying that *"not all my own modes of consciousness are modes of my self-consciousness"*.[1] The Kleinian theory of a phantasy life lived by the infant prior to self-consciousness and consciousness in the ordinary sense, and out of which the conscious world is constructed by projection,[2] would be a psychoanalytic parallel to the phenomenological notion that the world of the self arises out of the primordial ego-awareness. The self, in both cases, would be defined in terms of psychic activity. (Cf. the notion of the pre-scientific world in Husserl's *Erfahrung und Urteil.*) But while I think that something like the Kleinian theory is probably a correct account of the emergence of awareness, I do not see how either Husserl or Klein can save the phenomenalist self from assuming a special, non-phenomenalist status. For even the content of awareness at the primordial level differs from the subsequent object-content of later levels of awareness. Moreover, just because consciousness at this early level is not *self*-consciousness, the self has a reality independent of awareness. The self, whether empirical or transcendental, whether psychological or phenomenological, does not have the same kind of reality as the objects of the self. The phenomenalism of reality has excluded the self from its field of operations.

However, it might be said that, according to Husserl's or Klein's approach, the primordial ego is not really a self, that the self proper emerges, along with the object, out of subsequent awareness-processes. Awareness is preceded by physiological and behavioural reactions and adjustments to the stimuli of the environment. These reactions and adjustments prepare the organism for the later psychological stages of cognition. The self as well as the object emerges from this situation. Even when awareness first arises, distinctions between self and object are not drawn by the experiencing subject. Genetic psychologists have shown that both subject and object are products of learning, that in the early stages of awareness these two modes of experience are intermixed and only vaguely differentiated. Awareness of self as well as awareness of objects emerges from the context of experience. Experience becomes the basic and neutral factor out of which cognitive discriminations arise. Since the phenomenalist world constitutes a merging of cognition with reality, reality for the phenomenalist, whether

[1]*Cartesian Meditations*, p. 105.

[2]M. Klein, *The Psycho-Analysis of Children.* The essays in *Developments in Psycho-Analysis*, ed. by Joan Riviere, and *New Directions in Psycho-Analysis*, ed. by Klein, Heimann, and Money-Kyrle are also illuminating on this subject. Money-Kyrle's *Man's Picture of his World* applies the Kleinian concepts to epistemology and ontology in a very suggestive way.

subjective or objective, must be cognitive. As we learn about our world we learn about ourselves. For the self, reflecting, reality must always be coterminous with awareness. There can be no self, as there can be no object, whose reality antedates awareness. For the self the world begins with awareness. Subject and object, awareness and content are reciprocal and interrelated functions. Where distinctions can be made between functions it makes little difference which we settle upon as subject or object. That which is regarded as subject is its own object; each object is defined in terms of itself; all predicates are self-predicates. From the other point of view, the object is its own subject; the subject is defined in its terms; all self-predicates are object-predicates.

For both Kant and Hume, self and object are collections of perceptions. Kant, of course, retained the notion of the self behind appearance, the necessary synthetic unity for both self- and object-awareness. But the self as object to itself was ontologically on a par with the objects which comprise that orderly series called "nature." Kant did not work out the characteristics of the self which is known in experience. Whether he would say that the series of representations which make up the self as object is ordered by laws of a different sort from the series of laws of nature, is somewhat difficult to determine, although his concern with the realms of freedom and necessity suggest that the self as object conforms to the same laws as other sorts of objects. Space, of course, would be absent from the self series. There might be some categories involving space which would also not apply. But there would seem to be no insoluble difficulty for phenomenalism in working out the differences within the total content of awareness between those features which are self-ascribable and those which are object-ascribable. In the order of awareness, self- and object-awareness are correlative, interdependent processes. In the order of reality, there is one common sort of material. But just as different sorts of objects would be distinguished by the order and structure of the percepts which comprise them, so a series called "the phenomenal self" could be distinguished from all other objects by certain internal properties of that series.

Some critics of Hume have argued that the phenomenalist's ontology of the self founders on the question of identity.[3] Hume himself consigned personal identity to the function of imagination. No "real" connections can ever be observed between the members of the collections of perceptions called "objects" or "selves." Identity in both cases "is nothing really belonging to these different perceptions and

[3] D. M. Armstrong, *Perception and the Physical World*, pp. 70–79.

uniting them together, but is merely a quality which we attribute to them, because of the union of their ideas in the imagination when we reflect upon them."[4] The role of the imagination in identity-ascription appears to escape Hume's own characterization of what the self can be discovered to be; for what the self is and is thought to be is discovered by imagination. A unity of apperception, immanent rather than transcendental, is what Hume's imagination is. Hume's world is not populated only by perceptions in the sense of impressions and ideas; it also has faculties, processes of awareness, recognition, recollection, etc. We would ordinarily say that we can also be aware of these processes, even of the process of awareness, although we may agree with Ryle that this latter may involve a temporal lag. The imagination, or awareness in general, is not a super-sensible substance, though it may play a similar role: that of unifying the contents. The phenomenalist has taken awareness along with its contents as one of the givens of his analysis. Awareness is inseparable from the contents of awareness. But we have seen that the systematic elusiveness of awareness leaves one level of awareness free from the phenomenalist criterion of reality. However, the inseparability of awareness from its contents gives the phenomenalist a basis for asserting phenomenal identity of self. The "I think" does accompany every act of awareness. The self may not be a datum of consciousness for the Cartesian reflection, but the first-person perspective *is* given. It would inadequately express the truth of the cogito to say it shows that thinking is going on, for what is revealed in this reflection is a reflexive, self-referential awareness, not just "awareness." To speak of "my" awareness tends to lead us to substance, as Descartes' own predispositions immediately did. But the only legitimate analysis of the "my" for the phenomenalist is some sort of "ownness" which is immanent in the process which yields the "I think."

I do not think that the phenomenalist can give an analysis of the self-referential awareness which escapes solipsism. Husserl tried to do so but failed. Hume seems committed either to giving up empiricism or to accepting solipsism. The world for the phenomenalist is, as Husserl insisted, "for me absolutely nothing else but the world existing for and accepted by me" in my consciousness. (*Cartesian Meditations*, p. 21) But a solipsist awareness of self has been said to be impossible.

There would be no question of ascribing one's own states of consciousness, or experiences, to anything, unless one also ascribed, or were ready and

---

[4]Hume, *Treatise*, Everyman edition, (1939) p. 246.

able to ascribe, states of consciousness, or experiences, to other individual entities of the same logical type as that thing to which one ascribes one's own states of consciousness.[5]

Other-ascription is a necessary condition for self-ascription, and other-ascription, for Strawson, must be to an entity of the same type as the self. If "the things one ascribes states of consciousness to, in ascribing them to others, are thought of as a set of Cartesian egos to which only private experiences can . . . be ascribed," then, Strawson insists, we cannot make ascriptions to other such selves since we have no access to such unobservables. (p. 100) What Minkus calls the "dizzy extrapolation" of intellectual substance,[6] of pure consciousness, can play no role in self-ascription: only the phenomenal self is available for ascription. For Strawson, person identification is dependent upon the body. Even though the bases on which I ascribe predicates to myself may be different from those on which I ascribe predicates to others, any given self-predicate must have "both first- and third-person ascriptive uses," it must be "both self-ascribable otherwise than on the basis of observation of the behaviour of the subject of them, and other-ascribable on the basis of behaviour criteria." (p. 108) It would not be sufficient for self-ascription, if, as is the case in the phenomenalist's world, there is only *one* collection which can be a "self." The contrast with other objects is inadequate for self-awareness.

Strawson's claim that self-ascription requires "other-self-ascription" is rather dubious. The psychological work of people like Piaget seems to indicate that the otherness of objects is sufficient for the infant's acquisition of an awareness of himself. It may be that, if the Kleinian suggestion of a phantasy life prior to awareness is correct, other selves —at least *one* other self, for example, the mother—may after all prepare the infant's attitudes towards himself and his world. But Strawson's claim does not arise from any psychological material: it arises from a theory of language which rules out any unique ascriptions. The logic of "my self" is interconnected with that of "your self." The primitive concept for Strawson is that of a *person*, an acting organism. *An action* is not some pure mental process: it is a bodily movement for which I can give reasons, not just causes. The Kantian realms of causation and of freedom reappear in recent analyses of action, but devoid of any transcendental self. I think it highly questionable, however, whether these recent analyses (for example, by Anscombe, Strawson, Melden, Minkus) have come to grips with the full commitments of their notion

[5]Strawson, *Individuals*, p. 104.
[6]P. A. Minkus, *Philosophy of the Person*, p. 10.

of a person. They are still fighting off the twin enemies of mentalism and behaviourism, but the distinction between movement and action leads to some sort of mentalist psychology.[7] If other bodies are only instrumental for me in my other-self-ascription, I must be ascribing predicates of a different order and nature from object, that is, body predicates. I do not find that the concept of person is clarified; nor does Strawson explain what is the meaning of first-person predicates. If the meaning of first-person predicates is derivative from third-person predicates, behaviourism is the only possible result. If we learn the meaning of self-predicates first in our own case and then acribe them to others on the basis of bodily movement, first-person meaning seems primitive; at least, since my world is comprised only of object aware-ness and *my* self awareness—only, at best, of *other* self awareness, via objects—the only way in which Strawson has made self-predicates dependent upon other-self-predication is through the assumption that object movements of a certain sort are, in every instance, part of what we mean by a person. The notion of other objects mediates the notion of other selves.

If I am correct in my analysis of Strawson, phenomenalist awareness of and ascription to self depends only on other objects. But the pheno-menalizing of self and object is possible only within a non-phenomenal context. For what is the ontological status of experience, of the pri-mordial ego, which precedes awareness, which lays the foundations for the reality of self and its objects? Experience on this level, the entire pre-reflective context of organism and environment, seems to lie outside the phenomenalist situation, or to be included within phenomenalism only as the object for another awareness. Inter-subjectivity then becomes a prerequisite for a fully phenomenalist definition of self and object. The reality of the phenomenalist world is always more than can be grasped by a single self. The externality required is itself the content of awareness for some other cognizing self, and this transcendence is repeated and taken up in successive perspectives. But so far in our philosophical reflection, we have neither admitted inter-subjectivity nor justified the successive enlargement of the sphere of phenomenal reality. For the single self, for the solipsistic self, no escape seems possible from the duality of its total situation. The phenomenalism of its world is thus generated by a non-pheno-menalist world. Only if the realist existence of the objective world could be established, could the pre-reflective situation of organism and

[7]For a defence of this claim, see my, "Act and Circumstance," *Journal of Philosophy*, LIX, 13 (1962), pp. 337–50.

environment be validated as a source of knowledge; but if the realist objectivity of the world is established, phenomenalism is denied.

The solipsist self is unaware of this dilemma which arises only for the philosophic self seeking to delimit the character of a phenomenalist ontology. For this latter self, it is the ontological dictum which is basic. The questions raised by the philosophic self are not empirical questions; he does not seek for observational confirmation of the conclusions reached nor does he proceed, as Husserl claimed, by an unbiased observation of the processes under investigation. The rules of the game, as for all games, precede the analysis and control the performance. In this way, every ontological venture must be external: we proceed by first asking what the rules are. The difference between the psychopath who actually and fearfully lives an isolated existence and the philosophical solipsist lies precisely here: the latter has a reflective attitude. A philosophical ontology cannot be lived in the sense that the psychopath lives his experience. Philosophers have, however, claimed truth for their visions and have lived them as if they were as real as the psychopath's world. Thus, we must recognize the distinction between the philosophic and the meta-philosophic perspectives: there is a difference between the one who develops and defends a philosophical position and the one who examines that position critically. Before we can know whether our particular ontological attitude is consistent, self-adequate, or legitimate we have to be on the outside, at least in reflection, have to tender other positions. The possibility of raising questions of legitimacy or consistency requires the external point of view. It is, in part, just the demands of consistency, which play such an important role in philosophical theories and explanations, which mark some of the distinction between philosophy and science. Philosophical ontology cannot proceed in the fashion of science, by observing and noting the results of observation. A careful observational technique, utilizing all the familiar guides and safeguards of recent science, eventuates in empirical truth. A technique which is circumscribed in its application or limited in its results by prior commitments, as is philosophy, cannot lead to a true account of the world. (This point about the truth of philosophical systems is developed at more length in Part III.) But it is precisely because philosophy is concerned more with intelligibility than with truth (certainly not with empirical truth), that the rules of the game must be carefully respected.

Our reflections upon phenomenalism and the structure of the phenomenalist self must not be allowed to be distorted by the criteria of science. We must not insist upon being scientifically empirical. Rather, the task is more analogous to Kant's requirement: what are the structures necessary for explaining experience as it is? But we do not begin with experience and then seek to explain it; we begin with the explanation and strive to characterize the experience which conforms to it. We are not essentially concerned with the nature and experience of the world; the concern is with the implications of an explicit attitude towards our experience and the world. It is the analysis of the idea-thing relation which leads us to look to the nature of the self for an explication of the cognitive distinctions permissible within the phenomenalist situation. In thus turning to the self, we do not function as psychologists but as philosophers intent upon exploring the structure of phenomenalism. Specifically, we want to know what are the legitimate grounds within the self, within awareness, for distinctions between the objects of awareness. The self thus referred to cannot be the Berkelian mind or spirit, nor the Husserlian primordial ego, nor the Kleinian phantasy-forming self, since these have a non-phenomenalist structure: it can only be the phenomenalist self taken as the product of the same experience which produces the things as objects of awareness. The analysis occurs within the single self. We want to know what grounds solipsism can provide for epistemological distinctions.

Formulated in this way, it is clear that processes of retention, recollecting, and comparison are vital to the structure of the objective character of the phenomenalist world. Just as the continuity of consciousness unifies and initially organizes this world, so the specific and particular functions of the self serve to introduce distinctions of kind within this world. An object retained in memory differs from an object of immediate sensation. The objects of comparison differ from the objects of single sensations, although both agree in being universals; the former is a relation between properties while the latter is a property thus related. If we allow our individual self to have a mental structure and content similar to any ordinary adult, both the contents and the diversity of those contents immediately expand. Distinctions between religious objects, sub-atomic objects, emotional objects, artistic, mythological, and historical objects emerge. (The theory of objects implicit here is elaborated in Part III.) These divisions seem to appear (the phenomenologists insist on this) under an unbiased scrutiny intent only upon describing. But the claim of impartiality is always suspect. An effort at descriptive classification can be made to yield large areas of agreement between investigators armed with the same reflective or psychological tools, arising from the same historical and cultural world. That different responses result from the stimuli of diverse objects, is a simple observational remark. Moreover, the epistemological discriminations of the philosopher are frequently refinements upon the gross discriminations implicit in everyday behaviour. Furthermore, it seems likely that the unphilosophical self turned from action to reflection would draw some of the distinctions between kinds of contents that the epistemologist draws. But just as soon as reflection and introspection intervene in the development of the conscious organism, categories of thought, patterns of division, begin to insinuate themselves into consciousness, not as the simple products of experience but as the reflective attempts of the self to render its world intelligible. The language of organism and environment, of experience and action, is still applicable to some extent to the sophisticated areas of adult social and historical life. But the similarity between perceiving and thinking, even the overlap of these two processes, cannot be allowed to obscure the uniquely different role in conscious life played by the processes of action and reflection. Awareness itself arises only as experience becomes meaningful and intelligible; but reflexive awareness, with its conscious and deliberate attempts to organize experience in intelligible ways, adds new ingredients not possible on the early levels of awareness. The categories in terms of which experience is interpreted by the reflecting self may very well be themselves a product of the cultural context of that self, although there is no inherent impossibility in supposing that a genuinely isolated self could devise its own private set of interpretative principles.

The practical impossibilities of self-awareness arising in a context which is devoid of other selves are great. The only organisms known to reach the level of self-awareness do so in a social setting, where the speech and gesture of other self-conscious organisms aid its own development. Other selves appear to be an important aspect of that pre-verbal and preconscious environment of the phenomenalist self. But the realist basis of all self-awareness should not lead to the excesses of those who deny or overlook the role in awareness and language of the individual, private, experience. The individual, of course, has to learn to express his experiences in the public language of his society. From the point of view of communication, it does not really matter what the subject takes as the referent in his experience of the terms he uses. But if the terms he uses lack any reference to his own experience, that person is deprived of one important dimension of meaning for those terms. Pre-verbal experiences may even extend further than we think, if we accept the psychoanalytic account; but at some point the infant makes the transition from pre-verbal to

verbal experience. To call this transition one of "translation" is probably misleading. To capture at all the internal character of the pre-
verbal experience strains our credulity, especially in the instance of
psychoanalysis. But to be concerned to analyze the use of terms in
our language without giving any heed to the experiential reference
is to succumb to linguistic behaviourism, no matter how loud the
protestations against this charge from those who talk of meaning and
use. The recovery of pre-verbal experiences is always, I suspect, an
interpretation. There is no clear-cut evidence, free from guidance by
theory, in the various psychoanalytic recoveries. All talk about experience is talk; some is more interpretative, more theoretical than others.

The categories used in interpreting experience are always arbitrary,
never absolute or necessary, and never exclusive. They are always
functions of some reflective attitude, but no reflective attitude is closed
against change or opposition. Within the range of the phenomenalist
ontological dictum, the categorial divisions must always manifest the
correlation required by this ontology between object and awareness.
Moreover, the dictum also specifies that where there are differences
of objects there must be differences in the mode of awareness. Within
these limits, the phenomenalist can draw epistemological distinctions
quite freely. The operative controls then are transferred to intuition,
logical structure, or to language strata, and the debates as to the
legitimacy of such epistemic differences can arise independently of the
phenomenalist perspective. Where categories arise involving, from a
dualist perspective, the transcendence of experience, they must either be
reinterpreted as distinctions within the intention-fulfillment continuum
or they must be dismissed as illegitimate within phenomenalism,
as the empiricist criterion of meaning dismissed traditional metaphysics. The ontological dictum and the empiricist theory of meaning
work hand in hand, circumscribing the valid kinds of categories
admissible for the phenomenalist position. The empiricist theory of
meaning has undergone certain alterations, passing from a strictly
sensory to an intellectual base, from sense-data to theoretical constructs. These alterations are a recognition of the different role played
in cognition by the senses and the intellect, by perceiving and thinking.
The cognitive reactions of the organism to its environment may never
be purely sensory; cognition at every stage of development may involve
conceptual tools. But if we take the purely sensory responses as a
limit in cognition, we can characterize subsequent cognitive development as conceptual, meaning to catch the indirect awareness of the
world by this complex knowing self. There then arises for philosophical analysis a rather sharp break between physical (sensory) and

conceptual (symbolic) worlds. The phenomenalist is not the purely sensory creature, since he is already operating on the complex conceptual levels of cognition. This is the case for the phenomenalist who is also aware of his phenomenalism, for the self external to the phenomenalist self. It is even the case for the phenomenalist self itself, since many of its ideas, and hence many of its objects, are conceptual as well as sensory. But the aim of the phenomenalist self is to formulate its world as nearly as possible in sensory terms, in terms of percepts rather than concepts. Where conceptual elements enter to designate the relational and universal features of its experience, these elements must be carefully handled. So long as the conceptual component is rendered as an intervening variable rather than as a construct, the rules for phenomenalism have been observed. It is the language of construction which threatens to violate phenomenalism by leading to a realist conception, where constructs exist independently from awareness. In other words, it is precisely at the point where the intellectual elements in cognition take leave of the sensory that dualism appears. The transcendent meanings, the condensed inductions contained in certain words for the dualist, are products not of sensing but of thinking. The phenomenalist operates with the same tools of intelligibility as the dualist, but his task is to use the intellect in closer harmony with sensation than does the dualist. Where the phenomenalist finds it necessary to escape the sensory limitation, he can do so only by using the crutches of variables which intervene between one sensory content and the other. The crutches must be discarded as soon as possible and in no case must they be reified.

The rule against reification applies to both awareness and content, to self and object. Self can never be conceived of as a hidden substance, or thinking as a ghostly process. The self, like the object, is the conscious product of experience. The contents of self-awareness are intimately associated with the contents of objects; in fact, the two contents differ only functionally or epistemically, never ontologically. Once recognized, the difference in function between those sets of qualities referred to as self and those as objects leads to increased stress upon the differences. Essentially, the self for the phenomenalist is the centre of action and the focus of intention. The act of intending, of apprehension and fulfillment, leads to the reflexive-immediate distinction. Awareness develops from the early, primitive levels of response where self and object are not discriminated, to the more sophisticated epistemological discriminations of the adult self, only by the increase of the difference between immediate and reflexive attitudes. Where fully discriminate, the subject-object distinction implies the reflexive attitude, the awareness turned upon itself. There are two levels to the self: the early non-phenomenalist level of the indiscriminate monism of subject and object and the later level of full self-consciousness. Awareness and self-awareness are ingredient in the self and comprise one field of depth. From experience—which is not always, or at first, conscious—arises awareness. From awareness comes self-awareness and its twin products of self and object. Genetic, child, and psychoanalytic psychologists can help in the empirical effort to uncover the first levels of the awareness self but the self-awareness self can only be known and understood by each self which reflects upon itself, although both a knowledge of the world of objects and the early awareness self uncovered by psychology add to self-awareness understanding. Introspection sometimes leads to the dissolution of self either through religious or psychotic emphasis, but philosophical analysis of the self need not go to such extremes. What the philosophical analysis should reveal are the differences in the categories for understanding the awareness and self-awareness self. We should not invoke non-phenomenalist categories in our efforts at understanding and intelligibility. The question of the ontological status of subject or object is not an empirical question. It can be answered only when we have prescribed the rules for our answer. The stress within phenomenalism upon unity, continuity, and monism should not blind us to the validity and necessity for making distinctions within the self as sharp as those within the object. But every distinction must be a function of awareness, must be a distinction employed by cognition.

Here the rule for cognitive distinction does not enable the solipsist self to include within its domain the cognitive/non-cognitive, the experience-awareness distinctions; but because these distinctions are products only of the external point of view, we must not conclude that they are non-phenomenalist. We have discovered that there is no way in which the self can be defined phenomenalistically without violating phenomenalism directly (as Berkeley and Kant did), by making self and object two different categories, or obliquely, by reference to an experience which underlies both self and object, or, finally, by assuming (as does Hegel) that a totalistic point of view is possible within the self. One possible escape still remains but, as it turns out, it fails to meet the problem of incorporating into the phenomenalist requirements the background elements which we have discerned from our external vantage ground. We must look at this last alternative and understand why it fails.

3

The Realist Foundations
of Phenomenalism

THE PHENOMENALIST SELF reveals a twofold nature: the awareness self, which constitutes the basic and temporally prior ingredients, and the self-awareness self, which emerges from the process of objectification. Phenomenalist reality begins only with the emergence of awareness, with the awareness-self; but that reality is mature only when awareness has discriminated self from object, idea from thing. The specification of the object waits upon the embodiment of a fully self-conscious awareness. What is temporally prior—the awareness-self—must wait upon the self-awareness self before we find a phenomenalistically defined self. What presents itself to self-awareness is precisely what Hume described: a collection of ideas and processes. Only by allowing ideas to define and exhaustively characterize both subject and object can the ontology of phenomenalism be self-consistent, according to its own rules. Consistency, however, necessitates a compression of the realist time series into a dialectical flow of interconnected aspects of contemporary events. An even more radical alteration of realist dicta must be honoured before the phenomenalist can eradicate the awareness self and the still earlier non-cognitive experiences which originally generate the total phenomenalist world. Neither the awareness self nor the experiences underlying it seem amenable to phenomenalist inclusion.

These recalcitrant elements remain outside the phenomenalist orbit precisely because they are not contents of awareness for the phenomenalist self. It is only we who are examining the phenomenalist ontology who have discovered the non-phenomenalist structure at the bottom of this theory of reality. Though experience prior to awareness, as well as the early phantasy awareness, lies outside the cognitive world of the particular self (except that these may perhaps be recovered in analysis), I have raised the possibility of incorporating these elements into a phenomenalist ontology by expanding the sphere of influence of the phenomenalist self. Could the experiences of the solipsistic self become ingredient in another awareness, we could still preserve the essential *pour-soi* character of phenomenalism while moving outside the narrow confines of solipsism. The particular self must lend itself to colonization by becoming a content for some other awareness, bringing with it the non-phenomenalist elements of its world. What is required by this process of colonization is not a transcendence of solipsism by publicity, by intersubjectivity; inter-subjectivity can, in fact, arise for the phenomenalist only by means of monadism, by a plurality of particular selves, and this can be achieved only externally. Immanent to the phenomenalist self, there can be no publicity: the self and its contents exhaust the real. To talk in terms of a sympathetic transference of certain sense-impressions from myself to other selves aids the argument for other minds only after we have assumed the realist perspective and are seeking some rational justification for our beliefs. The externalization of qualities to constitute other minds no more transcends phenomenalism than does the differentiation of ideas from things. The delusion of retaining the realist talk of other minds by making them contents of the phenomenalist awareness is no more than a *tour de force* which fails because the concept of "other" becomes lost when absorbed into the contents of awareness of the particular, phenomenalist self. A publicity of selves cannot mysteriously be created from the tight phenomenalism of the particular self, simply because there is no principle internal to phenomenalism which could legitimize either public objects or public selves.

In the Fifth of his *Cartesian Meditations,* Husserl tried to show how phenomenological reduction does not lead to solipsism. Such an attempt seems, on the face of it, foredoomed; for Husserl has pro-claimed repeatedly throughout the *Meditations* that "The Objective world, the world that exists for me . . . this world, with all its Objects . . . derives its whole sense and its existential status . . . from me myself, from me as *transcendental* ego. . . ." (p. 26) The experience of otherness might arise for the transcendental ego as one among many contents of experience. All the contents of the self are analyzed as they appear. Thus, if we take the world of the adult self, certain objects do appear as other selves, I may experience intersubjectivity. But if "other subject" is a term whose meaning is constituted by me, a term—like all others—which must be qualified by the phrase "for me," either solipsism has not been avoided or it has been redefined. The main difference between the phenomenalist and the realist is that the seeming-being distinction has been eliminated by the phenomenalist; everything that *is* is a function of the constitutive activities of the self. Moreover, there are a number of passages in which Husserl defines his task as that of explaining what "intentionalities, syntheses, motivations" give sense to the phrase "other ego." (p. 90) In one of the final sections he reminds us that his theory "of experiencing some- one else . . . did not aim at being and was not at liberty to be anything but explication of the sense 'others'. . . ." (p. 148, #62)

Still, there is that obscure reduction within the reduction, the reduction to "*die Eigenheitssphäre*" (#44) which seems designed to yield more than a constitution of the *concept* of otherness. This reduc- tion follows the standard pattern: if you want to prove the reality of something—of an objective word, of other minds—you bracket the question of reality and examine the phenomena to see if there are criteria internal to the phenomena which will testify to their reality. But no amount of juggling, no amount of talk of "*immanente Tranz- sendenz*" (#48), can produce out of the "*Eigenheits*" reduction anything other than objects constituted by the self. The fact that in this case it is the primordial and not the transcendental ego that discovers the sense of "other" does not save phenomenology from solipsism. Van Peursen and de Waelhens are correct in stressing the ontology of meaning which characterizes phenomenology.[1] In giving meaning to myself—even in the sense of recognizing myself as myself— I transform myself from a mere thing into an acting agent, into an agent who gives meaning to being. Meaning becomes being; man is its revealer because he constitutes, makes, the intelligible world. The case of otherness is no different. Husserl's canvas may be larger, he may be able to take in more objects and events into his world, the solipsism may be a Leibnitzian monadism of plural selves: it is solipsism nevertheless.

Thus the kind of expansion required to render phenomenalism consistent by incorporating the primordial ego and its experiences in a larger perspective cannot be the realist plurality of selves. Even for the realist, the private experiences of each self are closed against each other. Intersubjective observation can only be behaviouristic. What is required for the expansion of phenomenalism beyond the idea of the single self is a perspective which can absorb the internal life of the solipsist as well as those background elements not included in the solipsist's definition of his own reality. We need, in other words,

[1]Vide their essays in Van Peursen, ed., *Rencontre, Encounter, Begegnung*.

a different type of awareness from the particular self. The philosophic perspective which we have been assuming in our examination points the way to a possible resolution of our problem, since we are discussing and analyzing just those features of the world of the phenomenalist self which *it* is incapable of raising to cognition. But succumbing to the temptation of allowing our critical perspective to play the phenomenalist game not only sins against the very essentials of the metaphilosophic point of view—that it remain impartial to the calls of divergent ontologies—it also renders impotent the critical assessment of any ontology. Even though we may discover that each ontology is closed against the other—in that we cannot move from one to the other without invoking external principles—it is clear that not only the evaluation but the critical formation of an ontology demands the externality of the philosophic perspective. To know whether any given claim is legitimate within an ontology we must know the rules for operating in that perspective. To have the idea of rules already takes us out of the primitive ontological attitude into that of criticism. Self-criticism, no less than other forms of criticism, demands an external point of view.

The critical perspective is requisite to our attempts to expand phenomenalism beyond solipsism, yet the requisite perspective for this expansion must be immanent and internal, though tested by the vantage point of externality. The perspective which will successfully enlarge solipsism while still adhering to the phenomenalist criterion of reality must, then, be seen as a natural extension of solipsism. The pre-reflective experience of the particular self must not only be contemplated, as we have been doing; it must also be lived and known. What for the particular self is by its very nature unknown must become idea for this larger perspective. To achieve such a transformation of perspective, the solipsist self must become divine.

There are two closely related ways in which the solipsist self can become divine: the way of Hegel's Absolute and the way of Spinoza's substance. If I, as particular self, view the works of nature and history, these are clearly not my products. But if I consider myself as *essentially* self, as mind or spirit rather than as *this* mind or self (*vide* Husserl's eidetic reductions), I can view history as a clear manifestation of the works of self. Nature can be included by strict adherence to the phenomenalist dictum. On this level, I as universal mind seek to understand the works of mind. Here, the general phenomenalist dictum—all reality is a function of self or knowledge—receives a different rendering. Solipsism is surpassed only in the sense that I now

encompass all the given world of nature and history without questioning its particular genesis. Phenomenologically, the world can be viewed
in this way without raising ontological questions, but of course an
ontology is presupposed in the process. Now those objects which
appear at first sight to be *en-soi*, different from me, are still phenomenalist objects. But phenomenalism of the individual self has been
replaced by the totalistic phenomenalism of a self viewing the whole
compass of particular objects. Divine intelligence (mind as universal,
as essential) considers the plural solipsistic worlds of individual minds
and claims them as its own. The individual minds are now viewed as
the contents of the divine mind. What each solipsist is from his own
perspective—master and possessor of a world—God is from his total
point of view. God is not separate from the world of finite selves: he is
the mind which holds these latter in reality.

If we give a more Spinozistic rendering to the divine point of view,
God must be taken as the totality of that which is: God and nature
are the same. On either interpretation, the divine differs from the
solipsist just as universal differs from particular. Whatever are the
attributes of the totality, the solipsist self knows only a few: just those
which it finds as common properties of its own world of ideas. If the
totality is viewed as a collection, we have nothing more than monadism,
an aggregate of isolated selves. In order to surpass monadism so as
to attempt a unification and phenomenalization of the particular, we
must universalize the collection after the fashion of Spinoza. Then,
the particularity of the totality will be the contents of the solipsist
selves, those collections of ideas which have acquired the status of
things for the phenomenalist self. The finite selves are contingent,
they come and go, and their contents stand in spatial, temporal, and
causal relations. These contingent, finite series of mental states are not,
for the Spinozistic conception, caused by the totality, but the universal
and particular must stand in some relation in order for the totality to
be more than a collection. The divine is *causa sui* because it exhausts
reality. It is not generated, has no beginning. But the universal
contains the particular and because it does, and because this contain-
ment is taken by Spinoza as logical entailment and deduction, the
universal is said to cause the particular. The causal series of the ideas
which are the contents of the finite self have God as cause insofar as
this causal series is part of the totality of the world. Causation as
applied to the divine means "no cause"; as applied to the relation
between divine and particular, it means logical entailment and deduction. To relate universal with particular requires, then, a relating of

logical order with empirical order. The logical order constitutes the *a priori* categories of the totality of which the empirical order is a member.[2]

In the divine, taken either in Hegel's or Spinoza's sense, the distinction between pre-reflective and cognitive experience disappears because nothing precedes the self of divinity. Although the passage from the particular to the divine succeeds in incorporating the non-phenomenalist pre-reflective experience into the phenomenalist ontology, has it not at the same time annulled the service performed by that experience on the level of the particular? It was only in virtue of the non-cognitive realist context of experience that self could be given a phenomenalist definition. In bringing this context to the level of idea, we seem led back to the dilemma of Berkeley and Kant: the self now appears not only omniscient but *causa sui*. Only because it is generated can the self be phenomenalist. The eternality of the divine self encompasses too much. The price of divinity is realism of self. The various ruses Hegel employed to cover up this self-realism—the distinction between particular and universal, the doctrine of absolute knowledge—fail precisely because they apply to particular consciousness as well. The identity of reality and knowledge holds as much for the particular as for the divine. The divine self is solipsism in a new guise. But for neither particular nor divine can we produce a phenomenalist definition of self without appeal to a realist context; the particular self *emerges* from a background of objects and other selves, the divine *has* a realist status because it is uncaused.

If these arguments and conclusions are valid, not only does externality appear in our analysis as a necessary ingredient in philosophical understanding: externality becomes a necessary foundation for the generation of the phenomenalist ontology. Internally, phenomenalism cannot progress to the publicity of objects or of selves, being enclosed within the walls of its own ideas. From the point of view of phenomenalist awareness, reality is exhausted by its own contents and the relations between them. But just as soon as we examine this perspective, we discover that not only is phenomenalist awareness a product of a realist situation but, in order to give a consistent definition of the self, realism becomes essential; no fully consistent definition of the self can be given within the terms of the phenomenalist ontology. Phenomenalism and realism as ontologies seem thus to be inextricably bound together, but only when we push phenomenalism to its fullest expression. For the particular self, solipsism yields all the necessary

[2]For a more extended discussion of these matters, see below, pp. 187–89.

cognitive distinctions internally, without extraneous appeal. Only when we, from our external vantage point, seek to render phenomenalism fully consistent, do we discover the inescapable reliance upon realism.

The interdependence of phenomenalism and realism operates the other way also: realist theories of reality have found it necessary to work with the immediate contents of awareness as media for contact with the realist world. The direct realist seeks to show that the immediacy of ideas reveals or is identical with the independency of things. The indirect realist fully admits the separation between ideas and things, even sanctioning a disparity between the two, and discredits the cognitive claims of ideas to yield accurate or full knowledge of things. Both the direct and the indirect realist use the phenomenalist distinction between ideas and things, but unlike either the direct realist or the phenomenalist the indirect realist finds it necessary to substitute representationalism, in some form or other, for immediacy. The indirect realist world is ontologically dualistic, incorporating the ideas of the phenomenalist not as conveyors of meaning of other ideas but as representatives of that which is not idea. Things for the dualist are not collections of ideas, even though for some (for example, the sense-datum philosophers) ideas do constitute part of the ontological character of things. It is the concept of things as transcendent of and different from ideas which marks the distinctive trait of the dualist-realist ontology. It is just this concept which renders such an ontology dependent upon the phenomenalist context of ideas. This relation between ideas and things renders the cognitive relation for the dualist rather tenuous. Whereas the major difficulty for the phenomenalist has turned out to be the consistency of his ontology, the *bête noire* of the dualist is the cognitive relation between ideas and things. He must show not only the possibility of ideas referring to things, but explicitly how this is done. Only then can we see whether the formulation and conceptualization of dualism is any more successful or consistent than phenomenalism.

4

Some Recent Misreadings
of Phenomenalism

A MAJOR CLAIM of these metaphysical analyses is that an understanding of any particular ontology requires both an internal and an external perspective. The need to view any ontology from within is obvious. To assume the external point of view is hazardous since externality usually involves a different point of view, with commitments of its own. I argue in some detail, in the conclusion of this book, the case for and the nature of a neutral external vantage ground. I have already been assuming this neutral stance in my reconstruction of phenomenalism. I have been careful to note where problems arise from the external view only, not internally to phenomenalism. In the final analysis, I am even prepared to admit that no perspective is entirely neutral, not even the meta-philosophical attitude of this book. But the biases—if they are that—of the neutral meta-philosophical perspective are of a radically different sort from the commitments of any particular philosophical position. I try to indicate this difference in the conclusion. What cannot be done, what leads to profitless analysis, is the attempt to explicate one philosophical position in the terms of another. Explication *does* involve translation from explicandum to explicans, but translation is possible only where there exist locutions in the explicans which do not violate their correlates in the explicandum. Most recent accounts of phenomenalism (and of dualism) have violated this basic translation rule, have used one set of ontological rules and one criterion of meaningfulness in the attempt to explicate phenomenalism. There is present here what might be called a *fallacy of translatability*. This fallacy is rather characteristic of the contemporary treatment of traditional philosophy.

The line of argument I have in mind takes the form of asking whether phenomenalism is an adequate translation of physical-object statements; or it seeks to show the inadequacy of such a translation: "every form of phenomenalism involves the thesis that anything we know about material things may be expressed in statements referring solely to appearances." (Chisholm, p. 189) A more general thesis about the translatability of one perceptual theory into another was vigorously defended by Ayer in his *Foundations of Empirical Knowledge*. Phenomenalism, naïve realism, and the sense-datum theories were claimed by Ayer to be equally valid theories, each one a variant of the common language of perception. I have argued the case against Ayer with respect to sense-datum theories in an earlier discussion.[1] The structure of my argument there took the form of saying that once we accept certain basic meanings for our physical-object words, phenomenalism is no longer possible. The fixing of these meanings within sense-datum theory leads to a dualist commitment. What I want to show in this chapter is that the phenomenalist fixes the meanings of certain key words in such a way that the translation of his language into any other idiom—especially into a realist idiom—is rendered impossible. Just as it is wrong to look at the sense-datum theory from the point of view of a language equivalent (or nearly so) to phenomenalism, so it is incorrect to think of phenomenalism as a linguistic (or ontological) variant upon dualism or naïve realism.

The function of contemporary forms of phenomenalism has been, in part (as Berlin has remarked[2]), to call attention to certain objectionable features of the new dualism which has arisen from the sense-datum theory. The sense-datum theories began by assuming naïve realism as true, but they ended with a dualism of sense-data and physical object. Not only do we have the dualism of sensible and non-sensible; we find efforts to justify an inference from families of sense-data, sensa, and percepts to physical occupants, scientific objects, and physical objects. The alternatives now seem to be either dualism or phenomenalism. But just as Reid and his common-sense realism sought to drive a wedge between such a radical alternative as Locke or Berkeley offered, so the recent move has been to invoke once more the realism of common sense. Mr. Quinton's recent discussion is designed to refute the premise from which both phenomenalism and sense-datum dualism derive, that is, "that we are never directly aware of or acquainted with objects."[3] Berlin invokes Dr. Johnson and common sense as advocates of the belief in objects having non-dispositional

[1] "A Defence of Sense-Data," *Mind*, LVII, pp. 2–15. Cf. also below, pp. 56–61.
[2] "Empirical Propositions and Hypothetical Statements," *Mind*, LIX, pp. 289–322.
[3] "The Problem of Perception," *Mind*, LXIV (1955), p. 29.

properties which can be and are sensed.[4] Austin wanted to know "what sort of thing does actually happen when ordinary people are asked 'How do you know?'," and he contrasted the philosopher's mistaken view of the world with "the world we live in."[5] Berlin rests his case against phenomenalism on the observation that "no direct translation from categoricals into hypotheticals is, as a general rule, and as our language is today ordinarily used, a correct analysis of, or substitute for them."[6] Warnock castigates all special philosophical vocabularies by appeal to the tried and tested language of everyday use.

It is, of course, always possible that any system of language may contain more or less latent contradictions and obscurities; but I think it could safely be said that a language in constant daily use is far less likely to be thus unsatisfactory than a technical vocabulary, devised rather *ad hoc*, which has never in fact been tested and shaped and modified by actual use.[7]

Armstrong writes an entire book[8] designed to defend direct realism against Berkelian phenomenalism.

Armstrong takes as the pivotal question of ontology, "What is the *direct* or *immediate* object of awareness when we perceive?" (p. xi) For Armstrong, this is not a scientific question "to be answered by observation and experiment, but is a conceptual question to be answered by the means appropriate to the discussion of a conceptual question, viz. philosophical argument." (p. xii) Conceptual analysis claims to be neutral with respect to what ontology will emerge from the analysis. Its method is that of revealing the commitments about the world contained in "the actual structure of our thought about the world."[9] The conceptual analyst starts with some system of thought, takes a few key concepts in that system, and then analyzes what those concepts mean, even what they *must* mean: he reveals the conceptual necessities of our thought. Like Kant, the conceptual analyst pretends that there is one system of thought (or language, in some generic sense), that this system is controlled by or has implicit in it certain formal, indispensable elements which determine the way we think about the world. It is claimed that the historical fact that the explications of most of the concepts in philosophy—"physical object," "self," "perception," "space," "time"—have given rise to so much controversy,

---

[4]*Op cit.*, pp. 295, 297–98.
[5]"Other Minds," in Flew, ed., *Logic and Language*, Second Series, p. 124.
[6]*Op. cit.*, p. 300.
[7]*Berkeley*, p. 239.
[8]*Perception and the Physical World.*
[9]Strawson, *Individuals*, p. 9.

to so many different answers, shows that someone is wrong, that most philosophers have not learned how to explicate the structure of their thought about the world.

This programme of "descriptive metaphysics" has grasped the contextual nature of philosophical concepts; it is provincial in claiming only *one* context for our thought about the world. The central concepts of philosophy have been embedded in different conceptual systems. In explicating his key concepts, each philosopher is trying to reveal the essential structure of *his* thought about how the world is, not the structure of some single system of thought shared by all. I would suppose that the philosopher, like all of us, is bound in some respects by the thought and language of his society, his period, his predecessors. But like the artist and the scientific theorist, the philosopher can break out of traditional moulds, can use the old concepts and terms of language to advance a new view of the world. Berkeley's concern over his term "idea" is a good example of a philosopher who wants to formulate an ontology different from the prevailing one but for whom the existing language is not wholly adequate.

The provincialism of talking in terms of one language, one conceptual system, and hence one ontology fosters the fallacy of translatability: it requires that the claims of any philosopher must be translated into this idiom or else be judged defective, even meaningless. The talk of descriptive metaphysics is a relatively recent version of this provincialism. Earlier, we heard talk of analyzing "the immensely complex vocabulary of perception in ordinary language."[10] Austin's programme was never to vindicate some one particular meaning to a word or concept. His forte lay in revealing the complexities and the varied meanings of our words. But his method in each case, for example, "know," "real," "object," was to explore the different uses of such terms in ordinary language. The word "real," for example, is "an absolutely *normal* word, with nothing new-fangled or technical or highly specialized about it. It is, that is to say, already firmly established in, and very frequently used in, the ordinary language we all use every day. Thus *in this sense* it is a word which has a fixed meaning, and so can't, any more than can any other word which is firmly established, be fooled around with *ad lib*."[11] The philosopher who tries to assign different meanings from those found in ordinary language is pronounced "wrong."[12] In the case of the ontological word "real,"

[10]Warnock, *Berkeley*, p. 246–47.
[11]*Sense and Sensibilia*, p. 62.
[12]*Ibid.*, p. 63.

"there are no criteria to be laid down *in general* for distinguishing the real from the not real. How this is to be done must depend on *what* it is with respect to which the problem arises in particular cases."[13] The question "Is it real?" should be replaced by some more specific one, "Is it denatured?" or, "Is it an allotropic form?".[14] Austin's ploy is always to move away from the general level to the particular and specific, to pin down the meaning of the word to some occasion of its use. But—and this is a strikingly important fact about the method of Warnock and Austin—the *philosophical* use of some term in the context of a particular ontology is never given a careful analysis in its own context! The philosopher is denied any technical area of problems or solutions. If he is asking intelligible questions, those questions, it is assumed, will not suffer from being translated into the context of the normal, day-to-day use of language.

Armstrong is concerned to defend naïve realism as the ontology implicit in our conceptual system. Strawson's *Individuals* produces a similar ontology. Warnock and Austin shy away from any particular ontology; the linguistic, not the ontological mode is their preference. Austin explicitly says he is not "going to maintain that we ought to be 'realists,' to embrace, that is, the doctrine that we *do* perceive material things (or objects)."[15] But Austin's reasons here stem from the multiple functions of "perceive": "There is no *one* kind of thing that we 'perceive' but many *different* kinds."[16] When the question is formulated in the language of phenomenalists and realists, however, the realist answer always seems to emerge from Austin's analysis. That is, phenomenalism is judged wrong. There are differences between Warnock's and Austin's approach to phenomenalism—Austin even makes several valid criticisms of Warnock's treatment—but that neither writer finds phenomenalism possible, lends support to the suspicion that behind their methods of analysis lies an ontological bent. We can witness the pull of realism most readily in Warnock's attempt to explicate Berkeley, for it is in just those places where Berkeley's phenomenalism fails to measure up to the naïve-realist demands that Warnock judges it defective.

Warnock's argument in favour of his own form of realism has both a negative and a positive side. Negatively, the argument insists upon the impossibility of dualism; more particularly, upon the impossibility

[13]*Ibid.*, p. 76.
[14]"Other Minds," p. 139.
[15]*Sense and Sensibilia*, p. 3.
[16]*Ibid.*, p. 4.

of formulating or saying dualism. Positively, the argument takes the form of drawing a distinction between statements of seeming and statements of being. It is in this linguistic distinction between these two different sorts of statement that what I am calling Warnock's realism controls his analysis. If we are going to argue that perceptual statements can take two forms, a form which states what seems or appears to an observer and a form which asserts what is the case, we have incorporated into our analysis of the complex vocabulary of perception in ordinary language the same distinction which, in a former day, was made by phenomenalists and realists.[17]

Warnock's realism is revealed in several passages in his negative critique of Locke. For example, in contrasting Locke and Berkeley on general terms, he says that Locke tried to find an entity named by general terms whereas Berkeley found the generality of words in their use. (p. 72) Like most recent philosophers, Warnock argues for a separation of meaning and reference. Locke's mistake was his failure to see that the meaning of most words lies in their use; he sought a reference for all words. Warnock paraphrases what can be called Berkeley's empiricist principle as follows, revealing himself very sympathetic towards it.

For our words can only be given sense by reference to things that human beings do and can experience; it is a delusion to suppose that we could speak intelligibly of 'objects,' if these were something quite other than the ideas that we do actually have. (p. 176)

More simply, words "can have reference only to what we do actually experience." (p. 82, cf., p. 85) To deny this principle is to leave the door open for the multiplication of entities, for the concept of substance employed by Locke. Warnock claims Locke's doctrine of substance to be the result of his mistaken views about language: "he interprets as a baffling fact about the world what is really a quite straightforward fact about language." (p. 107) Faith in the empiricist theory of language prevents Warnock from entertaining the possibility that Locke's analysis of general terms was motivated not by any theory of language but by his dualist convictions: the belief that the world is different from its appearance, that it has a nature or essence which does not correspond with our classifications. Because of his firm belief in the reality of substance Locke believed the perception of qualities to be an incomplete knowledge of reality: substance and real essence

[17]This is the same distinction which Kremer has recently made between solipsism and realism or between the relative and absolute theories of knowledge and language. (*Vide op. cit.*)

were necessary for the full understanding of nature. Warnock assumes a naïveté on the part of Locke which is unwarranted, which is, in fact, a function of Warnock's own mode of analysis. Because of the difficulties of saying what substance is, Warnock is led to conclude that dualism is impossible or at least unsayable. (p. 97) It *is* unsayable with Warnock's view of language.

Warnock also objects to dualism because it seems to him to deny us access to reality. But in explicating this objection, Warnock states the position of dualism in a distorted way. Locke, he says, makes it impossible for us to say for certain that we see any particular object. For example, can we say "there is an orange on the table"? Warnock tells us that Locke's answer is "no," because the real orange is not perceivable. But:

Oranges are not tasteless, intangible, invisible; it is often perfectly certain that we see an orange; it cannot be that in saying 'I see an orange' I am making a mere untestable guess at the presence of something I do not see and never could see. Such an account is worse than false; it is simply nonsense. (p. 178)

There are many problems embedded in Locke's doctrine of substance, many difficulties confronting the dualist, but neither Locke nor any other dualist has said what Warnock says that Locke said. Warnock treats Locke's argument about the unknowability of substance as applying to the phenomenal level, to the realm of nominal essence. Whatever the real-nominal distinction may be construed as saying, it most assuredly does not commit us to the position of not being able to say that there are oranges on the table or gold in my pocket. The oranges we eat, the gold we handle, are the collection of qualities we assume them to be. Lockean dualism does not postulate a reduplication of our phenomenal world in a noumenal realm, nor does any other dualism. His theory of substance and essence is offered as a way of understanding the world. What he denied to religion—that it contains mysteries—is affirmed of nature: it is not entirely amenable to a rational formulation, there is an aspect of reality which cannot be known by man. The language we use, the ideas we have, are limited, as Berkeley and Warnock say, to our experience; but the dualist tries to devise some way of using some of these ideas and words to refer to nature as unexperienceable, as it is in itself. Since Warnock's empiricist principle tells him that such an extension of language is impossible, when Locke talks about the real essence of objects being unknowable, Warnock construes him as meaning that we cannot say for certain that any group of qualities is an orange, gold, etc. But the words "orange" and "gold" refer to the same qualities in Locke's experience as in Warnock's. To be able to say "there is an orange on the table," all that is required is a knowledge of the meaning of our words and a check against illusion. Locke's dualism alters not one bit our ordinary discourse or our normal perceptual judgments. Dualism may be unsayable: it cannot be brushed aside by such a misreading of its claims as Warnock gives.

The burden of Philonous' refutation of Hylas' dualist concept of matter is that Hylas cannot speak intelligibly of matter, cannot characterize its nature, can only speak of it as the cause of his sense experience. For the dualist, matter cannot have any sensible properties because every sensible property is an object of immediate perception and matter is not immediately perceived. As Armstrong remarks: "For, if our immediate acquaintance is with sense-impressions alone, the onus will lie on anybody who says physical objects are quite distinct from sense-impressions, to explain what is meant by ascribing predicates like 'red' or 'round' to physical objects. There seems to be no way of discharging this onus which would allow of any intelligible description of physical objects as they are in their own nature." (*op. cit.*, p. 32) Armstrong says dualism is refuted because everybody knows that "we have a great deal of positive knowledge of the nature of physical objects." (p. 33) But just as in his polemic against phenomenalism so, in discussing dualism, Armstrong forgets that the dualist conceives of physical objects in a way different from the direct realist or the phenomenalist. Whatever knowledge the dualist may have of physical objects can only arise if he employs some *ad hoc* principles—of isomorphism, inference, and translation—such that he can take the data of his sense experience as informing him of some aspects of the unobservable part of physical objects.

Neither Warnock nor Armstrong discusses the various principles which dualists, for example, Russell or Broad, have constructed as a way of moving from sense-data to physical object. The dictates of his empiricist principle lead Warnock into arguing that Locke either was asserting something which could not be asserted or was saying something false and absurd. Locke was translated into Warnock's idiom and thereby shown to be wrong. Dualism *is* a hard ontology. It is threatened with—if not overcome by—a conceptual and linguistic failure. But there are important and fruitful moves which can be made before we conclude that dualism will not do. The conceptual and linguistic analysts, being commited to realism, cannot tolerate the notion of dualist matter, can find no place in their theory of meaning

for dualist reference. Phenomenalism, being closer to their own preference, should have received a more sympathetic analysis; but both
Armstrong and Warnock show themselves incapable of understanding
the phenomenalist's notion of "object."

In trying to explicate the meaning of Berkeley's definition of ideas
as the "immediate objects of sense," Warnock insists that the language
of seeming is an equivalent though more cumberous language. One of
his paradigm examples is "It seems to me as if I were hearing a sort
of purring noise." (p. 168) The language of seeming eliminates,
Warnock believes, any inferential factor from what we report and
thereby leaves us with that which is immediately perceived. The
problem is the one, familiar in contemporary theories of perception,
of finding a given which is indubitable, a datum without concealed,
condensed inductions. The language of sense-data—of round, red
patches—will not do, Warnock argues, for if I say "I see an oval, red
patch of colour . . . the observations of other people might establish
that there is actually nothing to be seen." (p. 174) Warnock is disturbed by Berkeley's seeming identification of ideas with sensations.
In part, his disturbance arises because of the solipsism imminent in
such an identification.

By saying that I perceive only ideas, and then regarding these ideas as
my own sensations, I seem to confine myself in a wholly private world—
a world, furthermore, in which there are no things but only *feelings*. (p. 150).

Warnock's way of avoiding solipsism within the Berkelian framework
(where "things" in the naïve-realist and dualist senses are banished)
seems to be to turn sensible qualities into things in a realist sense. He
distinguishes between the noise as it *seems to be* and the noise *as it is*
in fact. "The noise that I call 'purring' is in fact, as everyone else hears
only too well, deafeningly loud. . . . Of course, the noise sounds *to me*
mild and purring, but it actually is exceedingly loud." (p. 167)

In a similar way, Armstrong pronounces Berkeley "simply wrong"
when he fails to distinguish between "a thing's actual heat, and the
heat it feels to us to have on a particular occasion." (pp. 4–5) For
Armstrong, it "always makes sense to say that the object is not really
grey, but only seems grey to me," or "the water is not hot" when it
feels to me to be hot. (p. 6) Berkeley, of course, was arguing that it
never makes sense to draw these distinctions between seeming and
being. Berkeley's analysis of seeming may not be precise enough nor
exhaustive enough; there is some ambiguity over the term "immediate."
But any genuine attempt to understand his ontology from within could

not fail to see that there is no mistake, as Armstrong charges, when Berkeley insists that it is false to say "we hear a coach" when what we hear is a certain sound. Armstrong and Warnock talk as if the only possible meaning for "object" is the realist one, where appearance can differ from reality. Even the if-then formulation employed by Berkeley is misunderstood by Armstrong, under the control of his realist notion of object. When the phenomenalist suggests that there is a locution in his language which plays the role in that language which statements about unperceived objects play in the language of the realist, Armstrong tests the phenomenalist's if-then locution in terms of realist meaning. "For when nobody is perceiving a particular physical object, nobody is having sense-impressions of that object. It seems then that the phenomenalist must say that it is logically impossible for objects to exist unperceived, that the notion of unperceived physical existence makes no sense. Yet surely the notion does make sense." (p. 53) The sense which the notion of unperceived physical objects makes is realist, not phenomenalist. When the realist says "a certain unobserved object exists" he wants to say "that it *actually* exists." (p. 54) The phenomenalist is arguing that such a notion is meaningless, a manifest contradiction.

The phenomenalist seeks to elaborate an ontology where reality is defined in terms of mental contents, sense-data, or (in the language of Berkeley and Locke) ideas. There is an important sense in which the phenomenalist does turn sensible qualities into things, since what the realist refers to as a physical object is for the phenomenalist a collection or family of qualities. Moreover, the problem of introducing publicity into his world may be an insuperable one for the phenomenalist, as I have argued in the previous chapters. Solipsism may well be the strongest form of phenomenalism. The sensible experiences of the phenomenalist self just do define the scope and nature of his world. There is a realist element about such a phenomenalist world since the sensible experiences are grouped, ordered, and classified: families of such experiences are hypostatized and given independent status. But the independence is always from other sense experiences, such as pain and pleasure, and not from the self or mind. Warnock misses the point of this phenomenalist hypostatization and treats the qualities of sensible experience as existentially distinct from the sensations of the self. Berkeley's careful denial of the legitimacy of a distinction between sensation and its object is eliminated. In the *Three Dialogues*, Hylas tries to make just this distinction. It is not the dualist distinction of a substance over and above the sensible qualities, but just the distinction between a noise as it seems to me and the noise as it actually is. "The sensation I take to be an act of the mind perceiving; besides which, there is something perceived; and this I call the *object*. For example, there is red and yellow on the tulip." Berkeley (Philonous) is prepared to admit the tulip as a public object, so long as it is defined in terms of sensible qualities. He wants to deny the possibility of this collection existing independently of all minds. Thus, there is some ground for Warnock's split between what seems and what is within the phenomenalist world of sensible qualities; the split, however, is misleading if interpreted (as I think Warnock tends to do) as giving qualities a realist status.

The externality and hence distorting character of Warnock's language of seeming, as an explication of Berkeley, is much more evident when he deals with the appearance-reality distinction. Berkeley has taken care to indicate the ways in which he distinguishes between certain kinds of sensible experience and others, between what the realist calls dreams, illusions, or hallucinations and veridical perceptions. Berkeley offers various criteria for this distinction, chiefly, independence from our will, and the order and consistency of experience, an order and consistency in terms of past experience and expectations. Such distinctions are perfectly legitimate. The phenomenalist must be pictured as offering a kind of phenomenology of his experience, as sorting and classifying various parts of it in different ways. We must be cautious, however, in not forcing the phenomenalist's account of the world into the realist mould by asking for a phenomenalist translation of every feature in the realist account. The ontological rules for phenomenalism differ fundamentally from those of the realist. To be real for the phenomenalist means to be the content of some mind. To be real for the realist means to exist independently of awareness. The properties of objects in the realist world may find a formulation in the language of mental contents or sense qualities, but the realist independence of objects cannot be translated into phenomenalism. Warnock's use of the language of seeming distorts phenomenalism by looking at it only from the outside, from his own implicit, naïve-realist position. For example, he argues that the statement, "It seems to me and to God and to absolutely everyone as if there were an orange on the sideboard, but really there is no orange there," is not self-contradictory. (pp. 181–82) But this statement fails to be self-contradictory only for Warnock's realism, only for one who keeps seeming and being distinct. The point of Berkeley's phenomenalism[18] is that seeming *is* being: to talk of how

---

[18]Berkeley's phenomenalism of course is modified in the direction of realism once God is brought into the account. But it is not to Berkeley's total doctrine

things seem is to talk of how things are, allowing for consistency. We must talk of seeming only when trying to explain to the realist what the phenomenalist ontology is like. The "seeming" formulation which Warnock uses renders Berkeley's position clear only as it stands in opposition to realism.

The explication of the logic of "seeming" and "being" assertions does illuminate the nature of Warnock's realism. It misleads him about the nature of Berkeley's phenomenalism. It does not enable him to put Locke's position correctly. The assertion, "S_1, S_2, S_3 . . . S_n, therefore M," would be acceptable to Locke only after we recognize his prior acceptance of a dualist position with a causal theory of perception. The inference from the S statements to the M statement is controlled by Locke's beliefs about substance: he does not pretend to infer M from the S series alone. Locke's position is a combination of seeming and being, but Warnock fails to see the proper connection between the two aspects of Locke's ontology. He does succeed, on two occasions, in stating Berkeley's ontology more or less correctly. Recognizing that solipsism is the strongest form of phenomenalism, Warnock suggests that Berkeley should have argued his case from this point of view.

To show that sensible qualities are 'only in the mind', then, Berkeley should have attempted to establish that each of us can say *only* how things seem to *himself*; if this were so, no statement (in the present tense) about the 'sensible qualities' of an object could be made, unless that object were actually under observation at the time; and any such statement would also mention some person *to whom* the sensible quality 'appeared', 'in whose mind' it was. (p. 155)

The appearance language still persists in this statement, along with a reference to an object which appears; but if we overlook these parts, we have a fairly good account of what the phenomenalist must hold. More schematically, the phenomenalist position claims that "S_1, S_2, S_3 . . . S_n," *means the same as* "M," some statement about what the realist calls a material object. The material object statement is just a way of asserting the S series more compendiously. (p. 187) The inference which Warnock wants to place, for the phenomenalist, between the S series and the M statement is legitimate only after the phenomenalist has classified and grouped his sensible experiences to form things. But there is never a difference between asserting the S series and

that my remarks are addressed. I am concerned throughout Part I of this study to defend phenomenalism as an autonomous ontology, to free it from the interpretations of contemporary writers which make it parasitic on realism. It *is* parasitic on realism in the long run, but in ways different from those conceived of by current writers.

asserting the M statement. The contrast between the phenomenalist and Warnock's realist position is sharply exposed by this same schematism. Warnock says that it is possible to hold the statement "S_1, S_2, S_3 . . . S_n" as true while denying "M"; and that we can do this without accepting the dualist position of Locke. (p. 188) The alternative to both Locke and Berkeley is simply to stop using the language of seeming and use instead the language of being. But Warnock fails to appreciate that this is an alternative only if some form of naïve realism is previously accepted.

As for most other deviants from his own position, Warnock labels the failure to accept the difference between seeming and being a mistake. (p. 192) I am suggesting that his application of this distinction to Berkeley's phenomenalism is a fallacy, the fallacy of assuming the legitimacy of only one language or one ontology in terms of which all other candidates must be judged. Part of the trouble with Warnock's analysis is a use of "seeming" which is hardly ontological at all, the use which registers a psychological report. "I think that is a table but I am not sure" catches this use of the language of seeming. Of course it is correct to remark, as Warnock does, that the logic of such seeming-statements is different from the logic of statements of conviction: "This *is* a table." The difference is partially expressed by the difference between the judge's deliberations and his verdict. As Firth has remarked, it is not sufficient to say that statements of being have a "ritualistic function or represent some kind of ethical decision." That is, it is not sufficient when we are analyzing Berkeley's phenomenalism or taking phenomenalism as an ontology in its own right.

The theories of Berkeley and most phenomenalists are theories about our *beliefs*, and to refute them it is necessary to show that at least part of the belief or beliefs expressed by an M-statement cannot be expressed by any combination of S-statements. Even if it is true that M-statements or S-statements have linguistic functions other than that of expressing and inducing beliefs, this fact is irrelevant to such theories.[19]

This linguistic treatment of seeming and being statements is irrelevant because Berkeley's phenomenalism is more than a linguistic theory. But Warnock does implicitly invoke an ontology, that of naïve realism. So convinced is he of the truth of naïve realism that it is impossible for him to get inside Berkeley's position. The most he can do is to interpret it for realistically minded people. He is insensitive to the gulf which separates his realism from Berkeley's phenomenalism, a gulf almost as

[19]See Firth's review of Warnock's *Berkeley*, *The Philosophical Review*, Jan. 1955, p. 150.

wide as that between naïve realism and Lockean dualism. Whether Warnock is correct in his claim that the analysis of the vocabulary of perception in ordinary language leads to the sort of ontology he defends—whether, indeed, the ordinary language of perception has any ontology implicit in it—is an aspect of Warnock's general philosophical attitude (held not by him alone) which needs to be challenged. The kind of analysis which Warnock gives of the logic of seeming and being statements shows both Locke and Berkeley to have been wrong only because they both were trying to stipulate different uses of certain words. Warnock is certainly correct in pointing out that Berkeley, contrary to his own protestations, was not using words in the way that they are commonly employed. Unlike Warnock and Austin, I do not find this wrong or objectionable. There is no one use of words which is sacrosanct. The philosopher, the poet, the scientist all use some words in an extra-ordinary way, "it being unavoidable," as Locke pointed out, "in discourses differing from the ordinary received notions, either to make new words or to use old words in somewhat a new signification." (*Essay*, II, XII, 4) We may find some of these uses sterile, superfluous, pointless, or even meaningless. But if we wish to understand these extra-ordinary uses we must not impose an external criterion upon our interpretation of them.

Part II
DUALISM

In this part I am primarily concerned with sense-datum dualism, although the problems and difficulties here discussed are endemic to any form of substance theory. The sense-datum dualist is, in one part of his ontology, a phenomenalist. His dualism enters through his belief in realism, a realism where reality is not what it seems but is somehow related to appearance. The double concern with a Cartesian certainty and an acceptance of the reality of substance raises, for the dualist, ontological, epistemological, and linguistic problems. I explore these problems as they appear in Plato's theory of perception, in Russell's failure to resolve the linguistic and epistemic gap between sense-data and physical objects, and in Broad's more successful efforts at bridging this gap. Again, the intent is to understand dualism from the inside.

5

Sense-Data

SENSE-DATUM PHILOSOPHERS share several features with the phenomenalist. Both are concerned to give as careful an account as possible of the contents of experience *qua* phenomena. Both share an empirical heritage, a concern to tie human knowledge down to experience. There is an ambiguity around the term "experience."[1] In some cases, "experience" is taken in Hume's sense of "custom," of learning from the past. In this broad sense of experience, no particular ontological beliefs are paramount, although some form of phenomenalism is implicit: there is a realm of objects, either independent of awareness or as the contents of awareness, about which I acquire information. In other cases of the appeal to experience, there is concern with the nature, structure, and order of experience. Experience has been analyzed in terms of ideas, impressions, perceptions. The contents of experience were taken either, as by Locke, to be the source of our knowledge of a world of objects or, as by Berkeley and Hume, to be all we can say that objects themselves are. Locke and Hume are usually interpreted as doing a sort of psychology in talking of the contents of awareness as being ideas and impressions. Berkeley explicitly shifted from psychology to epistemology, asking questions of meaning: "what mean you by sensible thing?" He claimed that it was impossible to think of objects in any other terms than the terms of awareness. The dualist's substance is an impossible notion.

Another common ground between the phenomenalist and the sense-datum philosopher is the obsession with certainty. Descartes seems to have set the stage for this concern. The certainty of the cogito is peculiar in that it is very nearly analytic but also existential. It is nearly analytic because of the force of its denial; "I do not exist" is, while I utter it, an impossible truth. The truth of "I think, I exist" is

[1] Cf. my "The Concept of Experience in Locke and Hume," *Journal of the History of Philosophy*, I (1963), pp. 53–71.

unlike other analytic propositions in that its truth is not discovered by an analysis of the terms employed nor is it a function of some systemic set of axioms and definitions. Descartes said that its truth was grasped by a simple apprehension; when I perform Descartes' experiment in doubt I too discover the impossibility of my saying "I do not exist." The truth of the "I think, I exist" might be termed an "awareness-analytic" truth, to stress the fact that what is discovered is factual *but* certain.

I have already recognized that we cannot say that Descartes has established the existence of a thinking substance, but neither has he discovered merely that thinking exists or has taken place. What he has discovered is a first-person truth, a truth about himself, prior to determining *what* he is. I have also said that the phenomenalist begins his analysis with the cogito and its contents, and that the point of departure on the content side is produced through a scepticism controlled not by psychological principles but by epistemic rules. Those rules were Descartes' rules of the awareness-analytic. Descartes observed that there was a certainty to the contents of awareness also, if taken as contents only, as mental phenomena, although he did not explicitly make the connection with the certainty of the cogito. The sense-datum philosopher has been concerned with the Cartesian certainty directed towards the contents of awareness, not towards awareness itself. Husserl, of course, claimed certainty for the products of his reduction; his époché achieved what Descartes recognized but did not pursue—the separation of the contents of awareness from any referential claims they might have beyond themselves. But whereas Husserl encompassed the whole of the contents of ordinary awareness in his bracketed world, the sense-datum philosophers have felt that most of those contents play upon their pre-bracketed status. Husserl's reduced world contains condensed inductions which go beyond the contents of awareness. What sets the sense-datum theorist off from the phenomenalist is, of course, his conviction that reality is more than phenomenal; but he differs from the Hegelian or Husserlian phenomenalist also in circumscribing more stringently the contents of the phenomenal realm. Nothing is allowed in, save what passes the Cartesian test of awareness analyticity.

I   Sense-Data and Cartesian Doubt

Berkeleian phenomenalism is the main predecessor of sense-datum theories, but Berkeley's analysis of the datum for awareness was fixed not by the quest for certainty but by the historical context in which he wrote. The way of ideas had been firmly established by Locke; Berkeley saw no reason to break out of that tradition. He did support his analysis of the nature of the datum by a theory of proper sensibles. Moreover, his category of "immediate perception" is very much like the sense-datum philosopher's sense-data, in that it is not a psychological but an epistemic given. Berkeley's "ideas" are, like "sense-data," not the beginnings of perception psychologically and very probably never function at all in our actual awareness of the world; they are the analytic beginnings required by epistemology. Especially in the case of sense-data, it is a mistake to reject them because they violate the psychological analysis of what in fact we are aware of. Russell candidly admits the allegiance to Descartes in this matter of fixing the given.

What I am saying—and in this I am expounding part of Descartes's argument—is that there are some occurrences that I cannot make myself doubt, and that these are all of the kind that, if we admit a not-self, are part of the life of myself. Not all of them are sensations; some are abstract thoughts, some are memories, some are wishes, some are pleasures and pains. But all are what we should describe as mental events in me.[2]

For problems of perception, it is sensations which mark the necessary point of departure, although memories are seen to be necessary as a means for sensations to become recognized and identified. While perceptions "in all their fullness," that is, in containing beliefs and ingredients which go beyond immediate or indubitable sensations, "are data for psychology: we do in fact have the experience of believing in such-and-such an object," we cannot admit as data for theory of knowledge "all that an uncritical acceptance of common sense would take as given in perception."[3] The demands of strictness in knowledge curtail the scope of permissible data. Full-blown perceptual acceptance must be replaced by a rigid formulation of premises and conclusion. The nature of what is seen is prescribed by the requirements of knowledge. In seeking for indubitables in this peculiar Cartesian sense, what can be allowed as seen comprises only what cannot be doubted by the Cartesian methodology.

The Cartesian nature of the method employed by the sense-datum mode of analysis is even more apparent in Price's classic statement.

When I see a tomato there is much that I can doubt. I can doubt whether it is a tomato that I am seeing, and not a cleverly painted piece of wax. I

---

[2]*Human Knowledge*, p. 174.
[3]*Ibid.*, pp. 170–71.

can doubt whether there is any material thing there at all. . . . One thing however I cannot doubt: that there exists a red patch of a round and somewhat bulgy shape. . . . [4]

This special manner of being present to consciousness Price terms "being given"; but, although the description of the datum is the product of a close scrutiny of his own sense-field when in the presence of what is commonly called a "tomato," the *givenness* of the datum is a product of strict epistemological requirements, those same rigid rules to which Descartes appealed in the enunciation of his cogito. Price's own account of the nature of perceptual consciousness carefully extracts those ingredients in such consciousness which are psychologically given from those which meet the requirements of the Cartesian methodology. Psychological introspection is present throughout his analysis of the nature of perceptual consciousness, but it cannot be said to have entered into the selection of the data for analysis. There is a sharp difference between the methods for *fixing* the given and for *describing* the given.

Austin appreciated the role of the quest for certainty in the talk of sense-data. Pointing out that the sense-datum philosopher's use of "see" or "perceive" was special, he correctly spotted the motive at work.

Their real motive—and this lies right at the heart of the whole matter—is that they wish to produce a species of statement that will be *incorrigible*; and the real virtue of this invented sense of 'perceive' is that, since what is perceived in this sense *has* to exist and *has* to be as it appears, in saying what I perceive in this sense I *can't be wrong*.[5]

Austin thought the quest for incorrigibility was either for a goal which is unattainable or that incorrigibility is much more common than sense-datum philosophers allow. It is unattainable if the thought is that sense-datum propositions are incorrigible, because (1) the chance of making verbal mistakes in formulating what it is that I cannot doubt as contents of awareness is always present (p. 113), and (2) sentences as such are never incorrigible or fallible; it is sentences employed on particular occasions, under specific circumstances that may be incorrigible. The first point cannot be denied. It may be that the "I think, I exist" proposition is more incorrigible than content propositions, since the fact which the cogito proposition states does not hinge on language in the way that content propositions do. All that may be incorrigible in any given instance may be *that* I am aware and that I am aware *of* some content. *What* the content is, how it is to be

[4]*Perception*, p. 3.
[5]*Sense and Sensibilia*, p. 103.

expressed in language, may bring in the possibility of fallibility. Austin admits that under some conditions I could make an incorrigible sense-datum report.

If I carefully scrutinize some patch of colour in my visual field, take careful note of it, know English well, and pay scrupulous attention to just what I'm saying, I may say, 'It seems to me now as if I were seeing something pink'; and nothing whatever could be produced as showing that I had made a mistake. (p. 114)

But he claims that the same incorrigibility pertains to object reports as well, if the conditions are equally impeccable.

But equally, if I watch for some time an animal a few feet in front of me, in a good light, if I prod it perhaps, sniff, and take note of the noises it makes, I may say, 'That's a pig'; and this too will be 'incorrigible,' nothing could be produced that would show that I had made a mistake. (p. 114)

For Austin, the illusion that only sense-datum statements can be incorrigible is a result of thinking that there is a special kind of sentence which is *as such* incorrigible. I do not believe that the sense-datum philosophers have meant to say it was the sentence which is incorrigible. Just as the truth of Descartes' cogito statement is a function of his uttering that statement under the special conditions of wholesale doubt, so the determination of what content statement is incorrigible is a function of someone's experience. Equally, just as the sentence which merits the label of "incorrigible" in Descartes' experiment is a function not of a psychological doubt but of a doubt which plays upon the notion of logical impossibility, so the claim for indubitability for sense-datum statements is also a function of the Cartesian rules of logical impossibility. I do not think Austin appreciated this feature of Descartes' programme. It is not the case that Price is introspecting when in the presence of a tomato, asking himself psychological questions of belief and doubt, attending very carefully to what in fact he is aware of. Rather, he is asking what, if anything, there is in this experience which could escape the logically rigorous requirement of a denial being self-contradictory. The special sense of "see" and "perceive" introduced by the sense-datum philosopher is really not a case of seeing or perceiving at all: it is a recommendation of how we ought to analyze the perceptual situation, of how perceptual knowledge might be reconstructed. *That* there is an awareness with some content is a fact which cannot be denied, whose denial is logically impossible. If this claim is recognized as an instance of an awareness-analytic proposition, we may then be ready to talk in terms of those favourable instances where the chances of linguistic error in description are minimal. In fact, the fixing of the given by epistemic rather than psychological methods controls the description as well.

Once the given has been determined, the next step in the sense-datum programme is to rebuild—again following Descartes' lead—perceptual knowledge in such a way that the claim for independent objects can be supported. The epistemic given is formulated by Russell in basic propositions which constitute the primary epistemological premises in his reconstruction. In general, Russell considers all epistemological premises as having three main characteristics. They must be logical, psychological, and true, so far as we can ascertain. "Given any systematic body of propositions, such as is contained in some science in which there are general laws, it is possible, usually in an indefinite number of ways, to pick out certain of the propositions as premises and deduce the remainder."[6] This inferential order is what Russell understands by the logical aspect of epistemological premises. The logician, in other words, seeks for that minimum set of premises from which he can deduce the rest of the propositions in a given system. Russell as an epistemic logician attempts to apply this inferential order to epistemology; but he does not intend the deduction of epistemological propositions to be made solely from basic propositions. Within this range there must be certain primary propositions which form the epistemological, not the logical, basis for the other propositions of the class. I do not believe Russell anywhere says or means to imply that deductive inferences can be made from one epistemological premise to another: the deduction is from epistemological *premise* to *conclusion*. It is Russell's conviction that certain of these premises must be basic in order for valid inferences from the class of epistemological premises to be made. From the psychological side, such basic epistemological premises can be defined as those beliefs which are not caused by any other beliefs. "Psychologically, any belief may be considered to be inferred when it is caused by other beliefs, however invalid the inference may be for logic. The most obvious class of beliefs not caused by other beliefs are those that result directly from perception." (p. 132) But it is not the beliefs which *actually do* result from perception that Russell is concerned with; it is those which *should* result, epistemologically. When it functions as a premise for epistemology, such a fundamental belief is called a "perceptive premise." It might be thought that the belief expressed by a statement like "there is an eclipse" is a perceptive premise; but such a belief actually "goes

[6]*Inquiry*, p. 131.

beyond the mere expression of what I see" and hence cannot be valid for the sense-datum theory. "See" is here used in that special sense noted above. Epistemology demands, Russell is saying, a perceptive premise for which "there is never good reason to think false, or, what comes to the same thing, something so defined that two perceptive premises cannot contradict each other." (p. 135) Russell insists that what he calls "momentary empiricism" has to be the starting point for all empirical theories of knowledge, since it alone starts from that which I can know without dependence upon anything other than my perceptive experiences. Since such premises are going to form the basis for all other propositions in theory of knowledge, it is essential that they be independent of other beliefs and other propositions. They constitute the ground of later inferences and hence cannot themselves contain inferences.

Basic propositions are thus perceptive premises which are "a subclass of epistemological premises." They do not constitute the sum of necessary premises for an empirical epistemology but they form the basis of the system. Such propositions must be known independently of any evidence, "since there must be a perceptive occurrence which gives the cause and is considered to give the reason for believing the basic proposition." (p. 138) One of the questions which emerges from the relation of basic propositions to perceptive experience is "what do we know when we know that our words 'express' something we see?" That is, "when you see a black object and say 'this is black', you are not, as a rule, noticing that you say these words; you know the thing is black, but you do not know that you say these words; you know the thing is black, but you do not know that you say it is." (p. 60) However, when we are, as Russell is in the *Inquiry*, "studying the relation of language to other facts," we do take notice of the connection between the words and the non-verbal fact we are seeking to express. The nature of this connection is an important epistemological question which Russell has considered both in the *Inquiry* and, at more length, in the article, "The Limits of Empiricism."[7] However, the more important requirement for all basic propositions is that they "be of such a form that no other basic proposition can contradict them." These basic beliefs and their linguistic translations must be restricted to that which we can be said to know from sensation alone. We must avoid what Russell calls "condensed inductions," which go beyond the given or the sensational core, since these are not basic in the sense of being free from inferences. These inferences, these condensed inductions,

[7]*Proceedings of the Aristotelian Society*, 36 (1935–36), pp. 131–150.

are just those beliefs and acceptances which are eliminable through Cartesian doubt.

II THE CRITERION OF PHYSICALITY

Chisholm has seen that sense-data are products of reflection and not of psychological analysis. But he misunderstands the nature of the reflection involved. From some such statement as "He sees a boat," or "a boat presents him with an appearance," Chisholm says the sense-datum philosopher infers the statement "He sees an appearance." Such an inference is an instance of "the *sense-datum fallacy*."[8] But the sense-datum philosopher does not make this sort of inference. He asserts something like "He sees an appearance" because of the demands the Cartesian methodology makes for a beginning free from all possible doubt. Moreover, the appearance-reality distinction is reinforced by his initial belief in realism. This belief itself contains a criterion of physicality which is inclined towards dualism. Broad lists five characteristics of physical objects.[9] The object must have a "reasonable" duration and temporal unity, it must be extended into space to form a spatial whole, have causal characteristics, be multiply accessible to different observers and to different sense modalities of the same person; and it must have primary as well as secondary qualities.[10] The primary qualities are assumed to belong to some part of the physical object which is independent of observers, that part which Broad terms the "scientific object," the object of inference which is located in the constructed physical space. Price's "physical occupant" plays an analogous role in his version of the theory. Armed with this criterion, committed to Cartesian indubitability, the sense-datum philosopher then finds in the arguments from illusion, from the finite velocity of light, and hosts of other considerations, support for the sense-datum/physical object split. The sense-datum analysis is the best answer to the question of perception, given this methodology and this criterion of reality.

One of the earliest attacks on the sense-datum theory which overlooked the role of the criterion of physicality in the talk of sense-data, was Ayer's *Foundations of Empirical Knowledge*. Taking as the fundamental assertion of the sense-datum theorists that we never directly experience material objects but always sense-data, Ayer began his

---

[8]*Perceiving*, p. 151. Cf. his *Theory of Knowledge*, pp. 94–95.

[9]The way in which Broad's use of the criterion of physicality leads to dualism is discussed in chapter 8.

[10]*The Mind and Its Place in Nature*, pp. 146–47.

attack by discussing the argument from illusion. He argued that it was an invalid conclusion to draw from this argument that naïve realism is false; we can say naïve realism is "linguistically inconvenient" but we can never say, on the basis of this argument, that it is false. Such a conclusion would presuppose that naïve realism contradicts some of the known facts about perception. Put otherwise, the assertion of the falsity of naïve realism is invalid because such an assertion has and can have no empirical verification. The alleged facts upon which the argument from illusion is said to depend are declared by Ayer not to be facts at all, but only "subsidiary arguments" or "assumptions" made in order to facilitate the advancement of the desired conclusion. One such "assumption" is that "material things can exist and have properties without being causally dependent on any observer." (p. 12) Another is that a physical object cannot have contradictory characteristics at the same time. (pp. 14, 16)

These assumptions are, of course, part of the criterion of physicality with which the sense-datum philosopher begins his analysis of perception. The way Ayer treats these criteria is revealing of how the sense-datum theory was misinterpreted. With reference to the assumption of no contradictory properties, Ayer says:

I have shown that the ground on which it is maintained that there are at any rate some occasions on which we perceive sense-data which are not parts of any material thing is that some perceptions are delusive; and the ground on which it is maintained that some of our perceptions must be delusive is that if we take them all to be veridical we shall involve ourselves in contradictions, since we shall have to attribute to material things such mutually incompatible properties as being at the same time both green and yellow, or both elliptical and round. But here it may be objected that these contradictions cannot, in fact, be derived from the nature of our perceptions alone. If from one stand-point, I see what appears to be a round coin and then, subsequently, from another standpoint, see it as elliptical, there is no contradiction involved in my supposing that in each case I am seeing the coin as it really is. This supposition becomes self-contradictory only when it is combined with the assumption that the real shape of the coin has remained the same. (p. 14)

While it is true that the contradictions here referred to cannot "be derived from the nature of our perceptions alone," it is not correct to say that on the basis of these perceptions alone "there is no contradiction involved in my supposing that in each case I am seeing the coin as it really is." The term "coin" here is significant. If we attend only to our perceptions, it is unintelligible to speak of coins or any other similar object because the meaning of "coin" is something that is added by factors other than sensing or perception. If we attend strictly to our perceptions or sensings only, there should be no debates or questions at all, unless it be as to whether one person is having the same type of experience as another. The belief that our sense qualities belong to or are related to something else such as a class or family, or that they *are* one aspect of something like a coin, is indeed a supposition that cannot be conclusively proved true by an examination of our sensings alone. It is only after we have a theory about what appears that we can interpret the appearances. Unless we admit some meaning to the word "coin" there can be no debate. But once we have admitted a meaning to this and all similar object-words, then certain statements about sense qualities can be said to be true and others can be said to be false. The truth or falsity will be possible only in relation to the meaning of the word "coin," once we have a criterion of physicality, a theory of objects. Once we have accepted some meaning for physical-object words, some statements about sense qualities will be consistent with this meaning and others will be inconsistent. The phenomenalist fixes these meanings in one way, the realist in another.

Under the commonly accepted meaning of "coin," it *is* contradictory to say that "in each case I am seeing the coin as it really is," in the case cited by Ayer. It is contradictory because such an assertion is inconsistent with the accepted meaning of the word "coin," since this meaning contains the factor of *physical* existence and since part of the accepted meaning of physical coin, or any physical object, is that that coin or object cannot have contradictory characteristics at the same time. We might argue that the fact that from one standpoint I experience a round sense-quality of a certain colour and that from another standpoint I experience an elliptical sense-quality of a certain colour, does not afford us a basis for saying that we have been experiencing the same physical object. This would be a legitimate contention. But in the statement by Ayer he specifically assumes that the same coin is involved. For instance, he says "if from one standpoint, I see what appears to be a round coin, then, subsequently, from another standpoint see *it* as elliptical, there is no contradiction involved in my supposing that in each case I am seeing *the coin* as *it* really is." The italicised words make it clear that he means to say that the *same* coin is perceived from these different standpoints.

If by factual we mean only what the contents of our sensings reveal, Ayer is correct that naïve realism cannot be proven to be false. In fact, it cannot be proven either true or false, since the meaning and assertions of naïve realism depend upon constituents other than the contents of our sensings. The meanings of physical-object words may be exhausted by the contents of our sensings but more than sensing, more than awareness, must come into play in order to fix these meanings. Ayer, of course, tried to say that the meanings of physical-object words were fixed linguistically; he correctly saw that this operation is not a factual one. It is not entirely clear, however, just what his contention about language fixing the meanings of words in our ontological beliefs means; it should be clear by now that the meanings of physical-object words for the sense-datum philosopher are a function of his initial beliefs about physical objects. One's ontology may be a function of such initial beliefs; these beliefs may be acquired through one's society, even controlled by our language. It is a psychological question as to how these beliefs arise, what is the source of our criterion of physicality. But the other side to Ayer's linguistic claim— that it makes little difference which ontological language we talk, that indeed we can, more or less, translate from one to the other—is an instance of the fallacy of translatability. Furthermore, had the sense-datum philosophers proceeded as Ayer claimed, they *would* have committed the sense-datum fallacy charged by Chisholm. Both writers failed to note the role of this prior determination of basic beliefs— and hence of basic meanings—in one's interpretation of experience. Once we have established the meaning of some of our basic object words, choice of ontological languages is no longer free. When we start, as Ayer did, by maintaining that the sense-datum theory is not a theory at all but just one way of saying what we already know about the material world, certain conclusions follow which reveal the fallacy in Ayer's linguistic claim. (1) In order to make an accurate translation into the sense-datum language, we have to know the meaning of the material-object language: we have to know what it means to say "I am perceiving a material object." This involves some idea of what a material object is like, which means that we have some set of qualities which we take to be necessary characteristics of physicality. (2) Then, the translation must not contradict or oppose any of these criteria contained in our idea of what a material thing is like. Any translation which does, will be an invalid and faulty one, perverting, if not completely distorting, the original meaning. (3) Thus, from the beginning of our proposed translation, it is not just a verbal matter what language we use, since there may be some languages which do not contain the words necessary to convey the original meaning. The language used is determined by the meanings attached to our fundamental words, such as "coin," "physical object." (4) If we accept the commonly accepted criteria of physicality, one thing is at least certain: naïve realism cannot be used as one of our languages since the only way to save naïve realism in the face of these criteria is, as Ayer admits, to make certain assumptions as to the naïve realist's meaning which are inconsistent with these criteria; for example, to say of an object that it is seen or touched does not entail saying that it exists. We cannot say this about physical objects when we mean by "physical" what we do commonly mean. Any attempt to force this interpretation of naïve realism and to insist that it is an adequate translation of material-object sentences, amounts to an attempt to change the commonly accepted meanings of physical object words.

Ayer observed that the meanings in the criterion were not logically necessary. From this correct remark he concluded that the only way they could be validated was on empirical grounds. When he turned to the empirical evidence upon which the assumptions comprising the criterion are said to depend, Ayer claimed that the usual interpretation placed upon this evidence is not the only possible interpretation and that this evidence does not support exclusively the sense-datum interpretation. He tried to show that the empirical facts are able to support various "assumptions" about the nature of physical objects. He said that "it is in every instance a matter of our being able to establish a certain order among our experiences" which is the cause of these assumptions.

We say that an object seen in a looking glass is not really in the place in which it appears to be, because, when we go to that place, we find that there is no such object there to be seen or touched. We say that a penny which appears to have a different shape when it is seen from a different angle has not really changed its shape, because, when we return to our original point of view, we find that it looks the same shape as it did before. . . . We say, in the instance of the mirage, that the trees do not really exist, because we believe that people who were in what we should call a normal physiological state would not perceive them and because they cannot subsequently be perceived by the observer himself. (pp. 16–17)

Is it really because we are unable to touch the mirror image that we conclude that the alleged object seen in the mirror is not located there? Do we really conclude that the penny has not changed its shape from roundness to ellipticalness because when we return to our original position we still sense a round shape? Clearly, on the basis of the contents of our sensings alone, we should not draw these conclusions. Isn't it because besides the content of these sensings we have a criterion of physicality, that we draw such conclusions? We conclude that the mirror image is not a physical object located in the mirror because we believe such objects to be accessible to more than one sense modality and subsequent experience discloses that this is not fulfilled. We believe that the penny has not changed its shape because we believe that physical objects are permanent and not transitory as regards such qualities as shape. Thus, when we move about, we conclude either that there is no penny there or that not all of the changing shapes are the real shape of the penny.

These conclusions take the form which they do because we already possess a criterion, an idea of what a material thing must be like. Ayer is correct when he says that if we abandon this criterion and examine only the contents of our sense-experiences, we are powerless to say that one interpretation is better or more correct than another. But all that this means is that we need more than just the contents of our sensings before we can become perceptually assured of the nature and existence of material things, since without some meanings to physical-object words, we are limited to the individual contents of our sensings. What permits anyone to describe the sensible appearances in either the naïve-realist or the sense-datum language, is the presence of meanings for the basic words. The concept of factuality is subsequent to the concept of an object; "fact" is defined in terms of one's general ontology. The important truth behind Ayer's detailed analysis of theories of perception is that none of these theories is or can be empirical. In the instance of the sense-datum theory, it was the Cartesian methodology working in conjunction with a definite criterion of physicality which produced the theory.

III The Ontological Status of Sense-Data

The analysis of perception and the nature of the physical world offered by the sense-datum philosophers is, then, controlled by initial ontological beliefs and a methodology for producing a starting point free of doubt. Given the ontological beliefs and the methodology, it soon becomes clear that objects which would satisfy the criterion of physicality cannot be the contents of awareness, the only objects which meet the requirements of the methodology. The claim that what I immediately perceive, or what I am indubitably aware of are my own perceptions, yields the conclusion that I can never be aware *in this way* of physical objects. Sense-data do not only function in this normative fashion, telling us how we should talk about perception; they also play an important epistemic role in justifying whatever knowledge of the physical world I can be said to have. But a methodological datum can yield knowledge of an ontological entity only if there is some relation between that datum and the entity in question. In the sense-datum theory that relation is not only epistemic, sense-data are given ontological status. The relation of "belonging to" between sense-data and physical objects treats sense-data as ontological reals. A certain carefully specified family of sense-data constitutes an important part of the nature of any physical object for Price. It is through sense-data that we obtain whatever conjectural knowledge we have of the physical occupant or the scientific object, and it is only by including sense-data in our accounts of reality that we can give an exhaustive description of the real. Broad is more careful in this matter of the relation between sensa and scientific objects, preserving a fine distinction between them, even though he wants to conclude that tactuo-muscular sensa do reveal the correct geometrical shape of the scientific object. But sensible and physical worlds are meant by him to remain separate and distinct. However, since the qualitative nature of the physical or scientific world is known for Broad through Whitehead's method of extensive abstraction from the sensible world, we have a situation very similar to Price's more open acknowledgment that sense-data are ontologically members of the class of physical objects. Both Russell and Broad appeal to the postulate of structural isomorphism between sense-data and physical objects; in this respect they are more dualistic than Price. Broad denies that the ontological status of sensa is either physical or mental while Russell is content to make them mental. But in both cases, the geometrical properties which are taken as definitive of the structure of physical reality are extrapolated from sense-data. Whether part of the physical world or not, sense-data have ceased to serve as methodological devices and have come to have a status in the world.

The difficulties of such an ontological transformation of sense-data are explored in the following chapters, as they appear in Plato, Russell, and Broad. We can understand something of the problem initially by looking briefly at Price's efforts to move away from the strict dualism of Russell and Broad. In particular, the analysis of space which Price offers is typical of the way sense-data are given ontological status.[11] Price asserts that what he calls the "nuclear data," those

[11]I should remark that the distinction I have drawn between sense-data as the products of method and sense-data as ontological reals is not clearly marked in any of the sense-datum philosophers. I do not think that even they fully recognized the methodological nature of their given. A close examination of their analyses, however, supports this distinction and sheds light on some of the standard sense-datum difficulties.

which spatially synthesize and adjoin one another, do not "*merely* collectively *resemble* a certain solid, they collectively *are* a solid. . . ."[12] Presumably he is using the word "solid" in a physical-object sense, for a few pages later he says that the space of the standard solid is the same as physical or public space. But this physical solid is composed of data which are not in physical space and which only sensibly adjoin and are in front of or in back of each other. This means that in his earlier discussion of progressive adjunction the phrase "sensible visual solid" should be replaced by "physical visual solid," because the nuclear members of the family do not merely form a sensible or perceptual solid, as Broad maintained; they, together with their relations with other such solids, form a physical solid in physical space. The individual members of this nuclear solid are not in physical space, since for this to be so the individual sense-data would have to be related spatially to standard solids. But this is impossible since the relation between standard solids and nuclear data is never and could never be spatial. Rather, it is the relation of "being a constituent of." "Sense-data can be spatially related to other sense-data, and standard solids to other standard solids; but strictly speaking, sense-data, even nuclear ones, cannot be spatially related to the standard solids, nor standard solids to sense-data." (p. 250) How could they be so related if it is sense-data that make up the standard solid which is what is in physical space? But this is a very curious fact. While no sense-datum, nuclear or otherwise, can have a position in physical space (although nuclear data are sensibly related spatially to each other), collections of nuclear data do have such a position. Price must mean, when he says that individual nuclear data can be related spatially to other nuclear data, that the relation involved is a visual or sensible spatial relation, like Broad's visual whole which suggests real physical space but which is not in that space. If this is the correct interpretation, then space for Price is a collective characteristic. In other words, he defines physical space "as that in which standard solids are located," but since a "standard solid is defined as a group of sense-data related to each other by progressive adjunction," it turns out that physical space itself is defined in terms of sets of nuclear data. Unless some such data are related by progressive adjunction, "there is no physical space at all." (p. 252) While Broad defined physical space in terms of an analogy with sensible space, Price has taken certain aspects of sensible space and made them constitutive of physical space. Broad's perceptual object was only in space in a Pickwickian manner, but Price's nuclear

[12]*Perception*, p. 243.

solids, with their various relations, constitute what is meant by space. Price wished also to make it quite clear that common sense demands something more than this as constitutive of physical objects; his own theory tried to meet this demand by reference to a physical occupant which somehow inhabits the space thus defined by collections of sense-data. But the way in which the physical occupant occupies the space thus defined by sense-data and the way in which it can share the same space with the nuclear solid is never clearly specified by Price, nor could it be so specified so long as physical space is defined in terms of sense-data. The dichotomy between sensible and imperceptible has not been bridged by Price's efforts to bring physical and sensible worlds closer together. At best, physical occupation is marked out by tactuo-muscular sensations.

Apart from the difficulties which arise in Price's analysis of space and physical occupation, his analysis of space does indicate the onto-logical role he intends sense-data to have. What began as a non-empirical factor in the analysis of perception and reality turns out to have an ontological character. By what line of reasoning can the sense-datum philosopher make this transition from a non-empirical epistemic given to an ontological real? There would seem to be no justification for such a transformation. The difficulty which all sense-datum philo-sophers have experienced in trying to pass, either epistemologically or ontologically, from sense-data to physical objects arises from their failure to grasp the fundamental and totally diverse difference between sense-data and physical objects. One of the reasons for their lack of concern with the precise relations between psychology and philosophy has been, I think, their failure to meet the implications of their own Cartesian methodology. For if sense-data are not meant as violations of empirical psychology, they can only be the products demanded by the rigid epistemological requirements of their own methodology. Either sense-data are empirical, and then they are false, or they are non-empirical constructions, acceptable as one possible methodological point of departure for theory of knowledge. The sense-datum philo-sophers cannot have it both ways. There is a great deal of confusion in their own writings over the nature of sense-data. Price speaks repeatedly of "sensing a sense-datum," as if such language were justi-fied by empirical psychology. For all of his warnings in his first chapter about the need to reject, in theory of knowledge, the findings of empiri-cal science, he moves quickly from the formal, epistemological nature of sense-data to an empirical, ontological claim for them. His entire endeavour to determine the nature of the relation of "belonging to"

is actually a violation of the specifications of his Cartesian methodology. There is something most strange about the attempt to specify
the relation between a sense-datum as an epistemic given and a
physical object said to have ontological status in the world. The whole
movement within theory of knowledge which has championed the
sense-datum analysis has been guilty of this same error of abstraction.
What starts as a convenient tool for analysis and reformulation of the
structure of our knowledge, ends by becoming a basic ingredient in
the real. Philosophy as the logical formulation in a valid deductive
system of perceptual propositions has thereby been confused with the
psychological description of awareness and the ontological account of
reality.

6

The Ontological Status of Sense-Data in Plato's Theory of Perception

IF WE TURN FROM THE UNEASY ambivalence of sense-data as methodological and ontological ingredients to a more detailed examination of the role they might play as ontological entities, there are two tasks we must undertake. In the first place, we have the task of making clear just what sort of entities sense-data are. Are they particular existents, substances, or phases of substances? Are they attributes or modes, mental or physical beings? In the second place, we must give an analysis of the relations of sense-data to observers and to physical objects. The first of these tasks need not be carried out before we develop a theory of perception; for, as Price has remarked, the important aspect of sense-data for theories of perception which employ them is their relation to physical objects and to observers, not their precise nature and status. The first task is the more difficult part of the question about the ontological status of sense-data, but it is one which can be at least partially answered within Plato's theory of perception. The second task is easier to handle and takes a very interesting turn in the theory under discussion in this chapter. It is this question too which has a direct bearing upon the epistemic features of Plato's theory of perception. Before we can consider these questions, it is necessary to have before us a brief statement of Plato's perceptual theory as that is presented chiefly in the first part of the *Theaetetus* and in certain sections of the *Timaeus*.[1]

[1]The following abbreviations will be used throughout this chapter. *PTK* for *Plato's Theory of Knowledge* by Cornford, references being to Cornford's commentary and not to the text; *PC* for *Plato's Cosmology* by Cornford, the references likewise being to Cornford's notes and commentary; *RT* for Rivaud's edition of

I The Protagorean-Heraclitean Theory of Perception

The theory of perception developed in the first part of the *Theaetetus*, a theory which Burnet confidently ascribes to Socrates, while suggesting a Cratylian origin,[2] is developed in a way which Cornford calls dialectical (p. 30, 36, *PTK*) and Diès refers to as a method of reduction.[3] The young Theaetetus offers as the first definition of knowledge, "knowledge is perception." The first reduction or the first dialectical development of this definition is the identification of Theaetetus' definition with Protagoras' doctrine, "man is the measure." This is accomplished by pointing out that in saying "that any given thing is to me such as it appears to me; and is to you as it appears to you," Protagoras has said nothing different from "anything is as it is perceived to be." The wind appears and is cold to you and warm to me, and this statement is the same as saying that we perceive the wind to be both cold and warm and that it is both of these. Appearance and sense "are the same in the case of hot and cold and the like."[4] Things are as they are perceived to be.

It is important to notice that in this first reduction of Theaetetus' definition of knowledge as perception, Plato has introduced the distinction between sense object and physical object, for he has specifically said "when the *same* wind is blowing, one of us feels chilly, the other does not." (My italics) In using this example, Plato has, as Cornford observes, raised the question of how the several sense objects are related to the single physical object. This question is one of the two major questions we have to consider in this chapter. Cornford feels that Protagoras probably held that the physical object is both hot and cold, different observers perceiving different aspects of the same object. That is, Cornford suggests that Protagoras' own answer to this question about the relation between sense-data and physical objects is one of complete identification in every case. We will see that this theory is similar in many ways to the one worked out by Plato in the *Theaetetus*, but the distinction between the physical object and the sense object, between the wind which feels hot and cold to different people, makes certain characteristic differences between Plato's and Protagoras' theory. Before going on to examine these differences, it is

---

the *Timaeus*, in *Platon, Oeuvres complètes*, t. X, 1925; *T* for Cornford's translation of the *Timaeus*; and *TH* for Cornford's translation of the *Theaetetus*.

[2] Burnet, *Greek Philosophy*, part I, pp. 241–42.

[3] *Autour de Platon*, t. 2, pp. 454–56.

[4] Burnet, p. 238.

necessary to follow the further development of Plato's general theory of perception.

The second reduction or dialectical development of Theaetetus' definition of knowledge as perception is the identification of the Protagorean doctrine with the Heraclitean doctrine of flux. Protagoras' dictum says in effect, according to Plato, "that nothing is *one* thing just by itself, nor can you rightly call it some definite name, nor even say it is of any definite sort." The reason given for this implication of Protagoras' dictum is that, whenever we attempt to describe an object by saying it is tall or white or what not, we discover, in terms of Protagorus' doctrine of relativity, that it is also short, black, and many other contrary qualities at the same time. Nothing ever is *one* but always *many*. Regardless of what a given object may seem to one person to *be*, it is in process of *becoming* something else for another individual. In general, Plato asserts, "all things we are pleased to say 'are,' really are in process of becoming." (152D, *TH*)

It should be noted, however, that Plato cannot validly deduce Heraclitus' doctrine of flux from Protagoras' dictum, since to hold that things have many different and even contrary qualities at the same time does not mean that they are in becoming or in flux. On the theory which Cornford suggestively identified with Protagoras, objects would be defined in a manner different from that which is usual and they would have a different kind of existence. There is no impossibility in saying that an object is composed of all the sense qualities that all the observers in the world have associated or will associate with that object, while affirming that this object has an identity which is not that of an identity of process. However, there is evidence which supports Plato's interpretation of Protagoras' dictum. I shall develop this point when I come to compare Plato's and Protagoras' theories of perception.

The next stage in the development of Plato's theory of perception is the insertion of motion as the source of all this becoming. Grouping Protagoras, Heraclitus, Empedocles, Epicharmus, and Homer together, Plato asserts that they all held that "all things are the offspring of a flowing stream of change." (152E, *TH*) In other words, " 'Being' (so-called) and 'becoming' are produced by motion,[5] 'not-being' and perish-

---

[5]We should remember that the ultimate source of motion for Plato was the soul, the only thing which could initiate motion, capable of moving itself and other things. "How can anything which is moved by another ever be the beginning of change? Impossible. But when the self-moved changes other, and that again other, and thus thousands upon tens of thousands of bodies are set in motion, must not the beginning of all this motion be the change of the self-moving principle?"

ing by rest." (152E, *TH*) The third and final reduction of the original definition of knowledge makes Protagoras' dictum say that man is the measure, not of things which are, but of that which becomes.

In the sphere of perception, I am the measure of what becomes, but never is; and the Protagorean claim that 'perception is always of what *is*' gives place to the Platonic doctrine: Perception is always of what is in process of becoming. (p. 39, *PTK*)

With this development or reduction of Theaetetus' definition of knowledge as perception, Plato is now in a position to present his view of the relation between sense qualities and physical objects. If perception is of things in becoming, and if we are aware of sense qualities in perception which in some sense belong to the physical objects, then it is clear that sense qualities must also be in process and in becoming. No sense quality can "have its being in an assigned place and abide there" indefinitely. Their existence is momentary and arises in a process of becoming. White, sweet, hot, or any other sense quality "has no being as a distinct thing outside your eyes nor yet inside them"; it has no permanent location anywhere. Sense qualities for Plato have locations, but such locations are brief and dependent upon the entire process which generates perceived objects. The generation of perceived objects has a twofold cause: one part stems from the external, physical cause, the other from the organs of the percipient.

What we say 'is' this or that colour will be neither the eye which encounters the motion [of the external physical cause] nor the motion which is encountered, but something which has arisen between the two and is peculiar to each several percipient. (154A, *TH*)

This continual becoming and process is not limited to sense qualities. Both the external physical cause and the sense organs of the observer are subject to a continual flux. The sense organs must be subject to this constant change; for, just as it would be impossible for the object to be really white or large while at the same time becoming different in different situations without supposing that the object undergoes some change of its nature, so

if the thing which measures itself against the object or touches it were any one of these things (large, white, etc.), then, when a different thing came

---

(*Laws*, 894E, 985A) At 896A *Laws*, Plato defines the soul as "the motion which can move itself," indicating that the soul together with the secondary, corporeal powers which are able to communicate motion once they have received motion, "directs all things in heaven, and earth, and sea by her movements."

into contact with it or were somehow modified, it, on its side, if it were not affected in itself, would not become different. (154B, *TH*)[6]

What Plato is trying to do is to explain the becoming of qualities. If objects were really large, then when Socrates became taller than Theaetetus, an internal change would have to take place within Socrates himself, just as when we compare six dice with four, we cannot say that the six are more at that time and less when we compare them with seven, unless we suppose an internal change within the dice themselves. It is important to notice that Plato definitely rejects this possibility, the possibility which would say that objects do undergo constant change of this sort. The object he has in mind here is clearly the physical object which he earlier distinguished from the sense object. But, although the physical object does not itself change its nature each time relations introduce changes of the above sort, it is nevertheless constantly undergoing change of another sort. The object in itself has, as we will see, some distinct qualities of its own which are never perceived, but it is nevertheless constantly in motion. On the view of perception here being presented, the entire universe is nothing but motion. When the motion of the physical object and the motion of the sense-organs come into appropriate relations, the one exemplifies the power of acting while the other exemplifies the ability to receive action. The result of this relation is two new twin motions. One of each of these pairs generated by the action of the two motions "is something perceived, the other a perception, whose birth always coincides with that of the thing perceived." (156B, *TH*) The sense quality, which is what is referred to here as "the thing perceived" (it is not the physical object which is the object perceived), is generated along with a perception by the interaction of organ and object, both of which in turn are likewise motions.

As soon, then, as an eye and something else whose structure is adjusted to the eye come within range and give birth to the whiteness together with its cognate perception—things that would never have come into existence if either of the two had approached anything else—then it is that, as the vision from the eyes and the whiteness from the thing that joins in giving

---

[6]The same type of argument occurs in the *Timaeus* where Plato is arguing that the Receptacle, the recipient of all qualities and characteristics, must itself be without qualities. "Further we must observe that, if there is to be an impress presenting all diversities of aspect, the thing itself in which the impress comes to be situated, cannot have been duly prepared unless it is free from all those characters which it is to receive from elsewhere. For if it were like any one of the things that come in upon it, then, when things of contrary or entirely different nature came, in receiving them it would reproduce them badly, intruding its own features alongside." (50DE, *T*)

birth to the colour pass in the space between, the eye becomes filled with vision and now sees, and becomes, not vision, but a seeing eye; while the other parent of the colour is saturated with whiteness and becomes on its side, not whiteness, but a white thing. (156DE, *TH*)

The view of visual perception set forth in this passage, which pictures the eye and the physical object as producing through their interaction a third thing, the sense quality, was similar in many ways to the common opinion about visual perception in Greek philosophy. John Beare[7] has shown that the belief in the eye containing an inner fire which, when it comes into contact with streams of flame similar to it emanating from the object, results in sight, was a belief held in common by Alcmaeon of Crotona, Empedocles (with some variations), Democritus, and Plato. In the *Timaeus* (45B) Plato pictures the eye as being fashioned with a gentle fire, and seeing is accounted for by the meeting of this inward fire, as it streams out of the eye, with some like fire or light.

When the light of day surrounds the stream of vision, then like falls on like, and they coalesce, and one body is formed by natural affinity in the line of vision, wherever the light that falls from within meets with an external object. And the whole stream of vision, being similarly affected in virtue of similarity, diffuses the motions of what it touches or what touches it over the whole body, until they reach the soul, causing that perception which we call sight.

Ingenuous as it is, such an account of vision is by no means complete. There are several important factors in this account which are not explained. As Rivaud points out,

Platon ne s'explique ni sur la façon dont la lumière peut s'échapper continuellement de l'œil, sans s'épuiser, ni sur les conditions dans lesquelles elle rencontre, pour s'unir à elle, la lumière qui émane des objets. D'autre part, quel est le rôle de la lumière du soleil, dans la vision? D'après le mythe de la *République*, les objets n'ont pas de lumière propre: ils ne font que réfléchir la lumière solaire. En est-il de même, dans le *Timée*? (p. 105, *RT*)

II   THE NATURE OF SENSE-DATA AND THEIR CAUSES

Like many contemporary epistemologists, Plato has concentrated upon visual sense-data in the analysis of perception, but he indicates in the *Theaetetus* that the same account should be extended to all other sense qualities.

And so too, we must think in the same way of the rest—'hard,' 'hot,' and all of them—that no one of them has any being just by itself (as we said

[7]Beare, John, *Greek Theories of Elementary Cognition.*

before), but that it is in their intercourse with one another that all arise in all their variety as a result of their motion. (157A, *TH*)[8]

Similarly, at 156A, where he is describing the way in which the pairs of twin motions (the sense qualities and the perceptions) arise, he lists "seeing," "hearing," "smelling," "feeling cold," "feeling hot" as perceptions, indicating that each of these has its corresponding percept. He includes in this list also pleasures and pains, desires and fears, suggesting that the same kind of perceptual theory applies to the internal senses as to the external. The problem of the external sense qualities is made complex by these extensions, since Plato does not work out the details of the relation of "belonging to" of these other sense qualities. It is easy to see how Plato's theory can maintain that all sense qualities, of no matter what sense organ, arise only upon the occasion of the appropriate external stimulus meeting a specific condition of a given sense organ. In his account of vision, sense qualities are clearly pictured as being causally and existentially dependent upon both organ and physical object. But the interesting aspect of this theory is that the object, which was asserted as having no perceptible qualities in and by itself apart from perception, is now asserted to take on the sense quality which it helps generate in perception. In other words, the causally and existentially dependent sense quality becomes a part of the physical object. This identification at the moment of perception is understandable in the case of visual data, since Plato's theory of vision pictured the eye sending out streams of fire which meet similar streams coming from the object, the coalescence of which diffuses the object with the resulting product. But the identification is more difficult to see in the case of the other sense qualities. His account of the sense of touch, for example, given in the *Timaeus*, presents the common Greek notion that this sense modality extends all over the surface of the body and that tactile sense qualities are produced by the contact in the pores of the skin with particles travelling from external objects. The quality "hot" is a result of the sharp, piercing angles of fire particles entering our skin. The opposite, "cold," is a result of fluid particles

[8]This statement is rather confusing since Plato seems to be saying that "hard," "soft," "hot," and all other sense qualities arise in "their intercourse with one another." Such a statement is obviously false, for how could the sense qualities arise in their intercourse with one another, when it is *their* genesis we wish to explain? I infer consequently, that Plato meant to say that all sense qualities arise out of the intercourse of motions, as he has described in the case of vision. However, since an analysis of the other qualities (in the *Timaeus*) contradicts or limits this inference (since qualities other than vision are not presented there as entailing the twofold motion of object and subject), I may be placing the wrong construction upon this particular passage.

entering our skin and thrusting out the particles which are smaller than they and contracting the areas thus left vacant. The result is that these areas, which are naturally apart, struggle and shake in their efforts to resume their natural state. "This struggling and shaking is called trembling and shivering: and the name 'cold' is given to this affection as a whole and to the agent producing it." (62B, *T*)

In the case of these qualities, they are predicated of both agent and patient, whereas colour was restricted to the agent only. Hot and cold are both affections of the perceiver, the patient, *and* qualities of the objects, the agents, producing these affections. Unlike the eye which becomes a "seeing eye" and perceives colour *in* objects, the skin may become a "touching skin" but it feels and experiences as a part of its own nature the qualities thus perceived. The observer does not become red in visual perception of that colour but he does seem to become hot or cold in these tactual perceptions. This is a fundamental difference between visual and tactual qualities like hot and cold, but the outwardness or inwardness of sense qualities does not make any difference in Plato's contention that such qualities are relative to perceivers and to external objects. The external object can still be said to be hot or cold only at the moment of perception, but this quality is no longer uniquely the quality *of* the object of perception.[9] Moreover, there are no particles going out from the organ of touch to meet the incoming particles. The particles of fire come completely up to the organ of touch and penetrate inwards. This is also true of Plato's account of taste and sound in the *Timaeus*. A further difficulty is introduced in this extension of the account of perception presented in the *Theaetetus* by Plato's account of the qualities "hard" and "soft." These, he says in the *Timaeus*, are qualities which are purely relative to the resistance of our flesh. " 'Hard' is applied to anything to which our flesh yields, 'soft' to anything that yields to flesh . . . and hard and soft things are also so called with reference to one another." (62B, *T*) Cornford interprets this to mean that apart from any percipient, objects can be called hard and soft in relation to each other. In other words, whereas hot and cold, or any colour, belongs to a physical object only in relation to human observers, hard and soft belong to physical objects in relation to other physical objects. Hard and soft are also not applied to the patient at the time of perception, but only to the agent, the object. Thus, in one sense these qualities are more like visual

9Cf. Price, *Perception*, p. 229: "all normal tactual sense-data belong to two objects at once, viz. to the object which we are touching, and to our own body or some part of it."

qualities than like hot and cold; in another sense they differ in that an object can have these qualities apart from human perception. But even so, these qualities still do not belong to the object permanently: they are relational, although the relation does not have to involve human observers, and it is a relation which is just as changing as is the human relation.

Sense qualities of taste and sound are like those of vision and hard and soft, since they are essentially qualities of the objects and not of the observer, even though such qualities have a more intimate relationship with the observer in that the observer is directly aware of experiencing some alteration in his own condition at the moment of perception. Again, the sensations are due to external particles entering the organ, in the case of tastes, the tongue, and of sounds, the ear. Different tastes are caused by varying degrees of roughness or smoothness in these particles. Astringent tastes are due to rough particles, while acrid tastes are due to smoother particles cleansing the small veins of the tongue. Again, the sense qualities are, in a certain sense, predicated of both organ and object, but as belonging to the observer or the sense organ, the different tastes are affections, while the object tasted is said to be astringent, acrid, pungent, etc. Sound is identified with "the stroke inflicted by air on the brain and blood through the ears and passed on to the soul; while the motion it causes starting in the head and ending in the region of the liver, is hearing." (67AB, *T*) Cornford interprets Plato as saying that there are two motions; the external motion of the air caused by the instrument, the sound proper, and the internal motion which constitutes hearing. As in hard and soft, the quality of sound is identified with the object rather than with the agent, but the agent undergoes a definite affection. Moreover, were there no appropriate ear, there would be no sound.

Thus, of the sense qualities of vision, of touch, of taste, and of sound,[10] we can say first, that those of vision, sound, taste, and those of touch which deal with hardness and softness are similar to one another in that at the moment of perception they belong only to the physical object. The object becomes red, or loud, or hard, or sweet at that moment, and the sense quality thus belonging to the object depends for its existence upon both the object to which it now belongs

---

[10]I have not dealt with sense qualities of odours since they add additional complexities which are unimportant for the development of the general theory. Plato thought that odours could not be caused by any object in its normal state, but arose only "from substances in process of being liquified or decomposed or dissolved or evaporated. They occur in the intermediate stage when water is changing into air or air into water." (66DE, T)

and upon the sense organ which perceives it. Second, the qualities of heat and cold differ from these in that they belong to both organ and object. The first class of sense qualities differs radically from the second in this respect. Moreover, the mode of generation of all sense qualities, with the exception of visual ones, is the result of a one-way causal chain extending from the external physical cause to the sense organ. In vision alone, the causal action works both ways, and the sense quality arises not near the organ, as is the case with each of the other qualities, but mid-way between it and the external cause. And, finally, in every case Plato means for us to separate the affection of the agent from the quality perceived or felt.

With reference to this last point, Cornford refers to the testimony of Theophrastus that one of the main points of difference between Democritus' and Plato's perceptual theories was that "Democritus reduced all *sensa* to 'affections of the sense which undergoes alteration', whereas Plato did not deprive them of their independent reality." (p. 261, *PC*) In our survey of Plato's analysis of the organs of sense—touch, taste, and sound—we have found this separation being maintained, even in those cases where the quality is predicated of both organ and the object. For Democritus and many other pre-Socratics, sensation involved external causes striking the senses and producing in the organ certain affections or feelings which were the objects perceived. For Plato, the sense qualities present in perception are objective, even though they are causally and existentially dependent in part upon the sense organs of the observer. Taylor interprets Plato to mean that the sense qualities in perception are wholly objective and independent of the sense organ, asserting that "the objective fact of which we are directly aware in the sensation itself is 'that our flesh is being lacerated or pierced by the "hot" body,'" but this is clearly a wrong interpretation. (Quoted by Cornford, p. 261, *PC*) Hot is one of those qualities which Plato ascribes to both the organ and the object, but the quality of hotness would never arise were it not for the combined action of the external object and the appropriate condition of the appropriate sense modality. The sense qualities present in perception are objective for Plato, but not because they are independent of the observer. Their objectivity is limited by being partially dependent upon the observer who perceives them, but they are objective in that at the moment of perception, they belong to the object. We have followed his account of visual perception given in the *Theaetetus* and have seen that although the external object is not white prior to perception, it becomes "saturated" with whiteness when it is perceived and becomes a "white thing." As Cornford recognizes, Plato speaks "as if the object acquired, for so long as it is perceived, a quality which it does not possess at other times." (p. 261, *PC*) In his commentary on the *Theaetetus*, Cornford suggests that what Plato means is that the "flame or light belonging to the object cannot until this moment [the moment of perception] be called 'colour' or 'white'." (p. 50, *PTK*) Plato's analysis of the qualities other than vision in the *Timaeus* strongly supports the verbal predication suggested by Cornford. Plato repeatedly speaks of the cause of tastes, or of heat and cold as being "called" pungent, acrid, or hot, when the observer directly experiences heat or a pungent taste, etc. If this is Plato's meaning, he would be saying that objects cause certain affections in observers which lead to certain verbal ascriptions concerning the objects. He would not be asserting that ontologically the object became white, or hot, or hard, at the moment of perception. Certain motions entering the sense organs produce in the soul of the observer reactions which lead to certain verbal utterances, descriptive of the experiences of the observer. There is a difference between the following two statements: (1) X *is* white and hot but only for me from this position; (2) X is *said to be* white and hot because I am now experiencing white and hot. In the second of these statements, the object, even in relation to me, need only be certain causal powers leading me to have the experiences I am now having. It becomes a purely verbal convenience to transfer the contents of my feelings and experiences to the object and assert that it is white and hot. But the first statement asserts that even though the qualities of the object which are perceived are dependent upon a perceiver, they nevertheless are objective and belong to the object. The distinction between statement 1 and statement 2 is the difference between Plato and Democritus again. It seems dubious that this could be Plato's meaning, since he so clearly asserts statement 1 in the *Theaetetus*. Cornford is closer to the truth in the *Timaeus* commentary when he quotes Theophrastus than he is in the *Theaetetus* commentary when he asserts that Plato means to say that objects can be called white at the moment of perception. Not only are they called white, they are white at that time and for that observer. In some way which I try to make more precise later in this chapter, Plato asserts that the perceived qualities are a part of the physical object they are partially caused by. Extended to the sense-data of all the sense modalities, we can say that the object is white, hot, hard, loud, etc., in the perceptual relation, and only in that relation, with the exception already noted that Plato allows hard and soft to belong to objects in their relations with other physical objects.

Thus all of these sense qualities belong to the physical object momentarily at the time of perception. This means, as Cornford has noted, that the object acquires qualities in perception which it does not have otherwise. Plato asserts in the *Theaetetus* that the physical object by itself has none of the qualities which we perceive: these are all products of perception. But Plato did not mean to deny that physical objects do have some qualities. His point is that the object as known does not reveal any of these objective, non-sensible characteristics. The known object is the object endowed with the qualities and characteristics which have arisen as a result of the interaction of physical motion and sense motion. Shorey[11] describes the physical object of this theory in Mill's terms, as a permanent possibility of sensation, but it is clearly more than this. We know it has causal characteristics capable of helping to generate sense qualities, but we know still more about the physical object. Both the physical object and the sense organs are capacities of acting and being acted upon, and Cornford is correct when he points out that "this capacity must imply that my pen and this paper have some difference of property when not perceived, which would explain why, when I do see them, the pen looks black and the paper white." (p. 50, *PTK*) The fact that physical objects are motions which do exist when no interaction is going on, motions which are giving off streams of flame, and apparently particles of earth,[12] both prior and posterior to perception, indicates that they have some nature of their own. In the *Timaeus*, where the four primary bodies are constructed and where their transformations are described (53c–58c), these bodies appear to have qualities of their own independent of human perception, even if these be only geometrical properties. In his discussion of these primary figures, Cornford calls attention to the fact that Plato speaks of the contents of these basic figures as qualities or motions and powers.

The whole description of the warfare of the primary bodies in the process of transformation implies that these powers are actively operating. Without them the geometrical figures could not move at all or break one another down. The qualities are evidently conceived as existing in the primary bodies

---

[11]*What Plato Said*, p. 272.

[12]Whether the physical-object motions are constantly emitting particles of earth as well as streams of flame is not clear in the dialogues, but I see no reason to think that Plato meant otherwise. He would have a special problem on his hands if he tried to maintain that another causal relation sprang into being in perception which suddenly caused earth bodies to start emitting particles and to cease to do so when perception ceased. Such a view may be tenable and Plato may have held it, but we cannot determine this from the dialogues, so I choose to follow the former interpretation.

quite independently of the sensations and perceptions of any possible observer. (p. 229, *PC*)

Similarly, Rivaud, in his edition of the *Timaeus* says, "La théorie des figures élémentaires est destinée à expliquer comment l'ordre s'introduit dans le chaos mouvant des qualités. Par leurs propriétés définies et invariables, ces figures mettent une certaine fixité dans le devenir." (p. 80, *RT*) Since the physical objects of ordinary perception are composed out of the four primary bodies, we can infer that the physical causes of our various sensations have properties in themselves not unlike the geometrical properties of the primary bodies. This is amply supported by the discussion of the various sense qualities and their mode of production in the *Timaeus*.

For example, in discussing the quality "hot," Plato remarks that

we are all aware that the sensation [of fire] is a piercing one; and we may infer the fineness of the edges, the sharpness of the angles, the smallness of the particles, and the swiftness of the movement, all of which properties make fire energetic and trenchant, cleaving and piercing whatever it encounters. (61DE, *T*)

These are objects of inference and not of sensation. Likewise, while discussing the qualities of hard and soft, Plato makes the following remark:

A thing is yielding when it has a small base; the figure composed of square faces, having a firm standing, is most stubborn; so too is anything that is specially resistant because it is contracted to the greatest density. (62C, *T*)

These again are remarks concerning properties which are never sensed. In general, the causal explanation of the genesis of sense qualities presented in this section of the *Timaeus* attests to the fact that the physical causes of qualities have properties of their own which are never sensed, since in each case, the taste, the sound, or the tactile quality which is sensed is correlated with certain very definite microscopic structures in the physical causes external to the observer. Moreover, in the description of chaos in the *Timaeus*, we are told that "fire, water, earth, and air possessed indeed some vestiges of their own nature, but were altogether in such a condition as we should expect for anything when deity is absent from it." (53B, *T*) Plato is saying that, even if there had been men about in chaos to observe, they would not have been able to recognize these fundamental characters because they were so disorganized that they did not exemplify their true form. It was necessary for the god to step in and give these four primary elements "a distinct configuration by means of shapes and numbers," before they were able to take the shape by which they are commonly known. The structural properties of physical objects are necessary for the existence of their sensible qualities.

But a complication is introduced by this reference to the movement, out of chaos into order, of earth, air, fire, and water. These four are the primary elements of the world, but they are described also as the "qualities" which pass in and out of the receptacle. As such, they are contrasted with the receptacle which is permanent, while they are in constant motion, continually changing into one another, never standing still long enough to be designated as "this" or "that." The proper designation for these four primary elements, apart from their added structural characteristics, is "what is of such and such a quality." Like the sense qualities in the *Theaetetus,* these qualities are in flux. As characterizing the receptacle, these elements are described as being copies of Forms. (50B, *T*) Cornford insists that the copy referred to here is not the geometrical shapes of the fundamental bodies, but their qualitative, visible nature—visible, he argues, in that if someone were around, they would experience the familiar colours, sounds, etc., of fire, water, earth, air. At 61c Plato points out that he has been talking about the primary bodies and their various combinations with one another, and that he is now going to "try to make clear how it is that they come to have their qualities." Then follows the description of the qualities of the several sense organs which I have presented above. Cornford reads Plato as saying at this juncture that the previous account of the primary bodies has been conducted as if they were taken apart from sensation when after all "their properties could not be mentioned save in terms implying our perception and so anticipating the account, which has not yet been given, of the organs of sense and the sentient part of the soul." (p. 258, *PC*) But Cornford's own translation fails to support this interpretation.

Clarification of this particular passage is important for understanding the ontological status of sense-data in this theory, since the whole question of just what it is that is a copy of intelligible Forms passing in and out of the receptacle hinges upon this point. If Cornford is correct in his interpretation, then the Form is an archetype of the familiar, visible fire, water, earth, and air; the Form is not an archetype of the geometrical shapes of these bodies.

What we perceive is a certain combination of shifting qualities in a certain place at a certain time—the yellowness we see, the hotness we feel. Such a combination, whenever and wherever it occurs, is sufficiently 'alike' for us to name it 'fire,' and it is a fleeting copy or impress of an unchanging model. (p. 190, *PC*)

The copy, then, is the aggregate of sense-data comprising the familiar elements, the aggregate and not the separate individual sense-data composing the family. But is it possible to have a Form of fire, for example, which does not include all the qualities of fire? Even if the answer is negative, there is a very definite sense in which "yellowness," for example, would not have a Form, since there would be no *separate* Form for it alone. But if the Form of fire under which this particular quality is classed includes all the qualities of fire, yellowness would be taken care of in the intelligible world. Then, indirectly, at least, we could say that all sense qualities are copies of Forms. If all bodies are composed of these four primary bodies, in both their structural and sensible features, as the *Timaeus* clearly says, and if these primary bodies, in their sensible features, are copies of Forms, then another causative factor has been added to the generation of sense-data in Plato's expanded theory of perception. Not only are these features, in their recognizable shapes and patterns, dependent upon the structural features[13] and upon human observers with their appropriate sense organs, but they depend as well upon the Forms or upon the impression of the Forms. If we read the *Timaeus* as consisting of statements of ontology and not of logic alone, and if Cornford's interpretation of 61c is correct, Plato means to say, by the reference to Form and copy, that this relation has an important bearing upon the ontological status of sense-data. At least he would mean that sense-data are dependent upon the Forms existentially, if not causally. Just what the precise meaning of this relation is depends upon how we understand the theory of Forms itself. But some meaning would have to be given to this relation of sense qualities and Forms before we could fill out his general theory of perception.

However valid an interpretation this account may be, the transition at 61c seems to me to be misinterpreted by Cornford. What Plato seems to be saying at this point is that now he is going to turn to another topic, the way in which these primary bodies and their various combinations "come to have their qualities," where qualities means "sense qualities." This account will have to assume the human observer, since, as we have seen, a necessary condition for the existence of sense qualities is human sense organs. This account of the various

---

[13]Notice that there is an important sense in which these sensible qualities are independent of the structural features and exist, at least logically, prior to the structural features. Cf. with his account of chaos, *Timaeus*, 52D–53C.

qualities of sense is a causal explanation of these qualities involving the structural features of objects and the sense organs of men. If this is a new topic, what aspects of the primary bodies has he been considering up to this point in the *Timaeus*? Cornford gives the clue to the proper answer when he points out, as previously noted, that qualities which pass in and out of the receptacle (fire, water, earth, air) are also referred to as powers. In other words, Plato has been considering this aspect of the primary bodies in their *potential* capacities, their capacities to produce effects upon other bodies and upon human observers.[14] Cornford is correct, in so far as he says that the previous account of the primary bodies has been conducted as if there were men around to experience their powers (although this is not what Plato says at 61c); but I would suggest that Cornford is wrong when he says that the "things" which are copies of Forms are fire, earth, water, and air *as seen and experienced*. If he means to say that the copies are these various bodies in their potential capacities, then I would suggest he is correct, even though I am not sure it makes sense to say a potential power can be a copy of an intelligible Form. However, it is certain that in the absence of observers, the primary bodies would not exhibit any of the qualities they have when there are observers. The doctrine of the *Theaetetus* has ruled out any such unsensed sensibilia. But since the description of chaos presents fire, earth, water, and air as existing, if only in a hardly recognizable condition, and since the description of chaos precedes and is itself meant to precede the imposition of the geometrical patterns upon these basic bodies, it seems evident that independent of observers, the primary bodies consist of (1) certain powers or potentialities, and (2) definite structural characteristics. In the presence of observers, a third aspect of physical objects arises, namely, (3) the sense-data which become a part of the object at the moment of perception. These three characteristics would constitute a complete definition of a physical object for Plato. The actualization of 1 in their normal or usual conditions, that is the transformation of 1 into 3, is dependent upon human observers with their sense organs, as well as upon 2, the structural features. The demiurge had to impose 2 upon 1 before fire, earth, water, and air could assume recognizable form. But in the absence of 2, 1 would still exist as potentiality. It is 1 which Plato

[14]Rivaud's translation supports this interpretation, as indeed Cornford's own translation does. "Il faut maintenant nous efforcer de découvrir par quelles causes naissent les impressions que ces corps nous procurent. En effet, il faut bien toujours d'abord que les corps dont nous avons parlé possèdent le pouvoir de provoquer une sensation."

seems to be saying is the copies passing in and out of the receptacle; but, since it does not make much sense to speak of powers passing in and out, what his assertion amounts to probably is what Cornford says it does, the actualization of 1, which is 3. We could use Johnson's terminology and designate 1 a determinable and 3 the determinates of 1, to indicate the potential capacity of the powers of physical objects and the way in which Plato asserts that these powers can be realized in multiple situations. A physical causal chain involving the structural properties (2), the powers or potentialities of bodies (1), and the sense organs of human observers is needed for the production of the determinates (3). In the case of vision, this chain works both ways, from 2 to 1 to the sense organs and from the sense organs to 1 to 2. In addition, we have to include in these causal chains, the relation of 1 to the Forms. In some way, which Plato leaves unspecified in the *Theaetetus* and the *Timaeus* (but which can be filled in by any explanation of the participation of sense particulars in the Forms), the Forms are also necessary for the existence or the realization of 1.

III SENSE-DATA AS MULTIPLY LOCATED QUALITIES OF PHYSICAL OBJECTS

The method employed by Plato in giving an exposition of his theory of perception in the *Theaetetus* was, as we have seen, a dialectical technique by which he sought to derive his own theory from elements of the positions of Protagoras and of Heraclitus. In the course of this development, we found that Cornford indicated a point at which Protagoras would probably depart from the later development of this theory: the point at which Plato makes the distinction between the wind and two sensations of the wind. Cornford suggests, and Brochard agrees,[15] that, to the question "is the wind in itself both hot and cold when we feel it to be so?" Protagoras would reply that the wind is really both hot and cold. This view is, as Cornford recognizes, an attempt to save naïve realism, the belief that objects do have the qualities we perceive. Assuming for the moment that Protagoras did hold this position, it will be profitable for a complete understanding of the theory which Plato advances, to examine the details of this position and set it in comparison with the position held by Plato in the *Theaetetus*.

The view which Cornford identifies with that held by Protagoras agrees "with the doctrine of Protagoras' contemporary Anaxagoras,

---

[15]Brochard, V., *Etudes de philosophie ancienne et de philosophie moderne*, chap. III.

who taught that opposite qualities (or things) such as 'hot' and 'cold'
co-exist inseparably in things outside us, and that perception is by
contraries." (p. 34, *PTK*) Cornford thinks that the position held by
Protagoras and Anaxagoras was in the general Ionian tradition which
trusted the senses, opposed to the Eleatic position which made a
separation between the senses and real knowledge. Sextus supports
Cornford in this interpretation, since he testifies that

Protagoras says that matter contains the underlying grounds of all appearances, so that matter considered as independent can be all the things that
appear to all. Men apprehend different things at different times according
to variations in their conditions. One in a normal state apprehends those
things in matter which can appear to a normal person; a man in an abnormal
state apprehends what can appear to the abnormal. The same applies to
different times of life, to the states of sleeping and waking, and to every sort
of condition. So man proves, according to him, to be the criterion of what
exists: everything that appears to man also exists; what appears to no man
does not exist.[16]

It is clear from this statement that, if Protagoras did hold this theory,
he is saying that all of the qualities ever sensed by man and associated
with a given object already belonged to that object prior to sensation.
Man is the selector of various qualities or aspects of the object under
various conditions and at different times, but the qualities are causally
and existentially independent of man the selector. Cornford points
out that at this time in history such properties as hot and cold, "were
regarded as 'things'," not as qualities needing some other "thing" to
possess and support them. Thus, Protagoras would "deny that the wind
was anything more than the sum of these properties which alone
appear to us," and hence it (and all other physical objects) consists
of a group of unsensed sensibilia, since physical objects exist apart
from observers in the same condition as when an observer is present.
(p. 35, 36, *PTK*) The result of such a theory of the nature of physical
objects and of our perceptions of them is that physical objects are
defined in terms of large, perhaps infinite, groups or series of sensible
qualities which exist unperceived. The fact that the group is so large,
and that man's knowledge of this group is constantly growing, does
not mean that Protagoras has to be committed to the extension which
Plato derives from his theory, namely, that the physical object is
itself in flux. Sextus, however, and Brochard credit Protagoras with
holding to the flux doctrine. According to Sextus, matter for Protagoras

---

[16]"Pyrrh. Hyp." i, 218, quoted in Cornford, *PTK*, p. 35, n. 3; also in *Sextus
Empiricus*, ed. by J. G. Bury, vol. I, pp. 131–33.

is in flux "and as it flows additions are made continuously."[17] Brochard says, "la sensation changeant sans cesse, la réalité changeait avec elle."[18] If this is what Protagoras held, he is in close agreement with Plato, and Plato was justified in deriving this complication from the dictum of Protagoras. But Protagoras need not have held to this complication, for the physical object can be defined in terms of an infinite number of sensible qualities without, as a consequence, being itself in flux and constant change. Man's knowledge of the object does grow and develop; but there is no inconsistency in holding this doctrine concerning the infinitely large group of qualities composing a physical object and saying that the object nevertheless has an identity which is not the identity of a process. The object would be just that group of qualities which it is and no more. Even if this group is infinite, such a group would encompass the whole of the nature of the object. This would be its identity and there is no reason to suppose that all of these qualities would have to be in flux in order to belong to the object. In short, the statement, "X is in constant flux and motion," does not follow from the statement, "X is composed of an infinite number of qualities."

But whether or not Protagoras agreed with Plato in this respect, his analysis is in many ways identical with that of Plato. The main difference between the two theories lies in the fact that Plato is a dualist, in both the ontological and epistemological senses, while Protagoras is a monist in both senses. Physical objects for Plato are not reducible without remainder to groups of sense qualities, although such groups are an integral part of their nature. There is a structural aspect of physical objects which is never sensed and which is the partial cause of the sense qualities. But on the phenomenal level, Plato's analysis agrees with that of Protagoras, which is probably the explanation for Plato's deriving his theory from Protagoras. On this level, the level of perception, objects are defined by both men in terms of sense qualities. However, for Plato, these qualities do not belong to physical objects *simpliciter*, but only relationally, from a place and to an observer. Perhaps Plato found some difficulty in thinking of the same object actually having in itself qualities such as hot and cold, or round and square, which are usually thought of as incompatible. As it stands in Cornford's and Sextus' description, Protagoras' theory seems difficult to understand in this respect. How could the same object be, in itself, both hot and cold, or round and

[17]*Ibid.*
[18]*Etudes de philosophie ancienne et de philosophie moderne*, p. 25.

square, granting the possibility of unsensed sensibilia? The very idea of roundness excludes the idea of squareness, unless we add the qualification of "from a place" or "to someone." But Protagoras evidently was following the common tradition of the day which was capable of thinking of such qualities as existing together. Plato disagrees with this tradition, at least in his theory of perception. Where Protagoras sought to adhere to a straight naïve-realist position, taking even opposed qualities as belonging directly to the object and asserting the existence of unsensed sensibilia,[19] Plato advances a radically different theory of perception. The three fundamental differences are: (1) the physical object is not exhausted by its family of sense-data; (2) there are no unsensed sensibilia; and (3) all sensible qualities are causally and existentially dependent upon the observer and the structural features of the physical object.

Plato's theory is close to what has been called a "theory of appearing," but it asserts much more than the theory of appearing does, since, as we have seen, it claims that at the moment of perception the object does not merely appear such and such, but it *is* such and such.[20] The object does not appear to be red or hot, it is in fact red and hot, *but only from a place and to someone*. This important qualification brings Plato's theory of perception into close harmony with the multiple-location theory developed by Whitehead. The essence of this theory is this distinction between the qualities of an object which belong to it simply, in itself, and those which belong to it only from a place. On the perceptual level, Plato insists that objects are never anything in and by themselves: on this level, they are always what they are *to* someone or *for* someone.

Accordingly, whether we speak of something 'being' or of its 'becoming,' we must speak of it as being or becoming *for someone*, or of *something towards something*; but we must not speak, or allow others to speak, of a thing as either being or becoming anything just in and by itself. (160BC, *TH*)

This latter assertion is in part an overstatement since things do have

---

[19]Protagoras does not explicitly make an assertion concerning unsensed sensibilia, but if Cornford's interpretation of his theory is correct, sensibilia are implied by Protagoras' position. Neither is the assertion of unsensed sensibilia commonly associated with the naïve-realist position, but it is one of the ways in which such a position can be and has been defended.

[20]Brochard brings out the difference between Plato's theory and the theory of appearing, when he comments upon the *Theaetetus* that "il reste pourtant que cette existence du sensible, si fugitive qu'elle soit, est une existence: elle est autre chose et plus qu'une simple apparence subjective. C'est la matière qui, réellement et pour un moment, a pris telle forme, est devenue et est telle chose." (p. 27)

qualities apart from observers; but Plato is concerned in this section to drive home the novelty of his position concerning the perceptual level of objects. Even if Plato did mean this assertion to apply to *all things* in the universe, our analysis of the physical cause of sense qualities in the last section shows that Plato could not make this universal application and retain the important distinction between the sensible and the non-sensible features of physical objects. The modern version of the theory of multiple location, or of multiple inherence, attempts to define the qualities of an object in a similar fashion, as involving for the most part a triadic relation consisting of the pervading quality, the pervaded region, and what Broad has called the region of projection. The latter is nothing more than the particular perspective from which the human brain and nervous system views the so-called object. The qualities which are said to be inherent in the pervaded region are caused by the observer in the region of projection and, in some few cases—those which are not illusory—also certain characteristics located in the pervaded region. This theory allows for a great number of different qualities to belong to an object even though they seem to be opposed or contradictory. Any object has an infinite number of qualities and is never simply located here and now but takes its being *from* many different places. From the position of naïve realism, the most that this theory of multiple location seems to allow is a common objective constituent in the visual situations of many observers; but this constituent is a certain region of space which contains all those qualities which it appears to have to all the different observers viewing that region. In those cases which are not illusory, this region of space also contains "a set of microscopic physical events (movements of molecules, vibrations of electrons, etc.) which are the dependently necessary conditions for the pervasion of this region" by all those qualities.[21]

As Price has remarked, such a theory of perception combines most easily with what he has termed "the selective theory," where all of the multiply located qualities maintain their existence as unsensed sensibilia even when I shut off my senses. These unsensed sensibilia would all fit together "to constitute one unbroken, simple located, three dimensional surface."[22] However, it is clear that Plato's theory is not consistent with the selective interpretation of the multiple-location theory, since he has explicitly asserted that the qualities which *are* from various places, exist only temporarily when the combination of

[21]Broad, *The Mind and its Place in Nature*, pp. 163–164.
[22]Price, *Perception*, p. 56.

object-motion and sense-motion exists. Plato's theory really says that qualities inhere in a place not only *from* a place, but, to use a phrase of Price, "somato-centrically" from a place, indicating that they are of an evanescent nature and dependent upon a human organism for their existence.[23] But on either the selective or the connective interpretation of this theory,[24] Price finds it unsatisfactory as a theory of perception. To Price it is not evident that "one and the same entity can *both* be qualified from a place *and* be qualified simply or from no place." He argues that the visual and tactual qualities of an object are from a place, a particular point of view, but whether an object can have, as well, qualities from no place is not at all clear. It seems more reasonable to suppose that an object has all of its qualities wholly from a place. As we have seen, this is just what Plato asserted in the *Theaetetus* with respect to all sensible qualities, but he did say in the *Timaeus* (and such an assertion is implied by his account in the *Theaetetus*) that the structural, unperceivable qualities of the object are permanent characteristics of the physical object, existing independently of all observers. These must exist *simpliciter* and from no place. This aspect of the object is never known directly but only by inference. The object which is known is only the sense object, the single quality or the aggregate or family of sense-data; but for Plato the sense object becomes identified with the physical object at the moment of perception. The physical cause of these various sense objects has an existential independence of its own, but the sense objects have neither an existential nor a causal independence. The sense object is a fleeting product of two physical motions. But at the moment when it does exist, the sense quality would seem to pervade a region of space, or to pervade, inhere in, or saturate the area where the physical cause external to the observer is located. We cannot say, on this theory, that the sense quality ever is at a place simply, but only that it is from a place and for someone. Moreover, on Plato's version, we are not allowed to think of the place occupied as a fixed place which has permanent being; there is no single place which is *the* place of a given sense-datum. Like the sense-data themselves, the places of sense-data change with every new generation. More precisely, each sense-datum

---

[23]The sense qualities of hard and soft are exceptions to this somato-centric qualification, since they take their existence from a place occupied by other physical objects. They are still qualities which inhere in objects only from a certain perspective, but the perspective is not a human one in all cases.

[24]The connective interpretation is Price's way of designating the dependence or connection between the observer and the sense-data, as opposed to the selective form in which the qualities are independent of observers.

and its place is something quite definite and determinate, but since no sense-datum exists for more than a fleeting moment, the place of each datum is likewise just as fleeting. In fact, what Plato seems to be saying is that there are a series of places to match the series of sense-data. But he has said that the sense-data are parts of or belong to the physical cause at the moment of perception. If this relation of belonging to is one of identity, sense-data would have to be located in the places of their respective structural causes. This fact would entail the structural features, the physical motions, having no single fixed place either. Plato does make a further assertion concerning the constant movement of physical causes of sense-data: on his theory, the entire world is, as we have seen, motion. But since sense-data are multiply located qualities of physical objects, the places of the sense-data and of the physical structural causes must be identical or else the sense-data would not belong to their physical causes, if we take this relation as one of identity. However, difficulties arise as soon as the assertion of this identity of place is made, an assertion which Plato nowhere makes but one which he is committed to make if he means to interpret the relation of belonging to between sense-data and physical causes as the naïve realist would. Something very like the problem encountered by Price, when he turned sense-data into ontological entities defining the space of physical occupants, arises here for Plato. Space is a troublesome feature for any dualist who thinks of his substance as having spatial properties.

If it were possible, as is the case in hallucinations and the like, to experience all the sense-data we normally do experience without there being any physical cause involved in their generation; if, that is, something like phenomenalism were true, sense-data would exemplify spatial relations among themselves. If we assume a relational theory of space, we would say that such data have spatial relations. If we take an absolute theory of space, we would then say that these sense-data are located *in* space. On either view, there would be a space which was the space of sense-data. Where we introduce into our theory of perception a physical cause with definite structural characteristics which are unsensed, we have to find a location for this new factor since such causes presumably could not operate *in vacuo*. Here again, we can assume either a relational or an absolute space, and in either event, these physical, structural causes would have spatial relations. But it is at this point that a problem arises: what is the relation between the space of sense-data and the space of these physical causes? Are they identical or different? On a relational theory of space, it may be possible to have the space of sense-data and the space of their physical causes identical, providing we find no difficulty in saying that sense-data, which are private and fleeting, can be related spatially to unperceivable, permanent causes. The difference in the mode of existence between sense-data and physical causes, on a theory such as is advanced by Plato, might lead, on either theory of space, to the postulation of two spaces, a perceptual and a physical space. The fact that the one aspect of the object is multiply located only from points of view, while the other is simply located from no point of view, would seem to necessitate having two areas of space. But when we say, as Plato does, that the sense-data become parts of the physical cause at the moment of perception, is this not presupposing only one space, even in the absolute sense? To see how Plato answers these questions in his theory, or to decide how he might answer them, it is first necessary to examine his conception of space.

For most commentators, the receptacle of the *Timaeus* embodies Plato's concept of space. The receptacle is actually identified with space by Plato at 52B. Prior to this identification, the receptacle is described in various ways. It is introduced in the discussion when the narrator is ready to describe the production of physical bodies, the objects of everyday experience. As Rivaud points out in his edition of the *Timaeus*, "La théorie du lieu et celle des éléments n'interviendront que d'une manière incidente, et seulement dans la mesure où elles permettent de comprendre certains faits relatifs à la perception." (p. 64, *RT*) Plato then proceeds to describe the receptacle as the nurse of becoming (49A); as that which has a permanent being, in opposition to the transitory existence of the qualities which characterize it for appearance, and as being that *in which* becoming takes place (49E–50A); as the matrix of change (50C); as a mother, providing only the place for the offspring of the Forms (50D); as being free from all qualities but capable of taking on any quality (50DE); as invisible, characterless, all-receiving, and partaking of the intelligible in some strange way (51B); and, finally, as space, or that which provides a situation for becoming and that which is known only by a bastard reasoning (52B). The metaphors of the gold substance and the various objects which can be made out of gold, and the perfume base which is free from all odours before the desired odours are instilled into it, are employed to help convey the meaning Plato wishes to attach to the receptacle. From the outset, we must realize that the first of these metaphors is misleading if we take Plato to mean that the objects which become in the receptacle are made out of the

material of the receptacle. The receptacle is not matter, despite the
fact that Zeller, Robin, and Gaston Milhaud interpret it in this way.[25]
This interpretation, as Rivaud and Cornford suggest, seems to result
from taking the first metaphor too literally. On the other hand, if we
take the second metaphor in a literal way, we arrive at the conclusion
that the receptacle is a permanent substance underlying all change.
For Rivaud, neither conclusion is the one intended by Plato. Rivaud
rejects as well the interpretation which sees in the receptacle the
empty space, the void, of earlier pre-Socratic philosophers.

Pointing out that Greek geometers and atomists had "raisonné de
l'espace avec une précision qui ne laisse rien à désirer" and that "la
physique la plus ancienne s'était efforcée" to define the nature of matter
and to enumerate all of its properties, Rivaud argues, "Si Platon avait
simplement voulu nous faire entendre qu'il s'agit soit de l'espace vide,
soit de la substance matérielle des choses, peut-on admettre qu'il y
eût trouvé tant de difficulté?" (p. 68, RT) The receptacle is not, for
Rivaud, a new entity introduced into the discussion of the Timaeus.
"Le lieu n'a pas de réalité propre: ce n'est pas, à proprement parler,
une substance nouvelle, s'ajoutant aux deux substances du Devenir et
des Formes." (p. 68, RT) "Le lieu" is logically implicated in the
separation of the elements, in virtue of the fact that no two elements
can exist in the same place or can occupy the same position. The
receptacle is necessary in order to make the distinction between the
elements possible. Moreover, Rivaud does not believe that Plato
intended the receptacle to pre-exist, in a temporal sense, the elements.
The concept arises out of Plato's attempt to explain the nature of
becoming, to give a likely, rational account. For Rivaud, the receptacle
is more a logical, methodological fact than an ontological ingredient
of the world.

Le terme de χώρα avait alors servi à désigner non point tant l'espace que
l'intervalle logique qui sépare les contraires. Dans le Timée même, il est
soucieux de maintenir, malgré les emprunts auxquels il condescend, l'unité
et la continuité de sa pensée.[26]

The fact that the receptacle is the factor of necessity in the account
of the world suggests this interpretation to Rivaud, for the term

[25]The case of Zeller is well known. Robin clearly identifies himself with
Zeller's position in a footnote in his Platon, where he praises Zeller's interpretation
for connecting the extension of Descartes with the matter of Plato in the Timaeus
(p. 234, n. 1). He also refers to Milhaud's Les Philosophes-géomètres de la Grèce,
where the same position is maintained. Rivaud has given a thorough discussion and
refutation of this interpretation in his Le Problème du devenir, pp. 297–303.
[26]Le Problème du devenir, p. 311.

"necessity" in Plato's writings is usually applied to the necessity which attaches to the nature of something, without which that something would not be what it is. For example, "étant donnée la nature humaine, elle comporte des désirs inévitables, faute desquels l'essence même de l'homme ne pourrait pas être réalisée." (p. 65, *RT*) In the same way,

L'intervention de la cause nécessaire est inévitable, partout où elle rencontre une pluralité de termes, susceptibles de former un Tout. Par suite, elle doit se produire même à l'intérieur du Monde idéal et du Vivant en soi. C'est en vertu de la nécessité, que ni le Multiple, ni l'Un ne pourront exister séparément en un sens absolu, mais devront se mêler, selon des lois régulières, pour former un Univers. (p. 65, *RT*)

Reading the *Sophist* as asserting that "L'Idée de l'Autre" is necessary to provide for the connection and the separation both of the Forms and of different genres of being, Rivaud gives to the receptacle a similar function. From a physical point of view, "la nature du lieu va permettre, de même, la distinction des objets et leur alternance en une même place. La théorie du lieu apparaît, dans le *Timée*, comme la transposition physique d'une théorie dialectique." For Rivaud the elementary figures become Platonic Ideas encrusted with sense qualities, intermediaries between the pure ideas and the sensible world. The elementary, geometrical figures, in other words, make participation possible.

This interpretation of the receptacle tends to take it out of the physical world altogether and make of it a logical concept necessitated by the combination of the Forms and becoming. But if Plato meant to write a cosmology, as Rivaud credits him in his *Le Problème du devenir,* such an interpretation plays down the ontological aspects of the receptacle. The receptacle is introduced as preparatory to presenting the physical generation of perception. Thus, it would seem to have some status more tangible than that accorded it in Rivaud's interpretation. If the receptacle is necessary to account for physical perception, it must itself have some physical status. Rivaud recognizes this in his earlier book where he describes the receptacle as the theatre in which becoming is accomplished, "l'abîme immense et béant, dans lequel les formes vont s'ordonner," where he concludes that "pour la première fois, la spéculation des atomistes a séparé l'espace des réalités qui le remplissent."[27] But what kind of space is the χώρα ? For Demos, the receptacle is not space, "if we mean a pattern of definite positions," since Plato has explicitly designated it as indeterminate.

[27]*Ibid*, p. 314.

Definiteness is a product of the impression of the forms upon the receptacle. The receptacle can only be the potency of a definite space in which definite things occupy definite positions; as such it is indefinite extendedness. . . . The receptacle is wholly indeterminate; therefore, it can be identified neither with physical space, which is a definite pattern of positions, nor with actual motion, which is a measurable phenomenon. It must be rather construed as the potency of matter, and of space, and of physical motions; as that which, when impressed by the pattern, becomes matter, space, motion.[28]

If Demos is correct in these observations, we are again confronted with the problem of conceiving of a potency as existing prior to its actuality, since Plato has said that the receptacle is eternal. Although the receptacle provides a seat, a locus, or situation for events, it is not defined in terms of them. Although it is described as being wholly without qualities or characteristics, in order to be designatable at all it must have some being apart from the elements which give it recognizable shape and form. Can a potency fulfil this requirement?

Our analysis of Plato's theory of perception has revealed that prior to perception, the physical-object motions, the flame and earth particles and their structural characteristics, are in existence or, better, are in becoming. Since all becoming must, according to the *Timaeus*, take place somewhere, these physical-object motions, which are never sensed, must have a location. If the receptacle is the locus of all becoming, the physical-object motions must exist in the receptacle. If Demos is correct in saying that the receptacle is space only when it is qualified, we can now say that the receptacle becomes space independently of human observers, since the physical-object motions must qualify, in some way, the indeterminate receptacle. Thus, while the interpretation of the receptacle as potency might suggest that space for Plato is relative to perception in that the receptacle becomes space only with the imposition of sensible qualities, the fact of the existence of physical-object motions or of microscopic particles in motion prior and posterior to perception, shows that space is not entirely relative to perception. But now the question which arises is how do these unsensed aspects of physical objects acquire spatial properties? Do they acquire spatial properties by being "located in" the receptacle, or by having a place from which they can obtain relations with other physical-object motions? If the former, the receptacle would seem to be absolute space, a container of events in the physical sense. But the phrase "located in" is ambiguous, for, if the receptacle is only potency, how can we say that physical-object motions are located in the recep-

28Demos, *The Philosophy of Plato*, p. 32.

tacle? Until the existence of physical-object motions, there is no actual space; with the genesis of such motions, space is generated also. We seem driven then to take the second alternative and say that the receptacle is not a physical factor "in which" events are located in a physical sense, but that it is a way of expressing the ability of events, such as physical-object motions or groups of sense-data, to take on spatial characteristics in their relations with one another. Rivaud's logical interpretation of the receptacle is thereby vindicated.

The potency which is the receptacle becomes, on this interpretation, a potency of becoming itself; but we must not identify the receptacle with becoming: the potential and the actual are distinct. The receptacle becomes, then, the logical principle whereby, as Rivaud pointed out, events can be distinguished from one another and can assume definite locations, these locations being defined in terms of the relations among the physical-object motions. Since sense-data for Plato become parts of the physical object during perception, he seems committed to saying that sense-data belong to the same spatial field as do the physical-object motions. But on a relational theory of space, can a sensible be spatially related to a non-sensible? If sense-data belong to the field of relations consisting of unsensed physical-object motions, would they not have to take on the status of unsensed sensibilia, since this spatial field is defined in terms of non-sensible relations? As I have remarked above, sense-data (that is, visual and tactual sense-data) do have spatial characteristics but, on the denial of unsensed sensibilia, these relations depend upon human perception. The spatial field of sense-data is defined in terms of sensible relations. From the fact that sense-data are fleeting and constantly changing, the spatial relations between sense-data, or between groups of sense-data, are not permanent, as are the spatial relations of the structural qualities of objects. The structural spatial relations are of course changing within themselves but, unlike sense-data which pass in and out of existence taking their spatial relations with them as they pass out, the structural characteristics are permanent if not stationary. The permanence of the spatial field of unsensed causes is a permanence in movement, but the fleetingness of the spatial field of sense-data consists of more than movement: it consists of generation and destruction. Thus, to identify the space of sense-data with the space of their physical causes necessitates overcoming these two discrepancies: the fleeting versus the permanent, the sensible versus the non-sensible definitions of spatial fields.

There is some question, however, as to whether relations were explicitly recognized by the Greeks, so that my suggested reading of a relational theory of space in conjunction with Plato's theory of perception may not be the view Plato intended. But even if we interpret the receptacle as providing the place *in which* qualities and geometrical properties take on spatial characteristics, the same kind of problems arise. If the sense-data and their physical causes are situated in the same area of the spatial receptacle, there is some difficulty in conceiving of such fleeting and such permanent factors of physical objects belonging to the same area. There is also the difficulty of understanding how a factor which has its existence only when sensed can be located in the same place as those factors which are unsensible. On either interpretation of Plato's theory of space, the problems are the same although their solutions might turn out to be different on one interpretation rather than the other. Plato, however, was not aware of these problems and consequently did not work out any proposed solution. The whole of the discussion concerning the receptacle occupies only a very small section in the *Timaeus*, so that not only can we not be certain of his interpretation of the receptacle, and hence of his meaning of space, but it is impossible to determine how he would deal with this problem of the spatial location of sense-data. What is certain is that he distinguished two different aspects of all physical objects: the sensible aspect and the structural, non-sensible aspect. In addition, it is certain that he meant to identify the product of perception (the sense quality), especially of visual and tactual perception, with the non-sensible cause of this product. It is not clear from his writings just how this identity could be made, in view of the fact that the spatial relations of the two parts of physical objects appear to be so different. I am not sure we can bring together these two aspects of the physical object for Plato, but if we cannot achieve this spatial identity, sense-data will be located in a different space from the structural features of physical objects. Hence the relation of "belonging to" between sense-data and the structural features will have to be defined only causally and not as a spatial identity. If the bridge can be spanned so that the space of physical-object motions is identical with or overlaps the space of sense-data, then the conclusion Plato probably intended concerning this relation can be drawn: sense-data are related causally to the structural features of physical objects and also existentially, in the sense that physical objects can be said to be "red," "hot," "hard," etc., because they really *are* these qualities; "red," "hot," and "hard" are direct parts of the surfaces of physical objects.

IV CONCLUSION

We have now answered, in as great detail as is possible on the basis of Plato's own assertions, the second and most important question concerning the ontological status of sense-data: the relation of "belonging to" between sense-data and physical objects, on the one hand, and observers on the other. Even where the sense-datum can be located at the surface of the physical object, in a space coincident with the structural features of physical objects, the sense-datum is still a multiply located quality or attribute of physical objects: it still depends in part upon an observer, and his particular point of view. And even where the two spaces cannot be brought together, it is clear from Plato's analysis how he meant to answer the first question concerning the ontological status of sense-data, what kind of entities are they? Sense-data are not substances for either Plato or Protagoras. For Protagoras they were not phases of substances either, since the physical object was wholly defined in terms of sense-data. Sense-data for Protagoras were attributes of physical objects but the object was nothing over and above its attributes. The above analysis has disclosed that sense-data for Plato are also attributes of physical objects, but the object is no longer defined in phenomenalist terms, solely in terms of its attributes. For him, there is something besides sense-data composing physical objects, namely, the structural, geometrical, unsensed properties. Thus sense-data are attributes of something which is more permanent than they. If we are careful to avoid predicating of Plato's theory a material substratum which supports sensible qualities, we can conclude that sense-data for Plato are particular existents which are attributes of substances. The physical-object motions of the *Theaetetus* and the structural features of the *Timaeus* fulfil the function of substance, if we mean by "substance" that which endures for a time longer than an event such as lightning and which has an independent existence. Moreover, like later developments of the concept of substance, Plato's substance is unsensed, being, like the receptacle, an object of inference. In fact, Plato's definition of a physical object, which I have reconstructed, is very similar to that presented by Locke. For both men, a physical object is composed of three essential parts: a substance, a set of powers, and certain sensible qualities. Plato does not, as Democritus before him and Locke after him did, separate two sets of the sensible qualities, some of which have a more intimate relation to the physical object than others. Neither is Plato's substance a Lockean substratum about which we have no knowledge other than that it is necessary in order to account for sensible qualities. Plato gives us explicit information concerning the substance aspect of physical objects (although he does not indicate how he thought the inference from sense-data to physical causes could be made in the absence of his own characterizations of the latter), and, unlike Locke, I do not believe that Plato would say the structural properties of objects belong more properly to the object, are more of the nature of its essence, than the sensible qualities. Both are essential parts of the physical object, despite the fact that sensible qualities belong to physical objects in a multiply related way.

7

Linguistic and Epistemological Dualism

ONE OF THE MOST IMPORTANT problems within a dualistic ontology is that of justifying the language used in talking about the unobservable side of that ontology. Within the sense-datum theory, this particular problem is that of making the move from the given to that which is inferred, from sense-data to physical objects. In *Perception*, Price has offered an extensive analysis of this relation between given and inferred, but he was not concerned with the linguistic side of this problem: how to make the verbal transition from the basic propositions to the derived proposition about physical objects. Russell and Broad have been almost alone in attaching sufficient importance to this problem to devote any detailed analysis to it. In brief, the linguistic problem which arises on a dualistic analysis of our knowledge of the external world is as follows. It is recognized that many of our beliefs about the external world contain assumptions and convictions which are not revealed in any one experience, or even in any totality of sense experiences. Thus, a distinction is thought to be necessary between the given and the inferred elements of such beliefs on the assumption that whatever is found out is found out *either* by inference *or* by being something given. The basic epistemological problem issuing from this distinction is: what will justify our passage from the given data of our sense experiences to the inferred and accepted objects of our perceptual experiences? What probability is there for making such a transition? Whatever the answer be—and the answer is rendered especially difficult because the given is epistemic and not psychological—we must be able to state it in language which will not itself cloud the nature of the problem by failing to distinguish between the given and the inferred. We require one formulation for sense-datum experiences and one for perceptual experiences. We need, as well, statements showing or justifying the validity of making the transition from the first set of statements to the second. In other words, when we seek to verbalize the answer to the dualistic problem, we meet the same kind of issue on the linguistic as on the epistemological level. Can we construct statements of the two required kinds, and so construct them that we shall be able to provide for a verbalization of the epistemological transition from sense-data to physical objects?

I   BASIC OBJECT WORDS AND THEIR MEANINGS

Another way of pointing out the central linguistic problem of any dualistic epistemology is to raise the question "what linguistic form will adequately describe perceptive experiences?" where the term "adequate" applies in the epistemic and not in a purely psychological sense. According to Russell, perceptive experiences are the experiences described by basic propositions. Consequently, any description or translation of them must not go beyond the epistemic given in its linguistic expression. The total set of verbal propositions which describe perceptive experiences in this way constitutes a large and important part of that class of statements which Russell calls the "object language," or alternatively, the "primary language." He defines this object language as that language which consists wholly "of 'object words', where 'object words' are defined, logically, as words having meaning in isolation, and psychologically, as words which have been learnt without its being necessary to have previously learnt any other words."[1] These are words which, unlike logical words, do not depend upon a context for their meaning. This meaning is learned "by confrontation with objects which are what they mean, or instances of what they mean." (p. 26) Russell is content to explain man's understanding such object words in behaviouristic terms. For when a person hears an object word which he understands, his overt action, at least "up to a point," is that "which the object would have caused." (p. 68)

The object which is confronted is not always of the same type, for Russell explains that we can learn, in this confronting way, the names of people; class names, such as "man" and "god"; names of sensible qualities; names of actions, such as "walk," "run," "eat"; and relation words such as "up," "down," "in," and "before." Later in the discussion he makes it clear that words like "dog" and "cat" are also object words. The conjunction of physical-object and sense-datum words in the same

[1]All references to Russell in this chapter are to his *Inquiry*; this quotation is from p. 65.

list of words learned by confrontation is significant in that it shows that in his discussion of the object language Russell does not always keep before his attention the epistemological considerations which in other places seem to be directing his argument. In the presentation of what he means by the object language, he has not been concerned to introduce his causal theory of perception. Presumably, he either feels that what he here says is consistent with what he holds about the causal nature of perception or that a discussion of this theory of perception is irrelevant to the concept of an object language. However, in the above list of objects which give rise to object words, Russell could not be asserting that this list is consistent with the causal theory without some important qualifications. Basic propositions are a very important aspect of the object language, and the considerations of the causal nature of perception are quite relevant to a discussion of basic propositions, since it is their linguistic function to verbalize certain of our perceptive experiences. Thus, it is necessary to know just what we can be said to know in such perceptive experiences. We have already seen (in chapter 5) that that aspect of the object language which contains basic propositions must be epistemologically and not psychologically primary; if so, many of the object words which arise from the confrontation of such objects as Russell lists above will have to be dismissed on the grounds that they contain condensed inductions and hence go beyond the immediate epistemic given. On the purely descriptive level, there are many situations in our experiences which acquire names through the association of objects with verbal utterances. On this level,

all that is essential to an object word is some similarity among a set of phenomena, which is sufficiently striking for an association to be established between instances of the set and instances of the word for the set, the method of establishing the association being that, for some time, the word is frequently heard when a member of the set is seen. (p. 72)

For example,

If . . . in a certain situation, you are impelled to say 'cat', that will be (so long as you are confined to the object language) because some feature of the environment is associated with the word 'cat', which necessarily implies that this feature resembles the previous cats that caused the association. (p. 76)

But we acquire many object words in this way which do not stand up to the epistemological test: they are not restricted to what is epistemologically given in perceptive experiences.

Russell is aware of this fact. (cf. p. 152) He does not mean to construct an object language which consists only of those words which are free from condensed inductions. The object language is much more comprehensive; but, what is most important, its foundation must consist of object words which are free from *all* inferred factors in order for those sentences using induced words to be epistemologically acceptable. Thus, it is the concept of the basic linguistic proposition to which Russell appeals in order to escape such inconsistencies in his object language, although this appeal is somewhat implicit. There is a hierarchy of sentences within the object language. Here we find the first appearance of the problem: How do basic propositions furnish the ground for passing to statements containing object words which refer beyond the epistemic given? I deal with this problem later in this chapter (and in the following chapter also), but it is first necessary to pursue in more detail the linguistic aspects of basic propositions.

Since the function of basic propositions in the object language is distinctive and fundamental, it might be better, although Russell does not do so, to speak of two object languages, or two distinct aspects of that language. Thus, there is that object language which is used in common sense and by modern semanticists which purports to derive the meanings of its object words from the psychological given. On the other hand, there is that object language, basic in sense-datum theories, which is dependent upon the epistemic given in immediate perceptive experiences. It is the latter aspect with which Russell seems to be concerned in the *Inquiry* when he is discussing epistemology and the former when he is discussing language. It is only the second object language which can contain his basic propositions, since these have explicitly been asserted to be statements about the epistemic given. C.I. Lewis makes an analogous distinction without speaking of object languages. When we limit our language to the presented data, Lewis calls this the *expressive* use of language; but when we extend it beyond the presented datum, as when we say "there is a piece of paper," we are applying language in its *objective* use.[2]

Even after this distinction has been made, the difficulty remains of how words acquire their condensed inductive character. Such an inductive character cannot arise on the level of the basic propositions, since Russell specifically limits the components of basic propositions to the epistemic given. But if some situations contain a given which goes beyond the epistemic to the psychological given, how does this difference come about? According to Russell's analysis of the meaning

[2] *An Analysis of Knowledge and Valuation,* p. 179.

of object words, it is established through the conjunction of object with words heard, spoken, or read. In certain situations we have learned to associate the word "dog" with a particular object in our experience; in other situations, we come to attach words like "red" to objects in our experience. What is it in each of these situations which is named? Unless it can be shown how the name comes to mean more than is immediately presented in the epistemological sense, it would seem that all that is named in each case is a certain configuration of our perceptual field. Similar configurations come to have associated with them the same sounds or verbal tags. But if perceptual configurations exhaust the meaning of object words, the dualistic distinction between epistemological and ontological objects would never arise. We can, of course, make a distinction between given and inferred factors on a purely phenomenalistic interpretation, since the whole of any phenomenalistic object is never given in any one experience. Inferences must be made through the use of memory and past experience to further obtainable sense-data. But it is not this kind of inference which is characteristic of dualistic epistemologies. The word "dog" contains a condensed induction for Russell in the memory sense, but it also goes beyond experience in asserting the existence of an ontological object containing factors which are never directly sensed. These inferences from sense-data to the non-sensible factors raise a fundamental epistemological and linguistic difficulty. On his theory of the meaning of object words, Russell is unable to explain how this distinction enters our thought. Without it, there is no difference between the psychological and the epistemic given; but the whole purport of Russell's discussion of epistemological premises and their linguistic form is that in translating from internal beliefs to linguistic statements we must be constantly on our guard not to include references to that which is not epistemologically given. In other words, he assumes from the very beginning the above distinction which his theory of meaning seems unable to explain. It might be helpful for Russell to distinguish first- and second-order object words, the former being restricted to the epistemic given, the latter containing meaning-references to more than is given to us in this sense. But even this distinction does not account for the difference in meaning-content between first- and second-order object words.

This same difficulty is present in a slightly different form in Russell's elaboration of the nature of the object language. He insists that the linguistic form of object sentences must be what he calls "atomic." He defines "atomic form" in several different ways in the *Inquiry*. In the chapter where he first introduces this concept, he says "that a form of proposition is atomic if the fact that a proposition is of this form does not logically imply that it is a structure composed of subordinate propositions." (p. 134) What is single grammatically is not necessarily single or atomic in this sense. In another place, he defines atomic sentences more precisely, as follows:

A sentence is of atomic form when it contains no logical words and no sub-ordinate sentences. . . . Positively, a sentence is of atomic form if it contains one relation word (which may be a predicate) and the smallest number of other words required to form a sentence. (p. 95)

Russell considers it very important to make clear just what a sentence of atomic form is, since he has insisted that "all the sentences which embody empirical physical data will assert or deny propositions of atomic form." (p. 45) It follows that all *basic* linguistic sentences, like the derived-object sentences (those containing words whose meaning embodies a condensed induction), have an atomic form. The object language has been seen to include basic propositions, but the above definition of atomic sentences does not tell us all we need know about the words which fill out the *basic* atomic propositions.

Russell cannot mean to say, in the case of basic atomic sentences, that we fill in these sentences with any object word, since, as we have seen, not all object words are qualified to fill the requirements of episte-mology for basic object words. In the chapter on proper names, Russell constructs a language which consists of relation words and names. He purports to give a syntactical definition of "name" as any word which can occur in an atomic sentence. In the case of basic atomic sentences, however, the names must not extend, in their meaning, beyond the epistemic given. The object language which he discusses in this chapter seems to be what I have called the epistemological object language, concerned only with basic atomic sentences, although he does not bring out the distinction which I have suggested is necessary. The syntactical definition does not in itself tell us what sort of words can occur in the species "basic atomic sentences." What *are* the criteria for determining the proper sentential constituents of basic atomic sentences? The answer is, I believe, that the criteria lie in certain epistemological considerations which are paramount throughout the *Inquiry*. The words which can occur in basic atomic sentences are only those which are restricted in their meaning and import to what is epistemically given in momentary experiences, an epistemic given con-trolled by the Cartesian methodology. Russell has given an episte-mological rather than a syntactical definition of names, as applied to *basic* atomic sentences. Syntactical considerations are subservient to epistemological requirements. How the epistemological requirements arise Russell leaves unexplained in the *Inquiry*; on the basis of other writings we can say that these epistemological requirements—the criteria of meaning for physical-object words—are presuppositions throughout Russell's epistemological discussions. Like Price and Broad, Russell assumes, usually implicitly, that physical-object words contain a meaning-content which is never completely exemplified in experience. The implicit meanings for such words in his *Problems of Philosophy*, for example, were that physical objects cannot change as rapidly or as frequently as our sense-data and that physical objects are multiply accessible to different people and by different sense modalities. More-over, like Price's physical occupant and Broad's scientific object, Russell assumes that the atomic structure of physics is an important non-sensible ingredient in the physical world. These meanings are inconsistent with his theory of meaning set forth in the *Inquiry*, since there is no way they can be accounted for on the basis of confrontation. However, they are necessary to lend significance to the central problem of that work, that is, the construction of a language which will express our basic, perceptive beliefs without transcending the epistemic given. Since for Russell the result of the meanings commonly attached to physical-object words is the causal theory of perception (cf. chapters I–III of his *Problems*), it is the causal theory which is the silent, direct-ing hand in the crucial stages of the *Inquiry*. The effect of such direction is that many words which are usually taken to be names are incapable of occurring in basic atomic sentences. The epistemological meanings which Russell implicitly assumes throughout with reference to such words as "dog," "apple," etc., contain condensed inductions: they transcend the sensible qualities within experience both in time and in space, referring to the physical world as distinct from sensible qualities.

The need for this restriction in basic object words is very obvious in the chapter on proper names, where Russell makes it clear that the words which are to appear in atomic sentences (he again seems to be speaking of basic atomic sentences) can only be words which do not transcend the epistemic given. The only words which conform to this condition are the names of sensible qualities or sense-datum words. Russell is concerned in that chapter to work out a linguistic formula-tion which will express all that we can safely express concerning our experiences, without going into the inferred world of mediated experi-ence. Such a restriction indicates that he has unconsciously limited himself to the *basic* aspect of the object language. It is important to notice that his attempts to find a language which will be primary in the epistemological sense lead him into a phenomenalism which is strangely opposed to his causal theory of perception. One of the great merits of his basic atomic sentences, he believes, is that it enables us to use a language which is free from all epistemic doubt. In the common-sense language, statements of the form "this is red" frequently occur, but Russell feels that the force of the word "this" extends beyond the epistemic given and hence should be eliminated from our basic language. When "this is red" is considered as a subject-predicate proposition, the "this" "becomes a substance, an unknowable something in which predicates inhere, but which, nevertheless, is not identical with the sum of its predicates." (p. 97) Russell's concern to eliminate substance words like "this" suggests that he was advocating a phenomenalism, but the denial of the reduction of the physical world to sensible qualities is entailed in his own causal theory of perception. However, not being concerned with the origin of sensible qualities nor with their status in the physical world but rather with the construction of a language which will serve as the basic, primary language for epistemology, Russell is forced to remove the word "this" from the basic object language for the same reasons that "dog" is excluded. The statement "this is red" must be changed into the form "redness is here," where "red" is a name and not a predicate. When "red" is considered as a predicate, the introduction into our basic language of references to a Lockean unexperienced substance seems inevitable. On the other hand, when we consider "red" as a name designating some portion of continuous space-time in our immediate experience, we need not introduce the concept of a something over and above the sense quality. The dichotomy between subject and its qualities is thus avoided in our basic language. But unless Russell makes the further qualification that this is a language about epistemological objects only and not about the so-called external world of ontological objects, he is involved in a position which contradicts his own causal theory. The language which in some places he seems to feel applies to the external world has really been reduced to applying only to the phenomenalistic world of sense qualities. Can such a language serve as a link between perceptive experiences and derived propositions about the physical world?

II THE RELATION BETWEEN BASIC OBJECT SENTENCES AND DERIVED OBJECT SENTENCES

For Russell the linguistic statement form of any belief has two functions: to express and to indicate. Beliefs are expressed while "facts" are indicated. Language can fail in its indicative role when it purports to indicate what does not exist, as when I say "there is a dog" and there is no dog present. But Russell maintains that language when it is *spontaneous,* as opposed to when it is *reflective,* cannot fail to express the state of the speaker. Such spontaneous speech "may fail to communicate what it expresses, owing to differences between speaker and hearer in the use of language, but from the speaker's point of view, spontaneous speech must express his state." (p. 204) This concept of "spontaneous speech" is important in an analysis of the nature and function of basic propositions, since basic propositions for Russell must belong to the class of verbal statements which are spontaneous. If I am correct in identifying basic propositions and spontaneous propositions, there are some significant aspects of the role of basic propositions in Russell's empirical epistemology which are affected.

Russell explains that by spontaneous speech he means, first of all, speech which is evoked directly by sensation without interference by any other verbal intermediary. The statements "I am hot" or "I see a red patch" are offered as examples. He recognizes that the assertion "I see a red flower" is more naturally spontaneous than "I see a red patch," since most people do not converse in terms of sense-data. Thus, it is not so much the spontaneity of the verbal utterance which classes it among spontaneous statements as it is certain fundamental epistemological considerations. Spontaneous speech appears to be no different from the linguistic form of basic propositions. In both cases, the stimulus is a non-verbal occurrence which affects the person making the statement. But perceptive experiences evoke spontaneous verbal responses of two sorts: those restricted to the epistemic given and those which in their meanings point beyond it. "I see a red flower" is an example of the latter type. Russell excludes such utterances from the class of spontaneous propositions by inserting another criterion: what speech indicates and what it expresses must be identical. In other words, there are cases of verbal statements where there is no distinction between what is expressed and what is indicated. Expression and indication can be identical only where that which is indicated is a present state of the speaker.

If I exclaim, 'I am hot', the fact indicated is a state of myself, and is the very state that I express. The word 'hot' means a certain kind of organic condition, and this kind of condition can cause the exclamatory use of the word 'hot'. In such cases, the cause of the instance of the word is also an instance of the meaning of the word. This is still the case with 'I see a red patch', apart from certain reservations as to the words 'I see'. (p. 206)

Since questions of truth or falsity arise only with reference to the indicative function of sentences, it follows that "a spontaneous sentence which indicates what it expresses is 'true' by definition." (p. 215) Falsehood is possible only when what a sentence expresses is distinct from that which it indicates so that what it intends to indicate may not exist or may not occur. Thus, if basic propositions are spontaneous, as it seems they must be, considering all the characteristics Russell lists, they cannot be false. Unless he is willing to make sensible qualities part of the external world, as he cannot do and retain his causal theory of perception, Russell is committed to making basic propositions identical with spontaneous assertions. We saw in the previous section that, in the construction of his basic language, Russell committed himself to talking solely in terms of phenomenal sensible qualities. Since these, on his causal theory of perception, are personal and private, presumably what basic propositions express is identical with what they indicate.

This identification in itself, as far as I can see, would not necessitate any drastic revisions in his analysis of basic propositions and the foundations of empirical knowledge. Some revisions, however, may be required by the recognition of a problem which Russell does not consider. We have seen that the relation of ground and consequent arises within the object language itself, when we pass from basic propositions and their first-order object words to derived object sentences with their second-order object words. It is at this juncture that all of the difficulties of Russell's dualistic epistemology appear, since he is immediately faced with the problem of verifying beliefs of the type for which the verifier lies beyond experience. Russell recognizes the difficulty on this epistemological level; but no complete verbalization of dualistic epistemology can be made unless we can solve a similar difficulty on the linguistic level, the difficulty of making the transition from basic propositions which refer wholly to events within experience to propositions which refer to events outside experience. We saw this problem arise in connection with Russell's linguistic analysis of basic propositions: his theory of the meaning of object words does not allow for the derivation of condensed induced words from confrontation with objects. The meanings attached to object words of the second order ("dog," "cat," "table") were seen to have been surreptitiously introduced into his analysis without any account of their origin. The gap thus effected between basic propositions and derived-object propositions is just about as large on the linguistic level as the gap between sense-data and physical objects on the physical level of Russell's causal theory of perception. The physical dualism inherent in Russell's epistemology has, as might have been expected, emerged in his linguistic analysis. Epistemological dualism seems to be intimately related to linguistic dualism. Whether the relation is so intimate as to make the solution (if one is possible) of linguistic dualism applicable to the epistemological problems is a question which can only be resolved after we have examined Broad's attempt to answer this same question.

The transition between basic object sentences and derived object sentences would be a transition from one meaning level to another, from the level of the epistemic given, to that of the psychological given. In terms of expression and indication, this transition would be from sentences in which what is expressed and what is indicated are identical, and those in which these two modes of speech are distinct. This linguistic transition corresponds to the transition in belief from what is presented in sense experience to what is inferred or interpreted. This latter transition is the one Russell has dealt with in many of his books. His analysis in the *Inquiry* is committed to dealing with the former transition, although he does not do so in any great detail. He has insisted that we must, on the linguistic level, start with statements which indicate sensible occurrences since otherwise there will be no sound basis for epistemology. Basic propositions form the ground for all later inferred propositions by affording some ultimate empirical reference for epistemology. When the premises for an empirical epistemology are made explicit and are formulated in a language, Russell finds it necessary to form them into a hierarchy which may extend upwards indefinitely, but which must terminate in the reverse direction with some non-linguistic occurrence. As C. I. Lewis has said, the whole of empirical knowledge is a complex structure composed of many truths or statements which are substantiated by other statements, but

unless there should be some statements or rather something apprehensible and statable whose truth is determined by given experience and is not determinable in any other way, there would be no such thing as empirical knowledge.[3]

The relation of ground and consequent, of premise and conclusion may be all that Russell meant to establish between basic object propositions and derived object propositions since this relation is all that he does establish explicitly in the *Inquiry*. However, I believe we can find evidence which suggests that Russell really means to establish more than this relation. Moreover, a complete verbalization of a dualistic system demands a more extensive analysis. If my suggestion that

[3]*An Analysis of Knowledge and Valuation*, p. 171.

Russell has smuggled physical-object meanings into his discussion without taking account of their genesis in his theory of meaning is correct, we can see that the task he has been performing in the *Inquiry* has been mainly that of translating only one class of beliefs into statement form: those beliefs which are about the epistemic given. But since we know that in his dualistic epistemology there are two major classes of beliefs, we can see that for a complete linguistic analysis of his system, he would have to carry out a translation of beliefs about the interpreted or inferred aspects of our experiences. Once this has been done (and it is not a difficult task, since any proposition containing a condensed induced word is such a translation), the task of making a linguistic analysis of his system must first surmount the problem of the transition from the one class of statements to the other. It is this transition which Russell does not deal with explicitly in the *Inquiry*, although it is inherent in the dualism within his own object language.

Lewis has carried out an analysis of the linguistic aspects of empirical epistemology, wherein he deals in more detail with the linguistic relation between basic and derived propositions (or what he calls "expressive" and "objective" statements). While his analysis involves many factors which Russell would not wish to accept, I think it is in the main the sort of analysis to which Russell's dualism is committed. One of the main problems of such an epistemology has been the way in which sense-data can serve as evidence for physical objects which are never given in experience. Since the transition from sense-data to physical objects is analogous to the linguistic transition from basic object sentences to derived object sentences, the relation of these two kinds of statements involves the same problem of evidence and confirmation as exists with sense-data and physical objects. On this level, we are concerned with stating the evidence and the probability relation which obtains between these two classes of statements.

Lewis approaches this linguistic problem by first remarking that in the case of expressive language, "the cognitive judgment 'If I act in manner A, the empirical eventuality will include E', is one which can be verified by putting it to the test." (p. 180) This verification will be final and decisive "because nothing beyond the content of this passage of experience was implied in the judgment." As Russell would say, what the proposition expressed and what it indicated were identical. But, Lewis goes on to observe, in the case of objective judgments, the confirmation we have to compile is indefinite and hence we can never be certain of its truth or falsity. "This is so because, while the judgment, so far as it is significant, contains nothing which could not be tested, still it has a significance which outruns what any single test, or any limited set of tests, could exhaust." (p. 180) In this assertion, Lewis easily assumed what Russell has laboured to show, that sense-data, or presentations, can be evidence for physical objects. Although Russell might not agree with Lewis's analysis of the indefinite character of the confirmation process involved in using sense-data as evidence for physical objects, he has agreed that sense-data can be evidence for physical objects if certain further conditions can be realized. The problem which Lewis raises in this connection has been discussed by Russell in the *Inquiry,* where he deals with the existential propositions which, in their meaning, go beyond the given; but his approach differs slightly from the one employed by Lewis. Nevertheless, Lewis's analysis fits the requirements of Russell's causal theory. Russell's analysis of existential propositions was concerned with the verifiers of those propositions; he pointed out that as we pass from basic propositions to derived propositions, we travel correspondingly further away from the possibility of finding the truth verifiers of our statements. In the statement, "you are hot," the verifier is "hotness-there-now, of which I am not aware." (p. 231) The same is true of "the sun is hot," or "there is a dog." In general,

whenever an assertion goes beyond my experience, the situation is this: inference leads me to 'there is an X such that ΦX', and this, if true, is true in virtue of an occurrence which would be asserted by 'ΦX'. But I know no such occurrence. (p. 232)

Thus what any proposition which goes beyond the given indicates is a verifier which is not experienced but which is the truth condition for the sentence. The result of such an interpretation is that all propositions of this sort can never be verified and known for certain. All propositions which indicate something not in immediate experience contain variables which can be described but never named. We can know the physical world by description but never by acquaintance. However, all sentences have some constants which "must all be derived from experience." In the case of physical-object sentences, Russell argues that the constants bear some relation to what the variable describes. That is, the structural similarity between percepts and their physical causes is such that we can actually learn something about the physical world by examining our percepts. The meanings of the non-variable words in such sentences bear a significant relation to the variable words.

Lewis's analysis of two basic kinds of epistemological judgments seeks to meet the same problem which arises on the level of variable and non-variable words. This is the analysis which, I am suggesting, applies to Russell's epistemology. If there is the structural similarity between percepts and physical objects which Russell has argued there must be if we are to justify physical-object knowledge, then statements about percepts (or sense-data) stand in an evidence relation to statements about physical objects. Calling the judgments concerned with presentations, *terminating* judgments, and those concerned with interpretations, *non-terminating* judgments, Lewis asserts that the non-terminating judgments must be translatable into terminating judgments, since "only so could confirmation" of non-terminating judgments come about. (p. 181) The non-terminating character of these judgments "reflects the fact, not that the statement implies anything which is not expressible in some terminating judgment or other, but that no limited set of such terminating judgments could be sufficient to exhaust its empirical significance." (p. 181) Thus, linguistically, Lewis has distinguished between (*a*) statements about the epistemic given, (*b*) statements of terminating judgments, and (*c*) statements of non-terminating judgments. The first of these correspond to Russell's basic propositions. The second assert "some prediction of further possible experience. They find their cue in what is given; but what they state is something taken to be verifiable by some test which involves a way of acting." (p. 184) These are stated in the expressive language even though they "represent" predictions of future experience. The third class of statements makes assertions about objective reality and comprises "pretty much all the empirical statements we habitually make," from statements about pieces of paper and dogs to "the most impressive generalization." (p. 185)

Since Lewis believes that "the data which eventually support genuine probability must themselves be certainties," he seeks for such data in the given, since this, for him as for Russell, is certain. He does not wish to assert that no objective statement can find support either deductively or inductively from other objective statements, but only that in the last analysis all objective judgments must go back to something which is certain: "no empirical statement can become credible without a reference to experience." (p. 187) In other words, all the basic evidence for empirical propositions must be stated in the expressive language. When we place interpretations on presentations, Lewis says that we must know what we mean "in terms of experience" which we "can envisage, if the meaning is genuine." The full meaning of the interpretation consists in all possible implications which would confirm my belief in the interpretation. The interpretation, then,

dictates that the statement of this objective belief must be translatable into terms of passages of possible experience, each of which would constitute some partial verification of it; *that is, it must be translatable into the predictive statements of terminating judgments.* (p. 189)

In short, both the meaning and the verification of an empirical belief about an objective judgment "concern the predictions of further possible experience which the truth of it [the belief] implies." This theory of meaning and verification "makes the terminating judgment into which it is thus translatable centrally important for understanding the nature of empirical knowledge." (p. 190)

As I have remarked above, Lewis assumes throughout this discussion that sense-data do serve as evidence for physical objects. In fact, he insists that the meaning of physical-object statements is contained in sense-datum statements. Moreover, he asserts that "the terminating judgment itself *is* deducible from the objective judgment in which it is a constituent: from 'there is a piece of white paper before me,' it is deducible that 'if I turn my eyes right, this seen appearance will be displaced to the left.'" (p. 212) Of course, such is the case only if physical-object statements do entail sense-datum statements. Russell has raised this problem in his discussions of perception, being concerned to find some justification for accepting such an entailment. One way in which such a justification can be obtained, he has suggested, is if the principle of structural similarity is applicable. When we have accepted this principle and taken sense-data as evidence for physical objects, then sense-datum statements will become important, since the confirmation process will be stated in terms of the expressive or basic object language. Thus it seems that basic linguistic propositions are capable of serving as a link between perceptive experiences and derived propositions, only if the principle of structural similarity, or some other principle, is assumed. The structural similarity cannot be discovered since, for this dualist ontology, one side of the relation is unobservable.[4] This necessity of assumptions to bridge the gap between sense-data and physical objects has far reaching effects upon dualism and upon the analysis of truth.

III CONCLUSION

With the additional analysis of the relation of basic object propositions and derived propositions provided by Lewis's discussion,

[4] I should hasten to add that although I have used some of Lewis's analysis of the meaning of empirical propositions in this examination of Russell's dualism, Lewis himself was not a dualist in ontology. For a short statement of his attitude towards dualism and phenomenalism, see his "Realism or Phenomenalism," *The Philosophical Review*, LXIV, 2 (1955), pp. 233–247.

the apparent inconsistencies in Russell's theory of meaning can be mitigated, since it is now clear that in the completed linguistic analysis of his dualistic ontology, he has two theories of meaning. The one offered in the *Inquiry* is concerned with the meanings of sense-datum words; but within the dualistic system there has to be another theory of meaning which will account for the meanings of physical-object words. Russell fails to suggest any means by which these words, the ones he designates as containing condensed induced meanings, acquire their transcendent meanings. Apparently Russell has adopted the commonly accepted meanings of these words without raising the question of their genesis. It is these meanings which he has consistently been seeking to save in the face of all the refutations of naïve realism. He has been concerned to construct a theory of knowledge which would preserve as much of common sense as can possibly be made consistent with the facts, as well as with physics. He has not been concerned to question the fundamental beliefs of common sense except as they have conflicted with themselves or with physics. His whole epistemology has been a construction within this framework. Thus it is evident that his attention has not been directed upon the genesis of physical-object words. He has been interested in analyzing the meanings of sense-datum words, since they have been brought into focus by the methodological necessity of starting from some foundation which would serve as the ground of later assertions. Just how this analysis would be altered by an investigation into the genesis of physical-object meanings for condensed induced words is unpredictable *a priori* but it is clear that the analysis of the relation between sense-datum statements and physical-object statements which Lewis has offered is a necessary supplement to Russell's linguistic treatment of epistemological premises. That this supplement is inadequate by itself to explain physical-object meanings for the dualist arises from the fact that what the dualist means by "physical object" cannot be exhausted by any set of sense-datum statements. Phenomenalism can never be an adequate translation for the dualist's claims. The question for the dualist is whether sense-data can be taken as evidence for the existence and part of the nature of physical objects. But if physical-object statements contain a meaning which cannot be translated into sense-datum statements, the dualist must find some way of showing what that meaning is and how it arises and can be understood. If he cannot explain physical-object meaning, his dualism may, after all, be unsayable.

8

Dualist Reference

THE DUALIST OPERATES with a theory of objects which extends the meaning of "object" outside the usual empirical field. Those who seek to understand the dualist's ontology have to make this initial concession to the concept of object. In the case of reifications proper (groups raised to an ontological status which is different from that of their members), the task of understanding is simpler and easier. There are obvious ways in which certain groups have qualities not possessed by any of the members singly. France is composed of individual Frenchmen but France is a nation and a republic while no individual Frenchman is either. The dualist stresses the qualities of nation facts because he does not see the world in reductionist terms. But his analysis of the physical world leads him to assert the reality of entities not abstracted from sense particulars and not related to sense particulars in the way in which nations and individuals are related. He is led to posit substance.

The belief in substance expresses the dualist's conviction that the world is more than apparent, that things are not what they seem. He is initially inclined in this direction by three basic attitudes which control his philosophic reflections. He is not frightened by reifications and hypostatizations. He begins his reflections convinced of realism. His subsequent analysis expands the implications of a criterion of physicality, which he takes to be an expression of his realist belief. The phenomenalist takes as his point of departure his self and its contents. The elaboration of a world of objects emerges from the awareness of the isolated cogito. The dualist is on a more sophisticated and complex level of reflection, not because he can claim greater truth, but simply because his reflection arises as a questioning attitude towards phenomenalism. Phenomenalism is itself reified by the dualist; the phenomenalist's world is given independent (realist) status. Phenomenalism itself is found deficient on the grounds that it is

pable of expressing the principle of independent existence. Phenomenalist-realism differs from phenomenalism proper only in the principle of independent existence: for both positions physical objects are
nothing more than collections of actual and possible sensory contents,
but for the realist the contents exist independently of awareness. For
the realist, the phenomenalist is confusing existence with our evidence
for existence. The phenomenalist has no expression for independent
existence, except "independent of this bit of experience here and now."
Realist independence is no hypothetical if-then or interexperiential
affair: it is independence *from* experience. The world is as it appears
but is not dependent upon its appearances.

The dualist begins with this simple formulation of naïve realism.
But he begins also with his criterion of physicality. Physical objects
are spatially enduring entities accessible to sense perception through
their causal properties. They are also public, as between perceivers,
and quite independent of perception in their existence and activities.
The dualist is not only concerned with the evidential value of perception for physical objects: he wants to be able to state what the object
is in its independence. The very nature of dualist knowledge requires
knowledge of substance. The move from the phenomenal to the
dualist concept of object is motivated by reflection upon the nature
of the independent object. The principle of independence stipulates
that the object does not depend upon the perceptual situation for its
existence or for its nature. That nature could nevertheless be revealed
in perception, as the naïve realist believes, were it not for delusive,
illusive, and hallucinatory experiences. For, if we are to uncover the
independent characteristics of the object, we can do so by appeals
to the content of experience only if we have no grounds for suspecting
a discrepancy between content and characteristics. Non-veridical
perception provides the grounds for such suspicions: if the object's
properties are permanent and unchanging, how can we ascribe to that
object any of the changing properties of our perceptual experience?
The criterion of physicality says that the object is invariant to changing
experience. The phenomenalist can define invariance in relation to
experience, in such a way that these experienced properties are taken
as normal and characteristic of the object while those others are taken
as delusive. But realist invariance is not experiential invariance. For
the realist, phenomenalist invariance is arbitrary. The quest for an
invariance outside experience, one which is indifferent to the subjective
successions of perception, leads the realist to relinquish his naïve
belief in the reality of appearance. He now believes in the appearance

of reality, but the reality which appears becomes sharply distinguished from the appearing reality. Invariance is taken from experience. The real properties of the object become separate from the causal effects of the object on the perceiver.

The quest for an invariance outside experience—for substance—finds many diverse exemplifications, justifications, and reasons. Modern physics is seen as illustrative of substance in its talk of electrons, molecules, and sub-atomic particles. The phenomenal world is pared away and reality laid bare; but not quite bare, for the electrons, molecules, and sub-atomic particles are known only by inference from special perceptible data. Substance is also invoked as an explanatory concept, to account for the individuality of things and for the unity of experience. While the phenomenalist looks at the world largely in sensory terms, the dualist, in dealing with non-sensible invariance, is forced to place his reflections on the conceptual level. The phenomenalist's reflections are conceptualizations which seek to limit explanation to sensory contents. The dualist finds the bundle theory of individuation inadequate. He is not misled by the grammar of his language into thinking that there must be a referent for thing-words. He simply finds experience insufficiently illuminated by appealing only to congeries of qualities. His invoking substance is a conscious effort at rendering the world intelligible. But in foregoing the phenomenal structures of the phenomenalist explanation, the dualist becomes entangled in the complex problem of giving content to the concept of substance.

The peculiar nature of this ontology, which spilts reality into sensuous and non-sensuous, leads to a de-perceptualization of the physical world. Our talk and thought about the non-sensuous part of the world must avoid the phenomenalist locutions. But phenomenalist experience cannot be ignored, since the dualist finds phenomenal and real worlds related causally and epistemically. Dualist reference can only be maintained in language and thought by specifying the epistemic relations in such a way that some assertions based upon phenomenal experiences can yield some information about the non-phenomenal world. The information is not verifiable since verification can do no more than relate experiences: it can never move outside all possible experience, as dualist assertions must. Two alternatives are open to the dualist. He can think of the real world as comprised of atomic particles which are imperceptible, or only perceivable by very special and indirect techniques. Or, he can make the real world geometrically isomorphic with the phenomenal world by turning it into a geometrical world of points, lines, and geometric solids. Both approaches make the correlation of sensuous with non-sensuous worlds schematic and abbreviated: we can never have complete knowledge of the physical world, although some information does filter through into our phenomenal experiences. The information is informative only under the control of some explicit interpretative theory.

I   BROAD'S CONCEPT OF PHYSICALITY

Broad has variously formulated the concept of external physical objects. The composite picture yields ten different prerequisites for physicality. In "Phenomenalism,"[1] a physical object is said to require four conditions. (1) "It must be neutral as between various observers"; (2) "we must be able to talk of its remaining constant while many of the sense-data connected with it change, and *vice versa*"; (3) "we must be able to state causal laws in terms of such objects"; and (4) "there must be a sense in which they persist when I cease to be aware of the sense-data connected with them." In "The External World"[2] these conditions were shortened to (1) publicity and (2) the ability of yielding diverse appearances, with the added requirement that (5) the appearances of shape, size, and position must resemble that which appears. In *Scientific Thought*, these two lists are merged into one with another new condition added. The properties are referred to "a bit of matter." A bit of matter must (1 and 2) be independent of minds but "capable of being observed by many minds," that is, it must be independent and public (p. 229); (6) be neutral between the various senses such that we observe the same piece of matter by our different sense organs (p. 231); (4) persist and interact with other bits of matter whether observed or not (p. 232); and (7) have a permanent shape, size, and position in space in addition to being capable of moving from one position to another (p. 232). Condition (3) of "Phenomenalism" does not reappear explicitly either here or later. In *The Mind and its Place in Nature*, the list is reformulated and again increased. There the prerequisites are ascribed to physical objects. Any physical object is said to (8) be a strand of history which endures and has a unity and continuity; (7 and 9) be literally (as opposed to Pickwickianly) extended in space with a size, shape, and spatial relations with other such objects; (4) persist and interact with other objects when not perceived; (1) be perceptible by many different

[1]*Proc. Arist. Soc.*, XV (1914–15), p. 233.
[2]*Mind*, XXX (1921), p. 387.

observers and at different times; and (10) have other qualities besides shape, size, and spatial order, some of which may never be perceived. (pp. 145–47; cf. pp. 195–96) This last condition is meant to include more than primary qualities, although the additional, qualitative nature need not, and (he finds reasons for saying) usually is not the familiar secondary qualities of colour, sound, etc., but something similar, for example, mass or electric charge. (p. 207)

Prominent in this concept of externality is the distinction between appearance and that which appears, the distinction which in Broad's own theory is designated as that between sensa and scientific objects. This distinction is both a primitive and a derivative belief in Broad's account. "The belief that our sensa are appearances of something more permanent and complex than themselves seems to be primitive, and to arise inevitably in us with the sensing of the sensa." Neither psychologically nor logically can we work from appearances directly to that which appears. "On the other hand, there is no possibility of either refuting it [the belief] logically, or of getting rid of it, or . . . of coordinating the facts without it." (ST, p. 268)[3] But this primitive belief refers only to what Broad terms the "constitutive" properties of the physical world, that is, "that there are things which are relatively permanent, which combine many qualities, and which persist and interact at times when they are not appearing to our senses." (ST, p. 267) This primitive belief is covered by conditions 2, 4, and 8. The further specification of the external physical world, that is, all the other conditions but especially 7 and 9, is derivative and arises only late in the development of the individual or of the race. Neither physical space nor time nor matter is given; all three are constructed from the common experiences of man.

The common-sense notions of a single Space, a single Time, and persistent bits of Matter which exist, move, and change within them are by no means primitive. They must be the results of a long and complex process of reflection and synthesis, carried out by countless generations of men on the crude deliveries of their senses. . . . (ST, p. 228; cf. p. 95)

His criteria of physicality, which he offers as "the irreducible minimum of characteristics that a thing would have to possess in order to count as a physical object" (MPN, p. 146), cover both the primitive and the derivative components of the belief in an external world.

Although Broad has recognized and dealt with various ontological

---

[3]Abbreviated references to Broad's books in this chapter will be as follows: ST for Scientific Thought, PPR for Physics, Perception, and Reality, and MPN for The Mind and its Place in Nature.

alternatives as expressions of this elaborate criterion, has, for example, allowed that the distinction (which he thinks is imperative) between sensations, sense-data, and physical objects may be interpreted in a phenomenalist way by making physical objects functions of sense-data or sensations ("Phenomenalism," p. 228), he has himself consistently favoured at least the retention of sense-data and physical objects. He treats phenomenalism (in *Physics, Perception and Reality*) as derivative from naïve realism, just as his own form of realism is taken as an inevitable alternative to naïve realism in the face of the various arguments from illusion. Acceptance of the primitive aspect of the complex belief in external objects does not, by itself, lead us to a dualist-realist rather than a phenomenalist-realist ontology. This part of the belief only requires us to conceive of the world as independent of mind but revealed in perception. It is the derivative part of this belief which packs into the criteria of physicality the dualist-realist hypothesis. The distinction between literal and Pickwickian inherence (condition 9) brings this ontology into focus, since it is one way of saying that appearances differ *in kind* from that which appears, at least in their spatial properties. The further development of Broad's ontology includes a widening of the area of type-distinction between phenomenal qualities and the non-phenomenal world. There are good grounds for rejecting phenomenalist-realism in favour of dualist-realism, as Broad labours to show; but it should be recognized that the acceptance of a dualist ontology is not, in this theory, solely the result of arguments presented in the face of phenomenalist-realism, since the dualist ontology is implicit in the derivative aspect of the fundamental belief which Broad says arises inevitably in all of us. If this is the nature of our belief about the external world, it is strange that the familiar plain man should have for so long been interpreted as holding to the phenomenalist-realist ontology. If Broad has correctly formulated this ontology in his criterion, it has never been phenomenalist-realist, but always dualist-realist. Even in the earliest formulations of "Phenomenalism" and "The External World," with the clear distinction between appearance and that which appears, the dualistic nature of the belief should have been clear.

Broad purports to be expressing the conditions for physicality which would be acceptable for everyone, a kind of neutral ontology. But this proffered neutrality really masks the ontological bias of Broad (and of other sense-datum philosophers). On the level of ordinary experience, our ideas of physical objects are built up entirely on the

basis of phenomenal qualities.[4] We learn to distinguish veridical from
non-veridical experiences quickly, still within the phenomenal confines
of everyday experience. What we mean by a table in ordinary experience is precisely this particular collection of sensible qualities situated
in this particular place in my study; that brown, oval-shaped object,
made of oak, etc. From this particular specification of this table, Broad
goes on to generalize a concept of tableness or physicality. A physical
object then becomes what his various formulations of physicality claim,
that is, a permanent, public, independent object with shape and size.
It is only after he is armed with this conceptual abstraction from ordinary experience that Broad offers his arguments against a phenomenalist-realism. Appeal to the particularizations of physicality employed
in ordinary experience are no longer made. The abstracted criterion
replaces the phenomenological description of practical life. The experiences of ordinary life, relevant to the criteria, can no longer confirm
a belief in phenomenalist-realism: this is precisely the structure of
Broad's argument for dualist-realism. I do not wish to say that Broad
has misformulated the ontology of ordinary experience, since that
claim is not necessary for my argument that his criteria of physicality
already contain the ontology with which he concludes his many arguments against phenomenalist-realism. I think it is misleading to suppose
that there is an ontology of ordinary experience. What we as philosophers do is to impose various ontological frameworks upon our
everyday world. Neither Broad, nor any of the other sense-datum
philosophers, nor their critics, have recognized the status and genesis
of their respective ontologies. These ontologies do not emerge *from*
experience, they are interpretations *of* experience. Broad's interpretation is clearly embodied in his ten criteria for physicality. If we abide
by his formulation of the minimum conditions for physicality, the
situation is not that the plain man reluctantly relinquishes his belief in
phenomenalist-realism, but rather that he comes to realize the correct
nature of his basic belief. In short, with Broad's complex criteria of
physicality, it is impossible to accept anything other than a dualist
ontology.

However, there are passages in *Physics, Perception, and Reality*
where Broad writes as if he were using "object" in the phenomenalist
sense. He raises the question, "what is meant by 'one thing?' " This
question breaks down into two sub-questions: "What distinguishes it

[4]Martin Lean expresses this point well in his *Sense-Perception and Matter*,
18–25.

[one thing] at a given moment from other things at that moment?" and "What makes us call a certain succession of states the states of one thing that persists through time?" (p. 92) The answer to the first is "Homogeneity at a given moment of sense qualities within a definite boundary in space. . . ." (*Ibid.*) The fundamental notion in the concept of "one thing" is that of "certain sensible qualities having extension and shape." (p. 94) The answer to the second sub-question is simply that the changes of a state must appear continuous. Both questions, in other words, are given a phenomenalist analysis very similar in nature to the analysis in terms of families of sense-data which Price developed some years later. What makes the situation even more puzzling within the context of Broad's theory is that he says this analysis of the individuation of a "thing" is in accord with what common sense means by "one physical thing." Even conditions 1 to 4 of the early "Phenomenalism" article would seem to go beyond this phenomenalist reduction. However, he points out that inference is required to unify the sensible appearances defining a physical object in this way.

For . . . it is partly a matter of inference, and partly a matter of definition, to identify a seen with a felt boundary, either as to position or to shape. And then the identification is not a 'finding identical' of the objects of two different sense-perceptions, but a correlation of them with a third unperceived common shape through their correlation with each other. (*PPR*, p. 95)

The common unperceived space referred to here is not the constructed physical space of his developed theory, but the sensory or phenomenal space of perception; his point is that only after reflection upon tactual and visual sensible space orders do we come to identify them as one and the same order. Taken strictly, they are two different orders of space, but practically we learn to treat them as one. (pp. 16–29) Broad goes on in this context to deny the necessity of the idea of substance in the concept of one physical object, after the fashion of Russell's elimination of the substantival implications of "this."

What is true in the substance theory then has no special reference to the unity of a thing with a number of qualities but refers to the relation of instances to their universals, a relation which would hold in a case of a particular which was an instance of only a single universal. (*PPR*, p. 97)

To the usual arguments for substance from the reality of change ("X has changed" means "there is an X over and above its manifestations and it is the latter which has changed"), Broad replies with Hume that complete identity of successive states is not required for the concept of "one thing." "All that is necessary is that the successive objects of observations should be continuous with each other." (p. 103) Such continuity can be accounted for on a purely phenomenalist basis. Broad thus draws the conclusion: "For we now see that what constitutes one thing in the physical world is nothing of a deep or recondite character, and that its nature is just its qualities from moment to moment in the relations in which they constitute a thing." (p. 104)

The clear formulation of the phenomenalist-realist position on the nature of a "thing" is immediately sublimated in the subsequent discussion in *Physics, Perception, and Reality*. In the very next chapter on phenomenalism, he introduces the familiar distinction between perceptions and the objects of perceptions. Phenomenalism is said to hold "not merely that the objects of all our perceptions exist only when they are perceived, but also that there are no permanent real things with laws of their own that cause these perceptions and in some measure resemble their objects." (p. 164) Broad points out that the phenomenalist is forced to include in his ontology his own past perceptions as well as perceptions of other people, else his account of the world will be unduly restrictive and non-predictive. But once phenomenalism has been modified in this way, has, that is, been expanded beyond solipsism, the question is then "whether the processes by which the phenomenalist . . . arrives at his belief in all these other perceptions would not equally justify the plain man's assumption of a real world more or less like what he perceives." (*PPR*, p. 168; cf. 178) Broad's answer to this question is in favour of the realist, as opposed to the phenomenalist, assumption, in favour of a realism which goes beyond phenomenalist-realism to a dualist-realism. The clear formulation of "thing" in a phenomenalist-realist language in chapter two of *Physics, Perception, and Reality* served certain purposes in his discussion of causation; but what seems most strange is that he never shows any awareness that the language he there used in talking about the external world is inconsistent with the language used in subsequent discussions of the subject.[5] It is even inconsistent with his own formulation of the criteria of physicality 1 to 4 offered before the Aristotelian Society during the same academic year as the publication of *Physics, Perception, and Reality*. In his discussion of the ontology of phenomenalism

[5]Broad has recently recognized the ambivalence of some of his early works on the concept of object. But he assures us that it was dualism which he was always trying to explicate and defend. See "A Reply to My Critics," *The Philosophy of C. D. Broad*, ed. by P. A. Schilpp, pp. 811–812.

he seems not to have discerned that his account of "thing" in that book was an alternative phenomenalist formulation to the description of phenomenalism offered in his direct discussion of that ontology, although it is true that the formulation in chapter two is implicitly phenomenalist-realist rather than pure phenomenalist. The force of his own dualist ontology has obscured this lapse into phenomenalist-realism; it is a lapse which may perhaps be taken as a kind of presage of more fundamental difficulties within his system, the difficulties of an adequate linguistic formulation of his dualism.

There can be no doubt, however, that despite this peculiar discussion in *Physics, Perception, and Reality*, Broad's own preferences, even in that work, are for the dualist-realist ontology. He does not claim that this ontology can be proved correct, but only that it is the best explanatory postulate for our phenomenal experiences. "The notion of persistent physical objects is logically merely a hypothesis to explain such correlations between perceptual situations" as we commonly find in our experiences. (*MPN*, p. 152; cf. *PPR*, p. 180–85; *ST*, p. 278) This postulate is elsewhere described as a category or "innate principle of interpretation."

From the very nature of the case the notion of "Physical Object" cannot have been derived by abstraction from observed instances of it, as the notion of "red" no doubt has been. For the objective constituents of perceptual situations *are* not instances of this concept; and it is only in virtue of these postulates that we can hold that they are "parts of" or "manifestations of" instances of this concept. The concept is not "got out of" experience until it has been "put into" experience. (*MPN*, p. 217)

I think it important to note Broad's recognition of the categorial nature of his physical ontology, for this is just the point that needs to be emphasized against those critics of the sense-datum theory who argue that physical-object words can only be derived from our phenomenal experiences.[6] The meanings for physical-object words in Broad's dualist ontology are extra-ordinary and do transcend phenomenal experiences. No violation of meaning-genesis has been made so long as we properly recognize the source of these transcendent meanings, which lies in part in the criteria of physicality laid down by Broad at the beginning of his analysis. I am not at all sure that even Broad recognized the necessity, within his particular ontology, of deriving physical-object meanings from his criteria and not from phenomenal experiences; but this is a problem for the third section of this chapter. What is important to note at this point is Broad's insistence that the category of physicality as

[6]*E.g.,* Lean, *op. cit.,* 25, 28, 35.

formulated by him in his complex criteria presupposes a structural isomorphism between phenomenal and physical realms: "what is real but imperceptible resembles that which we perceive." (*PPR*, p. 222) More specifically: "There is a certain physical object and a certain part of it which can be called '*the* part of *the* physical object' which has this sensum as an appearance." (*MPN*, p. 183) Unlike Russell, who appeals to the same structural postulate, Broad does not seek the isomorphous features in all sense experiences but only in tactual experiences, which hold a privileged position in his analysis of our knowledge of externality.

Our conclusion, then, is that it is most probable that there is a real counterpart corresponding point for point to what is perceived in most (perhaps in all) tactual perceptions that we have of figure, though doubtless more differentiated than the tactual objects themselves; and that events in this reality are the causes of our visual perceptions. . . . (*PPR*, p. 265)

The concept of externality embedded in the criteria can thus only be elaborated by appeal to the doctrine of structural similarities between phenomenal and physical realms.

II   MATERIAL PARTICLES AND GEOMETRICAL POINTS

There are two separate tasks involved in any account of the physical world: an indication of the general conditions or prerequisites for physicality and the qualitative description of physical objects. The criterion, which in Broad's case has turned out to be an elaborate categorial imposition upon the data of ordinary experience, accomplishes the first task for Broad while the doctrine of structure renders possible the second. Although there are no reasons against assuming an isomorphism between secondary as well as primary phenomenal qualities, Broad argues that there is no need to postulate a correlation in the physical realm with anything other than primary qualities, for example, shape, size, or position. The secondary phenomenal qualities can be explained by a primary physical world. Tactual sensations bring us into contact with the external object, although it is rather difficult to state just what is known in such experiences. In *Physics, Perception, and Reality*, the importance of tactual sensations was stated in a tentative manner; if we ever do come into contact with the physical world, the coincidence of visual and tactual sensations may be considered one example. (p. 236) In his *Examination of McTaggart's Philosophy*, the experience is given a phenomenological description. "In tactual perception we seem to ourselves to be prehending the surfaces of independent material things, close to our own bodies, and to be exploring the latter and interacting with them."[7] In *Scientific Thought* the suggestion is advanced more positively. "When we actively feel a body we are trying to penetrate a certain region of the movement continuum from various directions, and are failing to do so. And our failure is marked by characteristic tactual sensations." (*ST*, p. 341) What Broad wants to be able to say is that physical or scientific objects are within the region thus marked out in the movement-continuum in a *literal* way: "the felt boundaries are the boundaries of a volume which is *in* the movement-continuum in the same literal sense in which a tactual sensum is in its tactual field. . . ." (*ST*, p. 341)

But what precisely do we learn from the tactuo-resistant experiences? Whatever is *in* the general area marked out in the movement-continuum of these experiences cannot be said to have "the peculiar sensuous reality that we experience" (*PPR*, p. 248), since the physical world of Broad's dualist ontology is a world without observers. Thus, it would seem that we can ascribe primary qualities to this world only in the sense that "it will agree in having distinctions where we perceive spatial [or tactual] distinctions and where other people agree with us in perceiving them." (*PPR*, p. 249) The objective is not so much to give a *qualitative* description of the physical world (since the term "quality" may itself apply to the non-phenomenal world in only a very indirect fashion) as it is to offer a *geometrical* formulation sufficient for the uses of science. Thus, besides locating the physical object in the movement-continuum, tactual sensations are said to reveal the correct geometrical shape of that object. (*PPR*, p. 262; *MPM*, p. 171–73) But Broad requires tactuo-resistant sensations to play another important role in delimiting and characterizing the physical world of external objects. In general, for all sensa the world of matter serves as partial cause of the phenomenal world. In finding our movements impeded by certain sensory defined areas in the movement-continuum, are we experiencing more than geometrical properties of the physical world? Condition 3 of Broad's criteria stipulated that we must be able to state causal laws in terms of physical objects. What is even more important, we must be able to state causal laws connecting physical and sensory worlds. In his discussion of causation in *Physics, Perception, and Reality*, Broad made it clear that he wished to define "cause" in a non-activist sense, that to, as uniformity. Thus to say that a certain tactuo-resistant sensation is caused in part by a certain feature of physical

[7]II, pt. 1, 62; cf. "Some Elementary Reflections on Sense-Perception," in *Philosophy* (Jan. 1952), p. 6.

objects means that the sensa stand in certain uniform relations with the physical object. In *Scientific Thought*, this uniformity is spoken of as a "fixing," according to general rules, of the filling of one region by another. A general formulation for causation takes the following form:

If any determinate c of the determinable C inheres in a region r of the Space-Time S, then a certain correlated determinate γ of a certain correlated determinable Γ inheres in a certain correlated region ρ of a certain correlated Space-Time Σ. (*ST*, p. 541)

In the case of physical causation, the region S and Σ are in the same space-time realm. There are other simplifying conditions for causation within the physical realm which need not concern us here, since the important question is what is involved in the causal relation between physical objects and sensa. Broad recognizes that the relation in this case becomes more complex because of the differences between the space-time realms of the two causal factors. But he insists that the causation of sensa does not differ in kind from that of physical objects. (*ST*, p. 542) Thus, presumably what he wants to say about physical-phenomenal causation is that, as with the other physical-phenomenal relations, for changes in the one there can be assumed correlated changes in the other. Causation is a primary quality since it applies to the physical realm, but it cannot be said, I think, that resistance sensations yield any insight into this primary quality since they disclose no more of the causal (that is, uniformity) connections between phenomenal and physical than do sensa such as colour, for secondary as well as primary phenomenal qualities stand in a causal relation with the physical world. It is only because of the assumption of structural similarity, and certain other special assumptions regarding tactuo-resistant sensations, that these sensa play any more determinate role than others. The causal relation in the phenomenal realm can be said to be similar to the same relation in the physical realm because the postulate of isomorphism stipulates a correspondence and because a uniformity principle can be stated to cover relations in both realms. But the causal principle does not thereby add any qualitative information concerning the physical world which was not already present in the structural postulate. In general, the belief that the physical world has the primary qualities in the same way that we experience them is replaced by the belief "that there is a one to one correspondence between perceived geometrical distinctions in the object of tactual perception and certain permanent ones in the reality events in which cause the perception." (*PPR*, p. 263)

The opposition between sensuous and geometrical plays a central role in Broad's attempt to elaborate his account of the physical world. He wants to maintain both that all we know of the physical world depends upon sensa, and that nonetheless the sensuous aspect of sensa must be eliminated in using them as descriptive indicators of the scientific, physical world. Like Russell, Broad has consistently maintained that the significant features of the physical world are constructed from the sensuous world of ordinary experience. His most detailed treatment of the constructionist thesis occurs in his various accounts of physical space. The question concerning space in the physical sense is whether we can think of the physical world as being a spatio-temporal whole analogous with the sensory whole of our various sense-histories. (ST, p. 454) The justification, as always for any feature in scientific formulations, is whether such a manner of thinking summarizes all of the data of our sensory world. Space-time is not an entity but a system of relations. "When we talk of the properties of physical Space-Time we are simply enumerating certain very general structural characteristics of that spatio-temporal whole which is the physical world." (ST, p. 457) More generally, for any space, whether physical or sensible, "We assume a class of entities which we call points and we assume certain kinds of relations between them and other relations which only relate certain selections of them."[8] A straight line, for example, is a selection of certain points in the space to which it belongs. Space-time in the physical world is a system of relations between the various components of whatever it is that inhabits that world. But the only account of the spatial or temporal relations of the physical world which Broad offers is geometrical. (ST, pp. 457 ff.) The requirement of abstracting the sensuous elements of experience before we arrive at a description of the nature of external physical objects is once again interpreted as a task for geometrical formulation. The analogy between the sensuous world of ordinary experience and the observerless world of physics lies in their corresponding geo-chronometries. But a geo-chronometry of the physical world, however useful to physics, is insufficient by itself to tell us what it is that has these spatio-temporal relations. Although there is a tendency in some passages for Broad to equate the physical world with the geometrical tools used in dealing with it, there can be no doubt that he meant to separate the two. In the early article on space already referred to, he very consciously distinguished between space and the matter which encloses it. To make such a separation "we must suppose that pieces of matter are related

[8]"What do we Mean by the Question: Is our Space Euclidean?" *Mind*, XXIV (1915), p. 465.

in a certain peculiar way to points of space." (*Mind*, XXIV, 466) We are thus confronted with two sets of spatial relations relevant to the physical world of matter: material and geometrical relations, the latter being unextended. We have, in other words, a sharp distinction between material particles and geometrical points. Spatial relations between material particles, or points in matter, cannot be stated without reference to the relations between the corresponding geometrical points and their relations to material particles.

The statement 'the material point A is twelve miles to the SW of the material point B at the moment t' means, 'the material point A is at the geometrical point a at t and the material point B is at the geometrical point b at t and the geometrical point a is eternally twelve miles SW of the geometrical point B.' (*Ibid.*, p. 466–67)

Geometrical points are timeless while material points are subject to time. Like the general concept of externality, space is a feature not given in experience but added to it by way of interpretation. (*Ibid.*, p. 470) Perceived shapes, sizes, and spaces are found in experience but physical space is not. Any physical space is "conceptual in the sense that" it is "constructed in order to deal with certain sets of experienced objects according to a certain definite plan." (*Ibid.*, p. 472–73) In the example just quoted, reference to geometrical points renders the material location precise. None of the perceptual data which is summarized by this precise spatial interpretation can be said to be *in* the physical space thus constructed. "This is because physical space and physical bodies are only constructed to deal with certain important data of sight and touch and not with all perceptual data even of waking life." (*Ibid.*, p. 474)

If we pursue this constructionist thesis closely, it would seem to lead us to the conclusion that all that is required in the concept of external physical objects is a precise geometrical formulation enabling physicists to manipulate and predict the features in the phenomenal world. The world of physical objects would be replaced by the world of geometry. Geometrical points would supplant material particles. Broad has raised the question about the reality of space, saying that this question has two possible meanings. It could mean "Are the points of physical space of the same logical type as particular sense-data?" or it could mean "Can all observable movements be stated as functions of physical bodies with the qualities that have been ascribed to them and of Space with the qualities that have been ascribed to it in the particular system of physics and geometry under discussion?" (*Ibid.*, p. 476) The first alternative is indeterminate, although Broad finds no reasons for an affirmative answer. The second alternative is the one he favours. Physical space is real in the sense of being a function of observable objects, but the space which is physical and the space which is geometrical tend to merge into one. For the geometrical points which are required to deal with physical position are themselves real in the same way that physical space is real: "in the sense that they are determinate functions of real series of actually existing particulars." (*ST*, p. 51) But Broad wishes to make the physical world something more than just a geometrical function of phenomenal events. In *Physics, Perception, and Reality* he remarks that all of the laws of motion are stated about what we perceive but are meant to apply to the imperceptible in the sense that "they are laws about that aspect of it [appearance] and its changes to which we believe there to correspond a real counterpart." (pp. 345 ff.) Mathematical analysis is held distinct from that which it analyzes.

Are we justified in supposing that the causes of the perception of a piece of wood and of a piece of iron of the same size and shape are differently aggregated collections of the same kind of small but finite real bodies differing only by their number and arrangement, and such that when, for purposes of the second law of motion, we make the mathematical analysis into particles, we can assume the same laws connecting configurations with acceleration, and explain the observed differences in terms of the differences of number and configurations? (*PPR*, pp. 351 ff.)

Particles in the sense of geometrical points must be carefully distinguished from *material* particles or the material qualities which are formulated by the language of mathematics. Strongly as the constructionist thesis is expressed by Broad, I think it correct to say that it never becomes so dominant as to lead him to deny an ontological realm of material particles which are the real counterparts of our phenomenal experiences. He considers the physical world to have various levels, where the levels are "stages where certain disintegrating agents, which have previously been effective, cease to be so." (*ST*, p. 401) The first level in the physical hierarchy is, however, not at all clear. "The sort of scientific object which is specially connected with a perceptual object, like a chair, may be called a *first order* object." (*ST*, p. 400) We are told that the first order scientific object is "supposed . . . to consist of a great many molecules arranged in a pattern in space" and these are called the *second order* objects. Does Broad mean to say that interposed between the molecules and the perceptual chair there is another imperceptible scientific object? His classification would seem to claim just this, but I do not see what kind of object he has in mind. Be that as it may, we move down in the physical scale by subdividing the molecule into atoms, "characteristically arranged in space and moving in characteristic ways in time." These *third order* objects are themselves arrangements "of positive and negative electrons, with characteristic types of motion," which constitute the *fourth order* objects in the physical world. The classification here is of an open nature, since Broad leaves the way clear to further disintegrating forces.

Matter and the geometry of matter, then, Broad means to separate. There is a realm of real objects classifiable in the manner just indicated, possessed of such qualities as position, motion, spatial arrangement, shape, etc. These primary qualities are referred to as material qualities. (*PPR*, p. 346; *MPN*, p. 592) In *The Mind and Its Place in Nature* he develops a precise terminology for referring to the material qualities possessed by the various order objects of the external world. Space and time are positional qualities, while colour and temperature are non-positional qualities. "Every particular existent is characterized by some determinate form of the determinable quality of Temporal Position." (p. 592) In addition, every instance of a non-positional quality "must *also* be characterized by some determinate form of the determinable quality of Spatial Position." These are the material qualities, distinguished from immaterial qualities which do not need to be characterized by spatial position. Under the impetus for mathematical precision in his formulation, Broad wants to say that every particular existent of a material sort must be both instantaneous and punctiform; that is, each existent is characterized by just one determinate form of the qualities of temporal position and spatial position. The result of this restriction yields point-instants which are the material counterpart of the geometrical points used in the mathematical formulation of physics.[9] Beside the single determinate form of space and time, each point-instant must have a determinate form of one or more non-positional qualities. (*MPN*, p. 593–94, 207; cf. *PPR*, p. 265) This is condition 10 of his criteria for physicality. Moreover, there are some qualities such as duration, shape, and size which can characterize only groups

[9]In his "A Reply to My Critics," in Schilpp, ed., *op. cit.*, Broad says that the terminology of point-instants to which I refer here was never meant to be a serious possible view. (p. 810) Broad is correct in saying that the only place where he uses this point-instant terminology is on pp. 587–603 of *MPN*. But these pages seem to me to embody only a particular and special way of talking about the conception of matter which I have discussed in this section of this chapter. The distinction between geometrical and material points is found, we have seen, in many places in Broad's writings. The problem facing the dualist—whether he recognizes its importance or not—is what language to use in formulating material particles.

of point-instants, not the particular point-instant itself. These qualities are dependent upon the particular relations between the individual members of such groups. Broad calls these Extensional qualities. They are so defined that they are the results of groupings of instantaneous, punctiform point-instants. In fact, Broad continues in this same context to build up a detailed definition of a material substance. (pp. 596 ff.; cf. *ST*, p. 215–17) Material particles, which themselves define material substances, are functions of material point-instants sharing the same determinate quality of spatial position, whose determinate qualities of temporal position "form a continuous series, so that the whole composed of these point-instants has a certain determinate duration," and each of which shares in the other necessary material qualities. With appropriate alterations in the conditions of the groups of point-instants, Broad extends this process of construction to the derivation of finite bodies with all the necessary features of a physical object as laid down by his criteria of physicality.

The various orders of objects in the physical world are imperceptible particles or groups of particles having properties of shape, size, position, mass, time, motion or change, and electric charge. These properties, or some of them at least, are formulated in mathematical and geometrical terms which are themselves derived from phenomenal experience in a manner I will examine shortly. If this account is anything like the picture of the physical world Broad had in mind, a special problem arises about the attitude he had towards the ontological status of the human body. In some passages he seems to have thought we could include our own bodies in the account of the physical world; in many places Broad treats these bodies as the paradigm of physical objects. He points out the special peculiarities in the relation we have to our bodies. The sense-object by means of which I am related to this object remains constant throughout my movements and adjustments with other sense-objects. In order to have contact-sensa of this object we do not need to move around since it is always within the contact area. (*ST*, p. 439) "My trunk is the *only* physical object which appears throughout the *whole* of my visual sense-history as a positionally uniform sense-object; and it is the only physical object which I can touch whenever I like. . . ." (*Ibid.*, p. 440) Moreover, tactual sensations of this object are accompanied by certain somatic sensations, such as the awareness that it is *my* body that is being touched.

My own body is thus known to me by tactual exploration as a closed surface which resists my efforts to penetrate it, like any other physical object. But it is marked out from the other closed surfaces that I feel by the qualitative peculiarity of the tactual sensa, and by the fact that I do not have to walk up to it and cannot walk away from it. (*ST*, p. 441)

Furthermore, the kinaesthetic sensations which accompany these sensa are taken by Broad as sense-perceptions of the inside of this particular body. We can never have inside sensa for other bodies. It is this peculiarity which suggests to Broad an empirical origin for our general concept of physical objects, although this is clearly not meant to supplant the *a priori* nature of the category of physicality. But assuming that we can take communication as involving more than a private soliloquy, we learn that other people have bodies of the same sort as we do, having insides as well as outsides, connected to our general sense field in the same peculiar fashion.

I thus come to recognize that there are plenty of other bodies besides my own, having internal processes; although I cannot *perceive* these processes in any body except my own. So the fact that I cannot perceive such processes elsewhere ceases to be any reason for supposing that they do not *exist* elsewhere. (*ST*, p. 443)

Since we can learn that somatically felt changes are correlated in this instance with optically experienced changes, we come to formulate the belief that what is optically filled in any instance is physically filled as well. But although this may be an accurate account of part of the psychology behind the belief in other bodies, there is a peculiarity about this account of human physical bodies which seems to escape Broad.

Where, for example, would we place this object in the account of the physical world in terms of imperceptible particles? Broad does not say that somatic sensa place us in contact with electrons or molecules nor that what we know in these special experiences are imperceptible but finite real particles. When we take somatic sensations as experiences of the insides of our bodies we are not using the term "inside" in the sense that we would were we to say that inside every physical object lies its imperceptible structure. Experience of pains, of hunger, etc., may be taken as different from experiences of tactual or visual sensations; but, if we are to use the vocabulary of "inside" and "outside" in this connection, it is comparable to speaking of the inside and outside of my desk. Inside my desk are hollow spaces filled with paper clips, notes, pencils, etc. Had I peculiar visual powers I could perhaps have experiences at the same time of the outside surface and of the inside of this desk. But whether we are inside or outside in this example, we are still in the phenomenal world. We have not left the world of sensa and penetrated to the physical world which stands as the postulated correlate to our sensa. We might be able to picture Broad's dualist ontology by saying that our tactual sensa bring us as close to physical objects as we can ever get sensuously and that this experience is almost like touching my desk or my body on the outside. But the situation is not the same with physical objects as it is with the phenomenal objects of our sensuous experience, since I can never penetrate beyond the tactual sensa and obtain a sensuous experience of the physical object which lies just on the other side. In fact, the notion of lying on the other side of my tactual sensa is misleading, since we are here dealing with two different kinds of space and hence of positional qualities. The inside of my physical body to which Broad refers is still a sensuously felt inside and hence part of the phenomenal world. In short, the attempt to place our own physical bodies on the map of physicality results in their being pushed out of the physical world into phenomenality. The phenomenal object called our body does have a peculiar and special role to play in our experiences, but on the particular dualist ontology advanced by Broad it cannot be taken as a *physical* object: we are no closer to the physical aspect of our bodies than we are to any other physical object. Broad has apparently forgotten, in these passages, the commitments required by his own ontology and by his other clear acceptances of the sharp separation between sensuous and physical. Like the phenomenalist-realist account of "thing" in *Physics, Perception, and Reality*, this attempt to single out the body as the paradigm of all physical objects has a strangely phenomenalist character totally inconsistent with his ontology.

His account of the relation between material particle and geometrical point indicates a concern to keep the material and the geometrical provinces separate; similarly, the material realm of physical objects must be kept strictly distinct from the phenomenal realm of sensa. The physical body we call our own cannot be placed in the physical realm so long as we mean by that body what Broad has clearly intended to mean, that is, the body we know through tactual and kinaesthetic sensations. Physical and phenomenal have been inconsistently blurred. It is the sharp separation of these two realms which is entailed by Broad's criteria of physicality. But the two examples we have remarked of his apparent transgression against the dualistic requirements of his criteria, are not the only tendencies in Broad's analysis towards the undermining of his dualism. The constructionist thesis which we have been examining in this section involves a twofold separation similar to that between physical and phenomenal. The construction of physical objects from punctiform, instantaneous particulars described in *The Mind and its Place in Nature* could not enable us to pass from the imperceptible world of physical objects to the phenomenal world of sensa. This construction, or any other one which will be faithful to the properties of that imperceptible world of particles, is and must be indigenous to the world of matter alone, although in order for the construction of finite material but imperceptible bodies to be useful and meaningful for the world of ordinary experience, it must be possible to work from the formulation to the phenomenal world. For example, while dealing with the meaning of causation, Broad says that it must be thought of as a relation between durationless states. He observes that it is no objection to say that these states cannot be perceived, for neither can the causal laws.

Both causal laws and the momentary states into which perceptually continuous change of quality is analyzed are discovered by reflecting upon and reasoning about what we do perceive. It then becomes quite irrelevant to the validity of causal laws whether the states in terms of which they are formulated really exist, so long as it is always possible to retrace one's steps from these durationless states to what we actually do perceive. . . ." (*PPR*, p. 117 ff)

Broad thought he had a method whereby this retracing could be achieved. But the problem here is one of working back from the formulation used in dealing with the external world to the world as we know it in sensuous experience. The constructionist thesis has, in other words, two forms within Broad's ontology. It assumes the form of a derivation of meaningful concepts to apply to the external world from the phenomenal world of ordinary experience. This derivation, which I shall refer to as the *linguistic construction,* is achieved by his use of Whitehead's method of extensive abstraction: it involves the defence of mathematical and geometrical concepts as formulations of the nature of the physical world. But the constructionist thesis also takes the form of a derivation of physical objects from instantaneous, punctiform abstractions. This *ontological construction* occurs wholly within the physical realm; whether Broad disowns this construction or not, some ontological construction is necessary for the dualism of his theory. The two constructions are of course closely related, since the material qualities used in the second construction are themselves defined in terms of the first construction, that is, in terms of the mathematical and geometrical language of physics. In fact, the problem for the dualistic ontology which Broad is trying to defend is actually how to keep the two constructions sufficiently separated to prevent the loss

of all meaning to his ontological concepts. It is debatable whether
Broad has been able to achieve this required separation; for the point-
instants used in the second construction to derive the world of physical
objects seem dangerously near to collapsing into the geometrical
points of the first construction. If we decide that this danger is not only
imminent in his system but also eminent, then I think we can say that
the constructionist element in Broad's physical ontology has triumphed
over the realist factors and renders invalid the concept of a realm of
matter distinct from our mathematical formulation.

III Linguistic Formulation and Phenomenalist Transcendence

Language should not be taken as a particular revealer of the structure of reality, but a theory of reality is meaningful and understandable
only if it can be formulated in a language. While there are difficulties
connected with formulating a language for phenomenalist and phenomenalist-realist ontologies, there are very special problems in a dualist-
realist theory which arise from the phenomenalist transcendence
required by such an ontology. Similar linguistic problems arise with
metaphysical or theological formulations: how can our words mean
more than is revealed in phenomenal experiences? Any theory of
ostensive definition is clearly phenomenalist in its restrictions, since it
is impossible to indicate that which is not directly experienced.
Physical-object words initially and ordinarily refer to phenomenal
qualities, but the requirements of the dualist's ontology necessitate a
non-phenomenalist language for physical-object words. The linguistic
construction for physical objects referred to in the last section represents Broad's attempt to offer such a non-phenomenalist formulation.
The requirement here is for a non-sensuous conception and linguistic
expression, a requirement which is achieved by looking through the
sensuous content of our phenomenal experiences to their geometrical
structure. The observerless world is interpreted as being geometrically
similar to the phenomenal world, and the linguistic problem becomes
that of deriving geometrical from sensuous terms. The danger,
remarked in the last section, of the second construction within Broad's
system—the construction of physical objects from point-instants—
coalescing into the geometrical formulation for physical objects, reappears on the linguistic level as the problem of determining whether
the geometrical formulation is an adequate linguistic description of
the non-phenomenal world.

The problems here and their proffered solutions can best be dealt with by first schematizing the various linguistic components employed by Broad for this task. Whether Broad was fully aware of the linguistic and conceptual difficulties confronting the dualist is not always clear; but his analysis provides us with an important contribution to the resolution of these difficulties.

LINGUISTIC MAP FOR BROAD'S DUALIST ONTOLOGY

I *Phenomenal Objects*	II *Transcendent Meaning Principles*	III *Physical Objects*
1. Quality words learned by direct acquaintance, e.g., red, extension, round	1. Criterion of Physicality	1. Geometrical words learned from mathematics and geometry
	2. Postulate of Isomorphism	
2. Statements comprised of quality words referring to groups of sense qualities	3. Principle of Extensive Abstraction	2. Quality words borrowed from phenomenal statements, e.g. extension, shape, size
		3. Statements translating quality words into geometrical words

The statements translating quality words into geometrical words (Linguistic Map, III:3) rest for their meaning upon the three meaning principles (II:1, 2, 3). The criterion of physicality (II:1) functions as a directive stipulating that our physical-object words must have meanings which go beyond the phenomenal realm; such words are to have an extra-ordinary meaning. The force of the postulate of isomorphism (II:2) consists in saying that besides the dualism of II:2, we must replace our quality words and statements (I:1, 2) by non-sensuous terms. That is, what the postulate calls for, with its emphasis on structural or geometrical relations, is precisely a non-sensuous language. But in order for the move from ordinary phenomenal statements to the abstractive statements of II:2 to be made, we need some principle showing that a transition can be made from sensuous to geometrical. Thus, we have II:3, the principle of extensive abstraction. It is this principle which plays the final decisive role in Broad's attempt to construct a meaningful language for his physical world, since it enables him to relate the formulation of physical laws to the perceptible events of our phenomenal experience, while at the same

time permitting him to say that the language refers to the imperceptible
world of electrons, atoms, and molecules. He borrowed the principle
of extensive abstraction from Whitehead, who used it, oddly enough,
to avoid the kind of dualism which Broad's ontology requires.[10] As
Broad interprets Whitehead's principle, it consists in defining the
geometrical terms—points, lines, and areas—as "series of converging
volumes." (ST, p. 45) The geometrical terms thus defined are not the
limits of converging series but are to be identified with the series
themselves, although unlike the series, the points or lines are not
perceptible. The only reality for such concepts is, as we have seen,
as functions of the converging series. Broad endeavours to give as
concrete a picture of the process of derivation as he can by showing
how far the geo-chronometry of an "idealized sense history" can be said
to be analogous to the geo-chronometry of the physical world. What
is involved is a careful but persistent elimination of the sensuous
properties together with a steady narrowing of the spatial and temporal features of the sense history. (ST, p. 459ff) We begin by extending, conceptually, the temporal and spatial field of a particular sense
history so that there are no limitations imposed by sensation or memory, for example, the sense history stretches indefinitely into the past,
and the spatial field includes what could be grasped could we see all
around ourselves at once. We then reduce this extended sense history
until we arrive at smaller and smaller slabs or slices, both temporally
and spatially. Thus, the history can be conceived of as composed of a
great number of instantaneous, punctiform slabs. Quality words are
thus transformed into geometrical words and we have the translation
required by III:3.

Broad never makes the distinction between the two components of
his constructionist thesis—the linguistic and the ontological construction—as clear or as decisive as I have argued that his position requires.
Thus, the derivation of the linguistic construction from phenomenal
experiences frequently appears as an ontological construction for the
physical world; but the fate of his realist ontology depends upon the
ability to keep these two constructions distinct. Even though the
linguistic construction can be legitimately derived, in the way Broad
intends, from phenomenal experience, the validity of this formulation

[10]Cf. The Concept of Nature, p. 30. "What I am essentially protesting against
is the bifurcation of nature into two systems of reality, which, in so far as they
are real, are real in different senses. One reality would be the entities such as
electrons which are the study of speculative physics. This would be the reality
which is there for knowledge; although on this theory it is never known. For what
is known is the other sort of reality, which is the byplay of the mind."

for his ontology requires that it be an adequate expression for the ontological construction while remaining distinct from it. But its adequacy
as a meaning-principle for physical-object words seems clearly to
rest upon the postulate of isomorphism, since it is this postulate which
specifies that the external physical world is an analogue of the
geometrical features of the phenomenal world. On the directive of the
principle II:2, Broad has reduced the physical world to point-instants.
This principle demands a geometrizing of the physical world; II:3
provides the meaning for such geometrizing while showing how the
isomorphous relations of structural features between phenomenal and
physical realms can be exemplified. Were it not for II:2, there would
be no justification at all for saying that III:3 applies to or is the
linguistic expression of the physical world; we would have merely
another formulation for the phenomenal world. In other words, it is
the postulate of isomorphism which enables Broad to escape an
unknowable-substance doctrine, but he escapes this doctrine only by
feeding into his meaning-principles the features required by his conclusions. Just as the dualist ontology he advocates as a necessary
modification of the ordinary view of the physical world was found to
be an imposition upon ordinary experience, so the specific form this
dualism takes is the result of the imposition of the postulate of isomorphism upon II:1. The logical status of both the category of physicality
and the postulate of isomorphism is the same: they are explanatory
devices capable of rendering intelligible our phenomenal experiences.
Like Russell, Broad has been motivated throughout his analysis of
perception and reality by a concern to defend the views of science and
of common sense. The latter requires some modification over what
Broad assumes it to be initially, but the realm of science and the
phenomenal realm are allowed to meet only on the grounds of geometrical similarity. The features of ordinary experience can then be
allowed to yield information about the external world, and some part
of the ordinary non-philosophical belief is thereby preserved. The
phenomenal world is related both ontologically and semantically to
the physical world by the abstractive process of rendering the sensuous
qualities into geometrical concepts.

When Broad is presenting the abstractive process required by the
principle of extensive abstraction, he does not always indicate that
he understands that the language thus abstracted from phenomenal
experience cannot be taken as a physical language for his dualist
ontology without explicit appeal to the postulate of isomorphism. But
the postulate is the implicit assumption behind the second part of

Scientific Thought, which tells us very little directly about the physical object words such as "shape," "size," "extension," or "motion." He assumes throughout that the appearances tell us about their physical correlates. In effect, the bulk of his analysis there is concerned with the quality words that refer to sensa; he leaves us, presumably, to make the necessary abstractions to physical reality. But there are many terminological slips in this and other of his discussions which could lead us to conclude that he has forgotten the requirements of his own ontology. He speaks of physical objects moving away from us and talks frequently of watching physical objects. (*ST*, p. 413) On his theory all that we can watch are sensa: the conclusion to physical objects is an inference based on his postulate of isomorphism and upon the experienced sensa. The same ambiguity attaches to some of the criteria in the category of physicality. For example, condition 1 asserts that physical objects must be public, perceptible to more than one observer, while condition 6 says that physical objects must be neutral between the different senses. But the intra-sensorial or interpersonal publicity allowed by Broad's dualism is at best only derivative from sensa and dependent upon the assumption of a similarity between appearance and that which appears. Interpersonal publicity is in effect phenomenal publicity, although Broad does not concern himself with justifying the belief in a common phenomenal world. If our phenomenal experiences are interpersonally similar, and if there is a world of objects behind the phenomenal world standing in a causal relation to this phenomenal world, then we can say that physical objects have a causal publicity, for example, that for similar phenomenal experiences there are similar or the same physical objects. In *The Mind and its Place in Nature* Broad violates the proper dualist mode of speech even more openly by arguing that the question of whether any given perceptual situation, besides having an epistemological object, has an ontological or physical object, cannot be settled by linguistic considerations alone: "the question can be settled only, if at all, by a careful enquiry into the nature and connexions of *things*." (p. 143) But it is one of the sceptical consequences of his own ontology that we can never enquire into the nature and connection of things in the physical sense: our enquiry is restricted to sensa. What these various terminological slips reveal is not, I think, a fundamental impossibility in the position Broad wishes to defend (as some of the sense-datum critics have claimed) but a failure to maintain the sharp distinction required by the phenomenalist and dualist modes of speech. The failure does, indeed, gloss over some important problems of verbalizing the dualist ontology and of assessing carefully the full significance of the postulate of isomorphism. It is also related to the other lapses into phenomenalist language remarked in the previous sections of this chapter.

IV   CONCLUSION

Are we to conclude, then, that Broad has been successful in keeping the linguistic and ontological constructions separated, that is, has avoided constructionism in favour of realism? A decisive answer cannot be given to this question. On the one hand, he has succeeded in offering a linguistic formulation which satisfies the phenomenalist transcendence required for his dualist ontology by providing a basis for physical meanings in a set of meaning-principles. He has not tried to pass directly from the quality words and statements of phenomenal experiences to the extra-ordinary physical-object words of the external world. On his system such a direct passage is no more possible linguistically than epistemologically. On the other hand, the linguistic construction thus emanating from the three transcendent-meaning principles presents us with a considerable conceptual problem. The physical world which is expressed by the linguistic construction is a world without observers and hence must be radically different from the world of appearances. But the task of conceiving what this non-sensuous world is like is hardly resolved by reference to geometrical formulations, since the components of such formulations are commonly taken to be points, lines, surfaces, and areas. When we abstract from any familiar phenomenal object and state its geometrical dimensions and relations, we do not ordinarily think we are dealing with other reals of an ontologically different sort from the phenomenal objects. As Broad admits, geometrical points are real only in the sense that they are functions of actually existing particulars. We cannot interpret the physical world of Broad's theory as having a reality like geometrical points, since this would reduce the ontology to a mere formulation. That Broad means the physical world to be a function of the phenomenal world in the sense that its geometrical features are the analogue of the phenomenal qualities is beyond doubt. But he just as clearly intends the physical world to be more than a formulation of certain abstract features of the phenomenal world. How then are we to conceive of it? We saw in section II the Broad relies upon physics at this juncture in his analysis: he presents a picture of the physical world in terms of the material particles—electrons, atoms, molecules—

referred to in physics. But he was not content with saying that the material particles, like the phenomenal objects of ordinary experience, have a similar geometrical structure. He found it necessary to make the material particles themselves constructs of point-instants, without making clear how a point-instant differs from a geometrical point. Is a point-instant another ontological ingredient in the physical real along with the other levels discriminated on his account of the items in the physical world? Presumably not, or he would have so specified them. Besides, it is clear, I think, that point-instants stand to the electrons, atoms, and molecules of the physical world in much the same relation as do the points and lines abstracted from the phenomenal world by the principle of extensive abstraction: just as the phenomenal world can be reached by tracing backwards along the abstractive process from the points to the qualities, so the physical objects of the external world are obtained by a constructive process from point-instants. If we take the point-instants in the ontological construction as distinct from the geometrical points of the linguistic formulation, then it would seem that we have in effect two different formulations, the one applying to the phenomenal world, the other to the physical world. If on the other hand, we interpret point-instants as identical with geometrical points, then we have one formulation for two different realms. But on neither alternative do we have a clear understanding of what is being formulated: we do not know how we are to conceive the components of the physical world apart from the formulation. Every attempt to conceive or to say what the physical world is like ends in a retreat to the abstract geometrical formulations of points or point-instants. We have a formulation without knowing what it is that is being formulated. In short, I do not think that the linguistic formulation which Broad offers for his ontology tells us how to separate the formulation from that which is formulated, the appearances from that which appears. A world of geometrical properties only (which his postulate of isomorphism seems to require) is indistinguishable from the geometrical formulations which apply to the phenomenal world.

The difficulties of Broad's analysis of the nature of external physical objects are difficulties of conception and not of formulation. We can follow him into his requirements of isomorphous similarities between phenomenal and physical and into his use of the principle of extensive abstraction. But our conception falters when we are asked to fill in the contents of the physical world while separating these contents from the formulation which expresses them. Broad has a notable predecessor in his suggestion that the contents are geometrical shapes and figures, for Plato, as we have seen, advanced the same suggestion in the *Timaeus*. Plato's spokesman in that dialogue admitted that the ontology advanced there was at best a fanciful or conjectural account. More recently, Descartes geometrized the physical world by characterizing its essence in terms of an extension which is grasped via the intellect and not the senses. The proof for the external world found in Descartes' sixth *Meditation* yields the conclusion, with much help from assumptions, that something exists which has the essential property of this sort of extension. Descartes did not establish the existence of the phenomenal world nor that of a physical world different from phenomenal and geometrical properties. Broad has the sanction of modern science behind his account of the physical world, but I think that he has not made the ontology of geometrical solids any more understandable than did Plato or Descartes. It is especially incumbent upon him to enable us to distinguish our talk about the physical world from that physical world itself. The alternatives for any dualist are a constructionism which denies the significance of this distinction or a sceptical doctrine of substance, the very meaning of which is threatened by conceptual difficulties.

Part III
MEANING AND TRUTH

The first chapter of this part argues that reference is an integral part of meaning. Reference comprises not just refer*ring* but also refer*red*. To understand the sense of a sentence we must know the sort of object that is talked about in that sentence. Epistemic or intentional reference must augment use in the analysis of meaning. The second chapter suggests some of the general ontological considerations of the theory of objects necessary for a dualist ontology; it develops the logic of non-empirical objects so that dualist reference can be better understood. The third chapter argues for correspondence as the basic truth-relation, but it points out that the terms of this relation are functions of particular ontologies. Truth is defined by ontological rules. Hence, truth cannot be ascribed to the ontological system itself.

The argument of this part thus has a common theme throughout its three chapters: referent is included in meaning, truth-conditions are contained in truth-claims, and what there is is a function of each ontology.

9

Meaning and Reference

ONE OF THE MORE FRUITFUL contributions of recent philosophy has been the stress upon a diversity of functions which sentences and expressions can and do perform in the context of language in use. It has become easy for philosophers to recognize a plurality of kinds of discourse. A subsidiary contribution has been to draw attention to language "as one human activity among others, interacting with others."[1] Still a third praiseworthy trait of recent philosophy is the stress upon the context of utterance of sentences and expressions. Sentences can be analyzed apart from their use on particular occasions only in the most formal of ways. The informal logic of utterance has come to replace the formalization of traditional and mathematical logic. The concentration upon the use of sentences in particular utterances has, however, had some deleterious side-effects. (1) The sentences and expressions analyzed have usually been those we normally use and meet in everyday situations; the utterances of philosophers have tended to be ignored or forced into the everyday mould. (2) The stress upon use has brought about a rejection of reference or denotation as an aspect of the meaning of sentences; reference is one of the jobs a sentence can be made to do but not part of its meaning.

This second side-effect is found in Wittgenstein, Strawson, and Ryle, but the rejection of reference from meaning is also found in most formal logicians—all those who have been concerned with intension rather than extension. The concern with modifying the traditional square of opposition so as to avoid the existential commitments of the A and E propositions is another aspect of the rejection of reference. The notion of meaning as use (and the rules of use) is most familiar from Wittgenstein and his followers. It is the followers of Wittgenstein who have talked as if reference has *no* role in the meaning of sentences. Wittgenstein only said: "For a *large* class of cases—though not for all—

[1]Strawson, review of Wittgenstein's *Investigations*, p. 72.

in which we employ the word 'meaning' it can be defined thus: the meaning of a word is its use in the language." (*Investigations*, #43) But almost the whole concern of the *Investigations* is to expose this large class of cases.

This claim for meaning without reference is extravagant; we cannot do without reference. The recognition of the dependence of meaning upon reference is especially important when dealing with metaphysical assertions. Metaphysical statements—certainly those of a dualist nature —must, if they are to have their metaphysical force, have more meaning than would be disclosed by attention to their use in their context. Attention to the contex of utterance is important in metaphysics as well as in all other forms of utterance. But we must realize at the same time that those statements mean more than is revealed by their interconnection in a system: they claim to make extra-linguistic refer-ence. This reference is an inseparable part of their meaning. Thus, the long-range value of a re-examination of meaning and reference lies in an explication of metaphysics.[2]

I proceed first by giving a brief summary of the view of meaning as use, as found in Strawson and Ryle. I then examine the charge that previous philosophers have identified meaning with denotation or reference. This charge may be true in the case of the early Russell, perhaps true of Frege, of doubtful truth as applied to Meinong, and clearly false in the case of Mill. This charge of what has come to be labeled the "Fido"-Fido Fallacy was motivated not so much by historical accuracy as by a fear of existential involvement by language. I want to take a look at this fear, to see whether it is well founded. There *are* existential commitments in metaphysics but these arise from and are to be analyzed in terms of ontological—not logical, or epistemological, or linguistic—considerations. The metaphysician has a theory of exist-ence and objects which it is the function of his language to express and formulate.

I   Meaning and Rules for Use

Wittgenstein has observed that "the meaning of a name is sometimes explained by pointing to its bearer" (I, #43), but the fact that a

---

[2]The rejection of reference from meaning is being frequently questioned now. *Vide*, Hampshire, *Thought and Action*, p. 200; J. Jarvis, "Definition by Internal Relation," *Aust. Journal of Philosophy*, p. 142, and "*Ethics* and Ethics and the Moral Life," *Journal of Philosophy*, p. 79; D. S. Shwayder, *Modes of Referring and the Problem of Universals*, p. 35; P. Ziff, *Semantic Analysis*, pp. 84–85; and J. R. Searle, "Meaning and Speech Acts," *Philosophical Review*, pp. 423–433.

sentence like "Excalibur has a sharp blade" makes sense even when the sword has been broken in pieces and destroyed, indicates that the meaning of a name (or of the expression using the name) is not to be confused with its bearer. (I, #39, 40–44) Strawson puts this point as follows: "The meaning of an expression cannot be identified with the object it is used, on a particular occasion, to refer to."[3] Meaning and reference are distinct. To "talk about the meaning of an expression or sentence is not to talk about its correct use, on all occasions, to refer or to assert." (pp. 30–31) The meaning of a singular referring expression "is the set of linguistic conventions governing its correct use so to refer."[4] Or, as Ryle puts the same point, "To know what an expression means involves knowing what can (logically) be said with it and what cannot (logically) be said with it. It involves knowing a set of bans, fiats, and obligations, or in a word, it is to know the rules of the employment of that expression."[5]

To give the meaning of any expression, then, I must give you the rules for the use of that expression. These rules *are* the meaning. This must mean that an utterance like "The dog is running," means something like the following: "if there is a four-legged animal with tail and a bark which is running, then this sentence may appropriately be uttered." If we ask for the meaning of the terms in this utterance, for example, of "four-legged," "bark," "running," you would have to give me a similar set of rules for their use; for example, when you hear a sound of the following sort (you then bark or arrange to have a dog bark), you may use the term "bark," etc. Some set of rules, fiats, conventions must be produced when I ask for the meaning of some expression since, we are assured, meaning is a set of linguistic conventions. If this account sounds odd, Strawson and Ryle would explain this reaction on our parts by saying that we may have been suffering under the mistake of thinking that expressions and sentences mean because they denote; even that their meaning *is* their denotata. They are concerned that we should not make the mistake of confusing meaning with objects in the world. Expressions and sentences are meaningful even in the absence of referents; hence their meaning cannot *be* the referents.

Although on Strawson's account expressions and sentences have meaning in the absence of referents, they do not (if they are potential-referring expressions and sentences) have meaning in the absence of

[3]"On Referring," in *Conceptual Analysis*, p. 30.
[4]Strawson, *Logic*, pp. 188–89.
[5]"The Theory of Meaning," in *British Philosophy in the Mid-Century*, p. 254.

rules for using and referring. Clearly, the rules for use would indicate when the expression would be appropriate and when its sentence would be true or false. To know the rules for use of sentences or expressions is *like* knowing whether there is a referent or whether the sentence is true or false. To give the meaning of some expression I do not have to give you the referent it refers to, but do I not do something very much like it when I give you the rules for using that expression in a referring way? Even Strawson said "Of course the fact that it [the sentence] is significant is the same as the fact that it *can* correctly be used to talk about something. . . ." (p. 32) Strawson even allows that the referring use of expressions and sentences *implies* a referent, at least as intended by the user. Moreover, Strawson also says that in the uniquely referring use we must specify *that* a referent is intended and *what* referent is intended. To know what referent is intended does not seem much different from saying that the referent is tied in with the meaning of the expression or the sentence.

II   RUSSELL ON DENOTING

Strawson wrote to correct Russell's analysis of denoting expressions; his objections to Russell's theory of descriptions was that Russell failed to distinguish between *asserting as if* the referent existed and *asserting that* it does, between *stating* that it does and *implying* that it does. Russell did not, in other words, distinguish between indicating the sorts of object assumed in certain expressions and sentences and making the existential move from sentence to existence. It is certainly true that in his discussions of meaning and reference prior to 1905 (prior, that is, to the essay "On Denoting" which I would suppose Strawson had in mind), Russell said many things which he took back or modified in 1905 and in subsequent essays. In *The Principles of Mathematics* (1903) Russell said "every word occurring in a sentence must have *some* meaning." (p. 42) Things are said to be what proper names "indicate"; all other words "indicate" concepts. (p. 44) The period of 1903–04 was one in which Russell saw himself especially close to Meinong. But the essay in 1905, "On Denoting," was written to correct some of his earlier excesses. In that essay, he found it "intolerable" to say, as he read Meinong as saying, that "the existent present King of France exists, and also does not exist; that the round square is round, and also not round."[6] Russell had by then viewed as dangerous any

[6]Reprinted in *Logic and Knowledge*, p. 45. I think it is doubtful whether Meinong *did* say that the entities talked about in propositions like "the present

such proliferation of entities, not only because some of Meinong's objects seemed to violate the law of contradiction but as well because Russell firmly believed there were no such entities. "There is," he wrote in *Introduction to Mathematical Philosophy* (1919), "only one world, the 'real' world. . . ." (p. 169) Russell was prepared to include in this one real world imaginations and thoughts, as well as the familiar physical objects; unicorns and Hamlet were excluded. Thus, Russell had his own ontological beliefs prior to his analysis of propositions. He wished to avoid any possible commitments in his language which his ontology did not sanction.

Those who charge Russell with identifying the meaning of an expression with its bearer[7] are correct in one sense: Russell had such a theory in mind, had perhaps even defended it prior to 1905, but, after 1905, wrote to avoid that possibility. Russell was afraid that if left unanalyzed, phrases like "the so-and-so," or even "a so-and-so," would lead us into saying that the object of such expressions exists. He even contrasts two analyses of these sorts of phrases. On the one hand, we might treat them as names "directly designating an individual which is its meaning."[8] On the other hand, we can follow Russell's own analysis of these phrases as descriptions, where we avoid the possibility of saying that their meanings are the objects which they designate. He himself wished to restrict names to those cases where the name does truly name some existent object, and this was determined by Russell's ontology, not by his logic. On Russell's strict view of names, of logically proper names, the existence of the designata is required, but Russell never thought of inferring existence from names. Rather, he made his analysis of names fit his ontology. Russell's theory of logically proper names (expressed in his essays on logical atomism as well as in the later *Inquiry*) hinges upon his belief that what we name ought to be a genuine particular; the only genuine particulars are, he believed, the objects of acquaintance. Nothing outside this area of acquaintance can be named.

It was the function of the theory of description to make certain

King of France" (uttered when France has no king) both exist and do not exist. In his *Gegenstandtheorie* (translated and reprinted in Chisholm's *Realism and the Background of Phenomenology*, p. 82) Meinong does say that the round square is both round and square, just as the golden mountain is made of gold.

[7]Besides Strawson's criticism which charges Russell with not distinguishing between assuming and asserting that the referent exists, the criticisms of P. T. Geach (*Mental Acts*, p. 48, and *Reference and Generality*, pp. 53–56) and Miss E. Anscombe (*An Introduction to Wittgenstein's Tractatus*, pp. 43–45) are relevant here.

[8]*Introduction to Mathematical Philosophy*, p. 174.

that our language does not violate the ontological belief in sense contents as the only genuine particulars, the only "particular particulars" as Russell called them. The theory of description, that is, took care to eliminate as names all expressions save those which named sense contents: "this" and "that" were, for Russell, the only logically proper names. The fact that they are "logically" proper names was, however, a function not of logic but of ontology. So the correct analysis of expressions like "the so-and-so," or the indefinite expression "a so-and-so," sought to avoid the possibility that the object spoken about might, as Russell said, "enter into" the expression or sentence.[9] Since expressions like "a unicorn" or "I met a sea-serpent" are significant though false, their meaning must lie elsewhere than in their denotation. Thus, in all cases of denoting phrases, the proper analysis is to treat them without talking about their denotation. ("On Denoting", p. 41.) A phrase may "be denoting, and yet not denote anything, e.g., 'the present King of France.'" (p. 41) This phrase has meaning, Russell said, providing the phrase, "the King of England" has meaning, but it has no denotation. (p. 46) Phrases like "the round square," "the even prime other than 2," or "Apollo," are "denoting phrases which do not denote anything." (p. 54) Furthermore, Russell announced at the beginning of his "On Denoting" essay that "a phrase is denoting solely in virtue of its *form*." (p. 41)

It is clearly incorrect to say, as Miss Anscombe says, that in Russell's view, "for a word or phrase to have meaning . . . it is necessary for what we mean by it to exist." (*An Introduction*, p. 43) At the best, what Miss Anscombe says here would hold only during the period of 1903–04; after that, what she says is true only for some words—for names—not for all words. Strawson comes closer to a correct account when he claims that the belief "underlying the Theory of Definite Description" is "that a genuine logical subject, a true referring expression can have a meaning only if there exists an object to which

[9]Of course, one strong motive for Russell's denial of referents as being involved in most expressions and sentences was the peculiar view of propositions which he held, inherited from G. E. Moore. (See Moore's "The Nature of Judgment," *Mind*, VIII, 30 (1889).) In the opening statement of his three-part article on Meinong (*Mind*, 1904), Russell said that perception has as its object "an existential proposition, into which enters as a constituent that whose existence is concerned, and not the idea of this existent." (p. 204) Even as late as 1911, "Knowledge by Acquaintance and Knowledge by Description" (reprinted in *Mysticism and Logic*), Russell was talking of physical objects being constituents of propositions. Objects in the past obviously pose a problem for such a view of knowledge, judgment, and propositions. The notion of a descriptive proposition whose constituents were not objects in the world was a pressing need for Russell.

it applies." (*Logic*, p. 188) But is it clear that names are the only type of referring expression for Russell? I am not even certain that Russell viewed naming as a denoting operation, but even if it was, his analysis of denoting phrases which are not logically proper names shows that he thought of them as denoting, even though they were also describing. The problem *is* complicated by the use to which Russell put the theory of description in his general epistemology. He insisted in "Knowledge by Acquaintance and Knowledge by Description" that *"Every proposition which we can understand must be composed wholly of constituents with which we are acquainted."* (p. 211)[10] And in "The Philosophy of Logical Atomism" he said that "the meaning you attach to your words must depend on the nature of the objects you are acquainted with." (Marsh, p. 195) The theory of names is controlled, in his epistemology, by his ontological views. He does not separate naming from truly naming. In order to know which terms are names we have to know what objects in the world can have names.[11] The operation of naming applies to the area of acquaintance, an area restricted, as we saw in chapter 7, to sense contents. Now if Russell had said that denoting phrases denote objects of acquaintance, we would still be unable to say that his doctrine was that the meaning of denoting phrases is what they denote. But so far as I can determine, Russell does not say even this, certainly not after 1905. In the essay "On Denoting," he speaks of the distinction between acquaintance and descriptive knowledge as "the distinction between things we have presentations of, and the things we only reach by means of denoting phrases." (p. 41) The denoting phrase does not, I take it, denote the presentations but the objects of description.[12]

Naming and denoting seem, then, to constitute for Russell two different operations. To name properly there must be objects to name. What can be named are only immediate sense contents. This process of naming may be a referring process, though this point is obscure in Russell's accounts. But there is another referring operation in which I use denoting phrases which are not logically proper names; they are open or disguised descriptions. The definite description talks about

[10]It is this principle of understanding and meaning which confronts Russell with those difficulties I have discussed in chapter 7 of formulating or saying dualism. With this principle, it is difficult to understand how we could ever understand any physical-object propositions. If all our terms find their meaning in sensory experience, what can even the descriptive proposition, "The cause of my sense-data," mean?

[11]Cf. his *Inquiry*, p. 97.

[12]Cf. "Knowledge by Acquaintance and Knowledge by Description," *Mysticism and Logic*, pp. 216, 222–23.

non-particulars, objects which cannot be directly sensed. The referring operation here does not require an object, since I can use these expressions without there being objects which the expressions purport to talk about. Another way of putting this point might be to call attention to the similarities between Russell's analysis in "On Denoting" and Strawson's in "On Referring." Both writers were trying to offer analyses of referring expressions which would avoid including the referent in the account of the meaning of such expressions. Russell does so by two moves: he severely limits the scope of names and he analyzes other denoting expressions in terms of descriptions. Strawson accomplishes the same objective by substituting, for the referent, rules for referring.

III   MILL

The mistake of thinking that the meaning of referring expressions *is* the object in the world which the expression denotes was traced to a preoccupation with names (especially with proper names) and naming. Since the word "Fido" stands for the dog in front of us, we might be led to say that the world means the dog. If we then assimilate most words and expressions to names, we may tend to think "that what a word means is in all cases some manageable thing that that word is the name of."[13] We would then find ourselves holding that meanings were things like dogs, towns, and battles. Ryle suggests that John Stuart Mill was close to such a view of meaning, although the essay in which Ryle seems to make this suggestion contains its own correction. The first few pages of that essay trace in outline form the points of the first five chapters of Mill's *Logic*. Ryle nowhere says outright that Mill held to the "Fido"-Fido theory of meaning, but he seems to imply that one who, like Mill, thought of most words as names is easily led to such a theory. Later in his essay, Ryle admits that with his distinction between connotation and denotation, Mill "virtually reaches the correct conclusion that the meaning of an expression is never the thing or person referred to by means of it." (p. 247) But this is not the conclusion Mill *virtually* reaches; it is the conclusion he *explicitly* and carefully states in frequent passages! In no sense can Mill be said to have confused meaning with the bearer of the name.

Mill distinguished between the meaning of a word and the "right use" of that word, between its signification and its purpose. (p. 11)

[13]Ryle, G. "The Theory of Meaning," in *British Philosophy in the Mid-Century*, p. 242.

Mill did say that a proposition "is formed by putting together two names" (p. 12) and that names are names of things, not of ideas in the mind. (p. 15) He did not say, or even suggest, that the meaning of names was the objects they named. For a name to have any signification it must, he said, give information about the object, for example, tell us something of its properties and attributes. (p. 20) Words are either connotative or non-connotative. "A non-connotative term is one which signifies a subject only, or an attribute only. A connotative term is one which denotes a subject and implies an attribute." (p. 20) It is important to keep in mind that a term which connotes does two things, it *denotes* or specifies some subject and *implies* (that is, tells us about) some of the subject's attributes or properties. The usual way of putting Mill's distinction, between connotation and denotation, is misleading, since connotation includes denoting. I think we could put Mill's distinction by saying that some terms only denote, single out a subject, while other terms both denote and give us information about the properties of the subject singled out. It is especially important to notice that Mill made a special point of saying that proper names are not connotative, do not both denote and imply attributes. Proper names only denote. Because they only denote, proper names have no meaning. (pp. 21–23) In general, "whenever the names given to any object convey any information, that is, whenever they have properly any meaning, the meaning resides not in what they *denote*, but in what they *connote*." (p. 23) An identifying chalk mark on a house or tree, put there to enable us to recognize that house or tree again, has a purpose but no meaning: "The chalk does not declare anything about the house; it does not mean, This is such a person's house, or This is a house which contains booty." (p. 23) By "learning what things" some word is "a name of, we do not learn the meaning of the name." (p. 24) Mill critizes Hobbes, as he reads him, for seeking for the meaning of names exclusively in what they denote, ignoring the proper locus of meaning, their connotation. (p. 62)

IV Existential Involvement

Mill was entirely clear about the mistake of saying that meanings are denotata, although he made the important and correct observation that meaning includes denotation. Russell saw the possibility of analyzing denoting phrases in a way which would allow their objects to constitute their meaning; he wrote to circumvent this possibility, certainly after 1905. Strawson and Ryle follow Frege's and, to some extent, Wittgenstein's lead in separating meaning from reference. To include reference in the analysis of meaning leads, they felt, to existential commitments. It *is* odd to say that objects in the world are meanings, but we have just seen that those charged with holding such a theory of meaning did not in fact hold to that theory. Some philosophers, like Russell, Strawson, and Ryle, have been afraid that someone has or might succumb to this view. Russell may even have thought *he* had succumbed to this view, although it is not clear that he did. But there *is* a fear of existential involvement by means of our language which a number of philosophers share.

I should think that the question of what objects there are in the world is not properly settled by epistemological, logical, or linguistic considerations. Philosophers have repeatedly been reluctant to engage in ontology. Where respectable at all, ontology has been the least respectable area of philosophy in the contemporary scene. But ontology has frequently masqueraded under other guises. Thus, Russell attempts to avoid Meinong's ontology through logical manipulations; Ryle replaces what he takes to be one metaphysic of mind by another through linguistic considerations; and Warnock's exposure of Berkeley's confusions is silently controlled by his own ontological attitudes. The easy rejection of reference as a part of meaning has issued from a misconception of logical and conceptual analysis. The fact that it has been possible to devise logical and linguistic techniques for dealing with denoting phrases which avoid the Meinongian commitments only shows that our talk can be so arranged that we need not accept an ontology where centaurs, round-squares, and negative facts are real. Whether we reify or not depends upon the demands of some particular ontology. The attempts of Meinong to produce a theory of objects which yields entities for every statement, as well as Russell's efforts to counter such reification must not be allowed to appear ontologically neutral. The move from purely epistemological or logical considerations to an empirical or to a non-empirical theory of objects can only be made with the help of specific ontological rules.

Philosophers fall, roughly, into two groups. There are those—of increasing rarity in the present period—concerned with the nature of existence, its kinds and properties. The larger group of philosophers are those who are obsessively concerned to avoid any existential commitments, who see potential inferences to existence in every sentence or expression. This second group wants to emphasize the mistakes in the ontological argument for God's existence; its members also hasten to spot other potential ontological moves. Even in such an area as formal logic, care has been taken to emend the traditional square of opposition so that the logician makes no claims for existence, certainly no inferences from a non-existential to an existential statement. Logicians have felt that "all" and "no" do not imply existence, while "some" definitely does. The move from "all" to "some" was seen as like that from idea to reality in the ontological argument. The relationships around the square were accordingly altered to avoid this move into existence. The criteria for validity do not sanction inferences to the truth-value of conclusions.

It is difficult to believe that logicians could seriously have thought that the truth-values of propositions could be fixed by formal moves. Just because the form of some proposition is the same as the form of sentences we do use to assert existence, we are not, of course, entitled to conclude that it is the *form* which determines what objects exist. Whether or not "a reference (spatio-temporal or otherwise) can be found cannot be determined by the syntactic form of the utterance."[14] This is always an extra-logical affair. If, by the rules of inference, from "all S is P" I can validly infer "some S is P," I cannot understand how anyone could have thought that I have made some claim for existence, that there *are* S's and P's. The *use* of a denoting phrase or sentence may very well presuppose, as Kneale remarks, "acceptance of an existential proposition."[15] Similarly, the drawing of the inferences around the square or from universal to particular proposition may also presuppose that there *are* entities represented by the subject terms. But these remarks reveal only that when I use a denoting phrase I *believe* there are denotata, or that, when I make logical inferences of certain sorts, I also *accept* the reality of what I am talking about. In this sense, logical *validity* may hinge upon factual *truth* or falsity. To know whether some particular inference is valid will then require some information or belief about the world. To determine whether the information or belief about the world is correct, we must turn away from logic.

When Quine speaks of one's use of language committing one to an ontology which includes all the objects covered by the values of one's logical variables, or says that the designative use of a substantive "commits us to the acceptance of an object designated by the substantive," he quickly adds that the commitment is to what we *say* there is, not to what there is.[16] All that we can conclude on the basis

[14]Paul Ziff, *Semantic Analysis*, p. 111.
[15]*The Development of Logic*, p. 601.
[16]*From a Logical Point of View*, pp. 13, 15, 16, 103.

of logic and language is the sort of ontology which the use of logic and language presupposes or leads us to assume. To claim that we could determine what the world is like by examining language is not to make a meaning or epistemic claim; it is already to engage in ontology. Such a claim would be saying that the nature of reality could be determined by *a priori* means. Quine does not make *this a priori* claim, but he does advance another claim which is *a priori* in a more sweeping fashion. Each language or formal system is accompanied by a conceptual framework which dictates how we substitute on our variables. We can change or alter our conceptual scheme; what we cannot do is to "detach ourselves from it and compare it objectively with an unconceptualized reality." (p. 79) To attempt to make such a comparison involves our looking and talking about this world as well as about our language; such looking and talking "must already impose upon the world some conceptual scheme peculiar to our own language." (p. 78) Hence, Quine concludes, "it is meaningless . . . to inquire into the absolute correctness of a conceptual scheme as a mirror of reality." (p. 79; cf. his notion of "myth," pp. 18–19)

Quine is one of those who distinguishes between meaning and reference. Theory of meaning deals with synonymy, significance, analyticity, and entailment. Theory of reference deals with naming, truth, denotation, extension, and the values of variables. (p. 130) But in the terms of Quine's meta-linguistic and meta-philosophic theory, the denotation or truth of our referring expressions and sentences never goes outside the bounds of our thought and language; theory of reference can never tell us what there is, only what we say there is. The truth-relation is always within language (or experience, perhaps). The question of existential import must be settled within thought and language. Quine's meta-philosophic theory commits him to a phenomenalism where "the world" is always "the world for some subject." Even in the case of a conceptual scheme which professes physicalism or dualism, Quine's theory reveals that these claims cannot be checked. I can *say* what there is; I can never claim I am right, because all ontological claims are conceptual claims restricted to what can be said in our language or within our experience. Reference is always inter-linguistic, inter-experiential. The referents of our ontologies cannot *be* entities beyond our experience. This meta-philosophic theory avoids existential commitments in its philosophy by making such commitments always fall short of the objective reality. Existential commitments have been introverted and therefore avoided, in the fearsome sense of committing ourselves to what there is.

In a recent important study,[17] Eric Toms distinguishes between the subject-matter sense of "exists" and the asserting sense of that term. (p. 66) The latter sense of "exists" presupposes the former. Toms' conception of "exists" goes even further, though he does not mark this further sense as clearly as he marks the other two. The elements of a logical system—the term and symbols—are existing elements. (p. 66) In this sense, formal logic cannot abstract from existence, though it is characterized by its abstraction from particularity. Toms wants to say that x indicates the scope of generality, not of existence. Similarly, $(\exists x)\ \phi x$ "means not that there is an x and it satisfies ϕ, but that ϕ is true of at least one of the given values of x." (p. 68) In the case of universal quantification, such quantification occurs after we have settled questions of existence: it "marks the point at which we decide to question existence no longer." A true proposition, no matter what its scope or generality, "must be credited with an existing subject-matter to which it somehow refers." (p. 74) Toms is quite emphatic about there being no inference from logic to reality. "To talk in terms of existing subject-matter and fact is not to make a *naïve* inference from propositions to an alleged reality beyond them, it is merely to take account of the 'inside view' of a proposition and of what is meant by an admission of its truth." (p. 74)

The worries over the existential import of propositions are part of a larger issue, the relation between logic and reality. Whatever relation we may conclude there is, it must be an ontological conclusion. To say that the real is rational is to make an ontological option. We cannot discover what the properties of the real are by logic, even to discover that the real does have logical properties. Our talk and thought about the real is bound by the rules of our logic and our language, though there is greater diversity possible than the defenders of conceptual analysis allow. We may follow the phenomenalist and say that no world is conceivable or speakable which does not conform to our logic and language. The dualist may be trying to say that part of the real lies beyond language, yet in some way is sayable or conceivable. These are very general issues relating to logic and reality. The question of existential import raises more specific issues: whether on the basis of logic or language we can conclude to what there is. The most general aspect of the relation between logic and reality concerns the claim that the metaphysician frequently attempts to move from the realm of logic to the realm of fact. "Deductive metaphysics" is

[17]*Being, Negation and Logic.*

supposed to proceed in this fashion, thereby committing the ontological move from idea to reality. Spinoza might look as if he did
proceed in this way, but proposition #28 in Part I of the *Ethics* makes
it clear, I think, that one cannot move in any logical fashion from
substance to the finite modes. Finite modes are particular things in
our ordinary world. Spinoza's proposition is saying, I would suggest,
that any attempt to make inferences from the necessary to the fac-
tually contingent is impossible: there is a gap between these two
realms. What Spinoza does say in his metaphysics is applicable to the
world in some way or other. There is some connection for him between
the realm of logic and the world as experienced. But he makes it very
clear that in order to grasp the world from the point of view of logic,
we have to shift from factuality to logicality. The move from ordinary
perception to the perception *sub specie eternitatis* is just the shift from
ordinary perception of the factual world to intellectual apprehension
from Spinoza's special logical (or ontological) point of view. This is
just one example of the metaphysical shift; it by no means explicates
what is involved in this shift, what is involved in seeing how the
metaphysical analysis applies to the world. The important point to
see, however, is that the metaphysical analysis does not apply in a
factual way. The metaphysician, if successful, can portray a way of
making the world intelligible which goes beyond the factual.

V   REFERENCE

To discover that the metaphysician has made the world intelligible
in extra-ordinary ways is not to discover the factuality of the world
in the metaphysical system. The metaphysician has not made a move
from the logically or conceptually necessary to the contingent. To say
that formally valid inferences depend upon or presuppose the existence
of the objects talked about in the propositions is surely *not* to say that
those objects do exist. To take particular affirmative propositions as
asserting existence is not to say that these propositions are true, that
what they assert is in fact the case. Denoting phrases may not denote
anything, if what they purport to denote does not exist. The lack of
denotata does not render such denoting phrases meaningless; what
has been overlooked in the recent analyses of meaning is that the
meaning of denoting expressions does not presuppose existing referents,
the objects that are talked about. As Russell observed, " 'I met a unicorn' or 'I met a sea serpent' is a perfectly significant assertion, *if we
know what it would be to be a unicorn or a sea serpent*, i.e., what is

the definition of these fabulous monsters."[18] This important qualification of knowing what it would be like to be a unicorn or a sea serpent is fundamental to understanding the meaning of these assertions. D. S. Shwayder has recognized this point: "The meaning which the rules give to the word is in no case the *referent*, even if the word always has the same referent; the meaning, if there is room for such here, is the *reference* to the object."[19] Because *reference* has been confused with *referent*, reference has been excluded from meaning, use has taken its place.

The sentence, "Odysseus was set ashore at Ithaca while sound asleep" has a clear sense but probably no empirical referent. But did the term "Odysseus" lack reference, the thought of the sentence would be incomplete. There is a difference of meaning between the sentence, "——— was set ashore at Ithaca" and "Odysseus was set ashore at Ithaca," just because the latter gives a definite reference and designation to the subject term. I might recognize a referring expression *as* a referring expression without knowing what sort of referent is being talked about. But I cannot understand what the referring expression says, what it means, what its sense is, without knowing the kind of referent involved in the expression. Frege's and Quine's insistence that the reference of an expression is the truth value of the expression (that is, the referent) overlooks the fact that the sense of an expression is parasitic upon the objects the expression is being used to talk about, to refer to, or to name. Frege was correct in keeping the idea or thought I might have when confronted with the expression distinct from the referent. When someone says, "The moon is smaller than the earth," it is not the ideas of the moon and the earth which are in question, but the objects, the moon and the earth. The actual referent does not, of course, "enter into" the expression; we are not making the existential claim that the referent does in fact exist. But significant reference does involve our knowing what the referent is that is talked about. In this sense, the referent does "enter into" our understanding and use of the expression, but it enters via thought. Frege was close to recognizing this point. He says that in the sentence about the moon, "we presuppose a reference," and he goes on to point out that we can be mistaken about the existence of the reference. "But the question whether the presupposition is perhaps always mistaken need not be answered here; in order to justify the mention of the reference of a sign it is enough, at first, to point out our intention in speaking or

[18]*Introduction to Mathematical Philosophy*, p. 168, my emphasis.
[19]*Modes of Referring*, p. 35.

thinking."[20] In another passage, while considering the sentence about Odysseus, Frege points out that the term "Odysseus" probably has no reference, adding: "Yet it is certain, nevertheless, that anyone who seriously took the sentence to be true or false would ascribe to the name 'Odysseus' a reference, not merely a sense. . . ." (p. 62)[21] I am suggesting that to anyone who takes the sentence seriously as having a meaning, as being meaningful, reference cannot be severed from sense. Truth or falsity could not be ascribed without determining whether the referent of a sentence or expression exists, but the thought of the referent enters into the sense of the sentence; otherwise we would not even be able to go about determining its truth value. Another way of saying the same thing would be to remark, as Frege was close to doing, that the *intentional*, not the *actual*, object enters into our use and understanding of the sentence.

St. Anselm worked with an ontology in which to have the idea of God in one's mind—as opposed to verbally using the word "God"— involved having God in one's mind. One achieves this condition only by prior belief in God. Critics of the ontological argument have tended to overlook these factors of belief and real existence. The ontological argument does not embody a cross-type inference. The inference is linear, from existence to existence.[22] To reject the argument we must reject the ontology underlying it, namely, that devout belief in God brings the reality of God to us. Recognition of the involvement of the referent in the meaningful use and understanding of referring expressions does not require the acceptance of any ontology, though it does require the acceptance of a view of thinking and intending: thought is thought *of* some object.

Meinong's theory of objects was not, I think, an ontology but rather an epistemology, although Meinong may not have been entirely clear about this distinction. In several passages of his *Gegenstandstheorie*,

[20]"On Sense and Reference," in *Philosophical Writings of G. Frege,* pp. 61–62.
[21]Sluga has recently suggested that Frege's notion of a function requires the concept of a *content* distinct from the reference and the sense of the expression. "The content is the information an expression carries about its reference." (p. 28) The reference is carried by the content. "In other words, the reference of an expression is a function of its content; that is, given the content of an expression, the existence and identity of the reference are thereby fixed." (p. 29) If Sluga's reading of Frege is correct, my suggestion about this passage in the "Sense and Reference" essay is reinforced. At any rate, Sluga's reading is what I would say is the correct analysis of the way reference is contained in the expression or sentence. *Vide* H. D. Sluga, "On Sense," *Proceedings of the Aristotelian Society,* LXV, 1965.
[22]Cf. my "Professor Malcolm on St. Anselm, Belief, and Existence," *Philosophy,* 36 (1961), pp. 367–70.

Meinong shows a clear understanding of the ontological neutrality of his "objects." "Blue, or any other object whatsoever, is somehow given prior to our determination of its being or non-being, in a way that does not carry any prejudice to its non-being."[23] When he makes a reference to his essay, *Ueber Annahmen*, he reveals the same recognition. In order "to deny A, I must first assume the being of A. What I refer to, so far as the being of A is concerned, is this something which is to a certain extent only a claimant to being. But it is of the essence of assumption that it direct itself upon a being which itself does not need to be." (p. 85) Meinong's insistence upon the givenness of objects prior to the determination of their being or non-being is usually overlooked; it is incorrect to ascribe to him, as Urmson does, the view "*unum nomen, unum nominatum*, the view that every noun must be the name of something having some sort of being."[24] The general thesis of Meinong's theory of objects is "That knowing is impossible without something being known" or assumed. It is the task of the theory of objects to go on from this point to determine or decide what kind of being the various objects of our thought have. One of the unsatisfactory features of Meinong's essays is that he was not always careful to separate his general claim about thought from his concern to sketch in some of the outlines of an ontology of objects. We *cannot* for long separate the ontology of objects from the epistemological claim that all thought requires objects; some analysis of the properties of the objects of thought must be made before we can know what we are talking about. Where Russell says that the *concept* enters into our thought of centaurs, and sea serpents, Meinong said that the object enters our thought, but he reserved for ontology the account of the object. Critics of Meinong reacted adversely on two grounds: they did not approve of what they took as an ontological move from thought to existence or being, and they objected to the kinds of being which Meinong allowed. There has been a strong prejudice against non-empirical entities.

The prejudice against non-empirical objects can be eliminated by a recognition of the necessity of ontology. The acceptance of my analysis of reference and meaning need not wait for such ontological enlightenment. The metaphysician must explicate "exists" and "object," the epistemologist need only insist upon epistemic reference. Two modes of analysis are possible for objects, the ontological and the epistemological. To reject reference and referents from the analysis of meaning

[23]Trans. in Chisholm, *Realism and the Background of Phenomenology*, p. 84.
[24]*Philosophical Analysis*, p. 189.

because it is believed that their admission into the analysis commits us to an ontology of objects is a fatal mistake for theory of meaning. Critics of reference have frequently made this mistake, even sympathetic readers of my analysis of objects have been eager to know the ontological status of intentional objects. To ask for the ontological status of intentional objects is to seek for a theory of objects. The doctrine of the intentionality of thought does not and need not involve asking such ontological questions. If my interpretation of Meinong is correct, he has not made a jump from thought to existence. He has only insisted that a theory of objects is a necessary complement to theory of meaning. To distinguish the theory of objects from the theory of meaning should enable us to recognize the indispensable role the referent plays in most utterances. To insist upon the referent as part of the meaning of sentences and expressions is not to make a "Fido"-Fido move. It makes no claim about language and reality at all. It only makes a claim about meaningfulness, understanding, and the conditions under which the utterances are made. Ziff suggests keeping referents and truth conditions distinct from conditions; he puts Meinong's point about the intentionality of thought and of language use (without speaking of Meinong, however) by saying: "It is impossible to refer without referring to something or someone (or some things or certain ones, etc.) But this is not to deny that one can refer to that which does not and never did exist."[25] Referring, Ziff argues, "is like pointing, not like pointing at a duck: one can point even if there is nothing to point at but one can't point at a duck if there is no duck to be pointed at." What one does in using a referring expression is "to indicate certain conditions. The conditions indicated in referring or in making a reference are said to be a 'referent.' "[26]

Toms' monograph marks a major step forward in the task of repairing the damage done by the over-zealous stress upon use in contemporary theory of meaning, but Toms himself has a tendency to run theory of objects and theory of meaning too close together. He ends his study by commenting that "there is no escape from being." (p. 121) Historical statements, assertions of non-existence, even negative statements are all talking about something. What is talked about *is* in some way. But even Toms frequently confuses the "is" in the subject-matter sense and the "is" of being. When dealing with logic and formal propositions, Toms says that two subject-matters are involved. The one, an *empirical* subject-matter, is not involved *essentially*, only vacuously. The other, *non-empirical* subject-matter, is involved

[25]*Semantic Analysis*, p. 84.
[26]*Ibid.*, p. 85.

essentially. (p. 70) I think that what he means by non-empirical subject-matter are the symbols, terms, and relations of logical propositions. In this sense, even formal propositions cannot escape from being since their terms and symbols *are*. The empirical subject-matter would be the actual objects talked about, not as epistemic referents but as objects existing in their own right. These do not "enter into" the proposition except as what is being talked about. Toms also draws a distinction between *external reality* and *reality as such*. "Reality as such includes all that is, and this includes mind. . . . Anything falling within reality as such will be an existence, e.g. a thing or a fact." (p. 100. Cf. p. 114) Thus, any wholesale denial of facts is self-contradictory: what I am asserting or denying is part of reality as such.

A corresponding distinction is that between history as historical *knowledge* and history as the *events* constituting the subject-matter of that knowledge. (p. 111) The problem of past events is often taken as similar to that of negative facts, in that we seem to be talking about non-existent entities: "any event which has ceased to be is preserved." (p. 112) The question, however, is whether the being of past events in present facts is the same as their being as events. I would not think it is. Toms overplays the difficulty here by failing to comment on this difference. "Present," in the following two uses surely does not have the same sense: "it is precisely the present fact of the non-existence of the individual past event which makes the event present." (p. 113) His main point seems to be that if we are going to deny existence in *any* sense, we must deny it in *all* senses. We cannot say that the object or event we are talking about exists in thought or in imagination, thereby thinking we have shown how non-existence is explained, for these are all modes of existence. It is existence in the total sense which must be denied if we are to deny existence. But it is just this denial which is impossible, once we admit the notion of different kinds of existence. Toms is not clear on this latter point. He clings to the paradox of non-existence, insisting that the denial of existence must be given in terms which exist. Toms is, in other words, a victim of his own theory about modes of existence. Because he wants to recognize the terms and symbols of propositions as themselves existing, and since he seems to overlook his own sound recognition of the fact that there is no escape from being, Toms ends by seeing paradox where I do not believe there is any paradox. Toms confuses the being of language with the being of what language talks about. To say "there *is* an object talked about" is a valid use of "is," but it is a use which is in need of analysis. It will not do to say that the "is" is the "is" of words, since this confuses language with what language is used to talk about. To say it is the "is" of an intentional object does, I believe, point the way out of the difficulties about non-existence and negative facts. Toms fails to appreciate this way out because he treats such objects in the ontological mode.

Meinong's insistence that the intentional or epistemic object is primary for us has been too little understood. Problems about the status of such objects arise only when we move into theory of objects. The initial givenness of objects is prior to any ontological determination, it is epistemic only. For the thinker or sayer, the thought-object or the said-object does not have status in being; those thought-objects can have being only for the person who thinks about them. At that time, there is a new epistemic object which is outside being. We are strongly tempted to see such epistemic objects as having status in reality, to go on and ask how they are related to other real objects. Any object, including the thought-objects, can turn out to be related to other actual objects. But to raise the question of the relation between thought-object and actual object is, if this question is meant in an ontological way, to misunderstand the nature of thought-objects. The relation is and can only be epistemological. We can ask about the adequacy of the former in relation to the latter, about the truth relation between the two. But epistemic correspondence must not be confused with ontological relations, lest we commit a serious category mistake. The role of sense-data in Price's theory of perceptual objects is an example, as we have seen, of such a category mistake: what began by having an epistemic role in his theory became a part of the physical object, not just the cognitive source for our knowledge of physical objects.

The mistake here can be brought out succinctly in the following way. Thinking of impossible objects, for example a round square, appears to be thought of something which is not. But to think of something which is not requires that thing to be something for thought. Similarly, when I think of a book, that book intentionally inexists in my thought. What is the relation between the intentionally inexisting book and the actual book? The one I can read, buy, take home under my arm, give to a friend, but this is not true for the other. In short, the intentionally inexisting book is not a book at all; the round square I think about in denying round squares is not a round square; intentional objects are not objects. What an intentional object is is the content of some thought. As a content, it does have mental reality, but in this it agrees with all other contents. The doctrine of intentionality should not lead us to multiply objects, to duplicate in thought the world of objects outside thought. Intentional inexistence is not existence.

Recognition of the epistemic status of intentional objects may free the way for admitting objects back into our theory of meaning. No existential commitment is made when we point out the role of reference and the referent in meaningful speech. The dispositional and behaviouristic theories of thinking in contemporary philosophy have tended to reinforce the ontological misreading of the referential theory of meaning. Many philosophers, until very recently, have looked at the *criteria* for thinking, understanding, and intending, rather than at the *processes* of thinking, understanding, and intending. Understanding as a cognitive act, no matter how that act may be analyzed—short of dispositionalism or behaviourism—presupposes more than use of expressions; the understanding of those expressions is not analyzable in terms of their use. Even those who have come to recognize the need for mental processes in our theories of thinking and meaning are still reluctant to launch a careful philosophical psychology which will bring out the nature and function of intention and understanding. When this is done I think it will become more apparent than it is now that epistemic reference—the grasping, in a mental act, of the referents talked about in our language—is a necessary condition for meaningfulness. To use the proper expressions on the appropriate occasions is not to use those expressions meaningfully unless I know what I am talking about; knowing what I am talking about requires an understanding of the referent. The objects of our talk enter into our thoughtful use of language but our thoughtful use of language does not determine what there is in the world.

The insertion of the referent into the analysis of meaning does not identify meaning with reference, which would be to take a too narrow view of meaning, nor does it restrict reference to the referring function of language, which would limit reference unnecessarily. In almost every meaningful expression (if not in all), we are talking about some object, state of affairs, persons, or conditions. Language cannot be used significantly without reference in this sense. Reference in this epistemic sense may not be the primary purpose of some particular utterance, nevertheless it enters into my intention and your understanding. To use language in a referring way is only to bring to the surface some epistemic reference, to single out for attention some one of the objects which have silently played a role in language use. The discovery of whether there are objects in the world relevant to our understanding of the objects intended is a function of some truth operation. The description and specification of the objects intended is a task for the theory of objects.

10

Theory of Objects

THE INCLUSION OF THE REFERENT in the analysis of meaning imposes a more stringent criterion of meaningfulness upon the metaphysician than the talk of use and rules of use does. To discover how to talk some metaphysical language is, in one sense, relatively easy: just immerse yourself in the language of that system. But to know what this language is talking about, what it says, requires more than attention to the use of its terms and expressions. Full cognitive meaning requires explicit object specification; referring rules must be enlarged by epistemic reference. This requirement need not take us beyond the familiar empirical realm. The analysis of all referents may rest with phenomenal entities. But if we are exploring within the framework of a non-phenomenalist ontology, within dualism, the demands of ontology will dictate the nature of the referential analysis. There is a sharp difference between the empiricist, intent upon keeping knowledge within reach of sensory experience, and the dualist, who sees more reality in our thought and language than is permissible in the empiricist philosophy. While the reductionist seeks to interpret the sensory and conceptual systems of man in common terms, taking the ordinary empirical sphere as the only valid scope for objects, the ontologist seeking to formulate a theory of objects will use just the reverse approach. He will seek to reify wherever possible, but in so doing he will be careful to specify that reification does not mean treating non-empirical objects as objects in the empirical sense. He will take care to indicate that the theory of objects is to be correlated with a theory of the real which allows levels or kinds of reality.

Before we can speak of objects, we must have a theory of reality which specifies the roles and nature of objects. Just as within phenomenalism objects must be separated from ideas, so in the general theory of objects we must not confuse objects with concepts or ideas. Similarly, epistemological and logical claims must not be confused with ontological ones. The claim for referents as a fundamental part of meaning is ontologically neutral. If I say "X exists," before I can fully understand this statement I must know what "X" is. I cannot talk meaningfully about any word or idea without knowing its meaning. In the case of some words and ideas, the meaning may just be their use, but use is an inadequate analysis of the meaning of all ideas or words. To know the meaning of some words and ideas is to know about their reference. But to have the requisite knowledge about the referents of such words and ideas, I must specify the ontological framework within which the statement operates. In the case of some concepts, for example, that of "the State," we can have at least two different analyses of the status of this object, depending upon whether our ontological framework is reductionist or not. Semantic and logical operations can be independent of ontology but cognitive considerations ultimately cannot. The consideration of contra-factual and negative statements cannot finally be sufficient by merely logical appeals. The queerness of such statements arises from the feeling that we ought to be talking about some object without knowing what kind of object (or seeing how it can be any kind of object) that is being talked about. The logical resolution of these puzzles must reflect an implicit ontological commitment or preference, to indicate how such objects are to be construed.

There can be no "science of objects" which is free from some prior conceptual scheme. A few general remarks relevant to the ontological analysis of the objects of some conceptual scheme can, however, be made. We can, for instance, say that the distinction between ideas and things must be made by any theory which seeks to talk of a world distinct from the cognizing subject. As we have seen, phenomenalism makes objects out of ideas, finding criteria internal to certain groups of ideas which set those groups off from others. If the philosopher wished to concentrate only upon the operation of cognition, he would not have to draw the idea-thing distinction. He would, however, have to recognize that thought and the content of thought differ: a subject-object contrast is another fundamental distinction required prior to a detailed theory of objects. The "object" on this cognitive analysis alone would be the contents of thought. Another general distinction independent of any subsequent ontology is that between thought and action, thinking and doing. Thought is, of course, frequently coincident with action, even *is* the doing, as Ryle and Price have pointed out in the case of recognitive and automatic action. In many other cases, the behavioural and action dimensions of the organism fail to describe the intending, purposive, thoughtful operations. Contemporary philosophers are still too much handicapped by the paramechanical fallacy to have elaborated a philosophical psychology adequate to intentional action. There is too much ambiguity, still, around the move away from behaviourism to mentalism. The ambiguity might have been resolved by a prolegomenon to a theory of objects which would have recognized these fundamental contrasts between thought and action, content and act, self and object. For such a prolegomenon would have to ontologize at least so much as to admit that any subsequent account of the terms of these contrasts must not deny the contrasts.

The ontology of objects can only be a function of some specific set of ontological rules. The greatest difficulty confronting the dualist is his claim for non-empirical objects as the referents of his dualist statements. In Part II of this study we have examined three attempts to formulate and to elaborate a theory of non-empirical objects. The results in all three cases disclosed a hard alternative: either the non-empirical objects are formalized, even geometricized, or they remain opaque to conception. This alternative may lead us to reject as impossible all dualisms, all ontologies having to do with non-phenomenal objects. The unsayableness and inconceivability of dualism may constitute that ontology's own just critique. Before rejecting dualism, however (and I shall not reject it in this study), we need to understand more carefully to what theory of objects the dualist is committed. In the course of elaborating the dualist theory of objects, we also gain an understanding of the referential features of metaphysics.

There is a minimum theory of objects required by the dualist ontology examined in Part II, a basic differentiation between kinds of objects which is required to explicate the demands of that ontology. Since the dualist begins his analysis with the familiar world of ordinary experience, there are at least three distinctions which arise from this level of experience. There are the familiar objects of our everyday world, the gross objects of normal perception: tables, chairs, etc. (physical objects). These can be broken down into smaller units, as the sense-datum philosophers have done under the controls of their demands for certainty. We can talk about such objects in terms of groups of colours, sounds, shapes, etc. (sense objects). These objects can be treated either as parts of gross objects or as a separate kind of object. For the sense-datum dualist, it is sense objects which provide the point of contact, however tenuous, with those non-sensible objects he seeks to characterize as physical. The universal-particular distinction applies here in the way in which the phenomenalist indicates: there are colours and sounds as well as red, green, C♯. The relations between universal and particular qualities reveal the third kind of objects of the ordinary world of perception (relational objects).

Physical, sense, and relation objects would seem to exhaust the components or features of the gross sensible world. There are clearly other kinds of objects, even in the empiricist's world. Without prejudging the question of the differences or similarities between sensing and feeling required by some epistemological or ontological system, it seems correct to say that aches and pains differ from sense objects, although to state these differences may not be easy. I can have an experience of sound which, besides giving rise to the awareness of the sound as heard, for example C♯, gives rise also to definite feelings, such as pain if the sound is shrill or piercing, or sadness if it arouses certain associations. The same holds for other sensations. The sensation—the heard sound—appears to be more independent of us than the feeling, but this difference must be capable of further classification. That there is a difference has not always been recognized by sense-datum philosophers.

The most important distinction in the dualist's world is that between empirical and non-empirical, that is, between the three kinds of objects already named and metaphysical objects. Metaphysical objects are not just relations between empirical objects, although they frequently arise out of and refer to such relations. A metaphysical object is a reification of some relation or quality discovered among gross sensible objects, or it is an entity with an ontological status of its own. The dualist's physical object is such an object; the entire fate of his ontology waits upon a satisfactory analysis of the nature of metaphysical objects. The dualist is careful to specify that empirical is somehow conjoined with non-empirical object; it is not just epistemologically related but causally dependent upon the metaphysical object. The difficulty for the dualist is not only how empirical can be joined with metaphysical object; a more searching difficulty arises in specifying the kind of reality the metaphysical objects have. They cannot, for the dualist, be like the empirical objects in respect of sensible properties. Only formal properties are left to constitute any similarities between empirical and non-empirical objects; and these, in the case of the dualist's physical object, are difficult to specify. What does the dualist mean when he says that such objects exist or are real? The theologian has the same problem: what are we to mean by God's existence? The reality of God, like the dualist's physical object, is always realist: God and physical objects must have an existence independent of any cognitive relation.

There is a major difference between certain kinds of non-empirical objects, such as the general will, absolute spirit, or the state, and the dualist's physical object. The former are reifications proper, abstractions from perceptual experience hypostatized by the demands of ontology. It is just because this kind of object is rooted in empirical experience that the reductionist is able to present his case for dispensing with the reification. But the possibility of reduction need not be turned into a plea against creating these objects as entities on their own merit. The demands of a particular conceptual system may quite legitimately require the extraction of certain empirical features of our world and the transformation of these features into ontological objects. It is in this sense that non-empirical objects depend upon a concept system for their reality. The peculiarity of the dualist's physical object is that, while it is in one sense a function of his concept system, in another and more important sense it is independent of his system. The absolute idealist may claim that the reifications of his philosophy are quite independent of his conceptual orientation; the hypostatized abstractions must then find their place within the theory of objects alongside the dualist's physical object. But the inability of the sense-datum language to replace the physical-object language reflects the difference in nature between physical objects and other sorts of non-empirical objects. The sense-datum language can replace the physical-object language only when physical objects are taken as nothing more than a collection of sense qualities. On such an interpretation, physical objects can still be construed as objects different in status from normal empirical objects: they then become reified products of our concept-system. The dualist finds inadequate this kind of objectification precisely because a physical object for him is always more than any collection of sensible qualities. Like the theologian's God, the dualist's physical object cannot be extracted from gross perceptual objects, no matter what its relation with such objects may be.

But the independence of such non-empirical objects as the dualist's physical object or the theologian's God cannot be of the same sort as the independence of empirical objects for the phenomenalist-realist. For him, as for the reflective layman, the gross object of perception are accessible to our sensory organs though they are existentially independent of our perception. The full comprehension of this perceptual world, of its many interrelations, its uses, its qualities may require the force of understanding and the aid of complex conceptual structures. But the objects examined by the conceptual tools of the understanding are never believed to be dependent upon this or that concept system. Conception may refine and disclose what, to sensation, remained unobserved; but the relation between concept and object always remains, for the phenomenalist-realist, an external relation. For the dualist, on the contrary, physical objects are first revealed and conceived through the ontological constructs of his philosophy. Something not before considered is revealed but the revelation becomes a creation. Out of the materials of empirical objects, another sort of object emerges as a result of the structure of theory. The theory arises because of a deficiency felt in the world of empirical objects; the theory seeks to render intelligible, in a way not envisaged before, the nature and relations of other levels of reality. Created by ontological conception, such non-empirical objects as these are nevertheless not functions of concept systems in the usual phenomenalist way. Once conceived, they are offered as independent realities in the realist manner. God does not depend upon man's conception for his reality, physical objects for the dualist are more than groups of empirical objects, even though God and physical objects owe their conception to the complex intellectual products of science, philosophy, and religion. The realism ascribed to common sense is raised to a new level. Whereas for common sense and the phenomenalist-realist, what impinges upon the living organism in the form of sensory stimuli is noted, formulated, and accorded independence, for the dualist and the theologian sensory stimuli are replaced by conceptual projection.

This theory of objects rests upon an epistemological distinction between sensing and conceiving. The phenomenalist attempts to define reality in terms of sensory contents. Internally, as far as it goes, phenomenalism is an empiricism. In this it is unique among ontologies since it allows one to get or to be inside without having also to be outside: it can be formulated without reference to the philosophical point of view, although we have seen that it cannot be *fully* and *consistently* formulated without getting on the outside of that position. The very attempt to make it consistent leads to its own transcendence. It is transcended either by the divine perspective, which seeks to gather up the individual and finite perspectives into an all-embracing phenomenalism, or it is transcended by some form of dualism, which is motivated by the conviction that reality is not what it seems. The dualist is one who has gotten on the outside of phenomenalism by taking the philosophical perspective, thereby raising the question of the legitimacy and adequacy of phenomenalism. This act alone—of raising questions of legitimacy and adequacy—converts the phenomenalist into a conceptualizer. The philosophical perspective is, then, ineluctably non-empirical. Just as soon as concepts begin to function in awareness, awareness ceases to be purely empirical. Phenomenalist awareness is as close to empiricism as one can get. But just as soon as we are able to regard phenomenalism as a theory of reality, as well as a point of view taken toward the world (the difference between interpretative and action categories), phenomenalism can no longer be seen as empirical. No theory can be empirical since all theories employ concepts, and concepts, by their very nature, are non-empirical. An empirical theory is one in which the conceptual constructions are offered as fitting, representing, or mirroring reality. The philosophical perspective reveals that concepts cannot stand in such a direct and straightforward relation with reality. Forsaking the level of action for the level of interpretation forces us into a non-empirical theory. Every non-empirical theory of reality finds itself driven into the creation of objects to fit the concepts of theory. Concepts cannot fit sensations or the world of sense: they must carry their own objects with them. Once blown into being by conceptual construction, the non-empirical objects of theory begin to elude the fathering concepts: we find it difficult to express in language or to conceive in understanding the reals generated by our theory.

To the non-empirical ontologist, objective autonomy is the crux of the theory of objects. To the empiricist critic, objective autonomy is the illegitimate abstraction insufficient for sustaining the ethereal weight of the theory of objects. Man has begun action with his automatic and sensory-motor awareness. Although the passage to rational, intellectual modification and interpretation of sensory data has frequently been rapid, it has often been the intellectual, the theoretician, who has measured his projections against the rough shores of common sense. The appeals of the Aristotelians against the Platonists, of the Ockhamists against the metaphysicians, of the logical positivists against the unempirical have all echoed the primitive, romantic pleas of the sensory creature. Contemporary empiricists urge their analyses as clarifying techniques for the complex intellectual structures of science. Sensation is offered as a gloss for intellect, whereas the correct order is just the reverse: intellectual constructions of theory, even of empiricist theory, are interpretations of sensory experience. The artist, the philosopher, and the scientist each seek to render our world intelligible in terms of diverse conceptual and ontological devices.

To insist that an empirical interpretation of the world is alone valid or meaningful is to undercut the force and nerve of all three. But to appreciate the ontological nature of the artistic, philosophical, and scientific accounts, we must recognize the necessity of a non-empirical theory of objects.

To understand what a non-empirical object is is to see the possibility of objective autonomy outside the province of empirical objects. What is required is not the incarnation of abstract and elusive properties in concrete bodies. The transformation of epistemological or semantic objects into ontological objects is a much more subtle and complex operation than the empiricist's appeal to clarity and Ockham's razor reveals. The reified objects of Hegel's logic or of Bosanquet's theory of the state are not abstractions given empirical and sensible dress. They are abstractions rendered independent and objective in virtue of theory and experience. "The State" in modern political theory and action has frequently become something more than a term or concept summarizing a collection of people: it has become a monster or a god decreeing, absorbing, directing, and forming the lives and actions of individual men and women. "The State" as monster or as god is revealed through the actions of particular individuals, and the attempt to produce it for measurement, classification, or description will yield only the individuals forming and formed by this abstraction. But the refusal to accord objective independence to such an abstraction characterizes only the short-sighted and legalistically minded who seek to pin blame or praise for the actions of "the State." Political and social phenomena can be interpreted by other kinds of objects, by the "general will," or the "class struggle." In each case, the interpretative principles must be seen as functioning by means of objects transformed from empirical and epistemic areas into ontological entities. The full characterization of such ontological objects can be done only with the help of the particular rules of some specific ontology. Understanding the rules of ontologies may, for those trained in the empirical persuasion, require imagination and analogical extension. But ultimately analogy is insufficient for making clear the nature of metaphysical objects. Our language may prove incapable of formulating in non-analogical terms the properties and status of non-empirical objects; but unless we can understand and present at least a partial formulation of our understanding of the ontological status of non-empirical objects, the dualist's claim for the intelligibility of his ontology must be rejected.

The theory of objects marks the philosopher's concern with what there is; such concern does not arise out of an interest in compiling an inventory of the items of the world. Some of the items which interest the philosopher could possibly be inventory-entries. But the peculiarity of the philosophical account of what there is is that the list of items depends, for the most part, on a prior analysis of the *nature* of what there is. The philosopher settles the question of the nature or essence of what there is before he determines *that* there is anything which fits those essences. Descartes tells us what the essence of body is before he justifies the assertion that there are bodies. Spinoza gives us a careful account of the nature of substance before affirming that it must exist. More contemporary philosophers have sometimes tried to begin with an inventory of what there is, but just as soon as they have tried to describe the nature of what they have said there is, the inventory begins to change. Other philosophers have been concerned with only what they can *justifiably* say; frequently their criteria of justification—of good reasons—have restricted their list of items in the world to what can be said with *certainty* to be. In short, the philosopher is always concerned more with what can be *said* to be than with what there *is*. He claims that at least for the sorts of items which interest him, what items appear on his list are a function of justification and of the analysis of the nature or essence of those items.

Some items appearing on the philosopher's inventory have been put there because of their explanatory value. The world and our experience are intelligible if (perhaps even, in some cases, only if) we talk of monads, or of forms, or of prehensions and actual occasions, or of space, time, categories, schemata, syntheses, etc. The very fact that these items are strange-sounding and unfamiliar to all but the trained philosopher indicates that these items on the philosopher's list cannot be found by examining the world of our experience. But it would be unfair to the philosophers who have talked of such items to say that these items are *only* theoretical constructs, or have *only* an explanatory status. For they are meant to have ontological status as well, to be, in some sense, real items of the world. The precise sense in which they are real items in the world is one of the more difficult questions in metaphysics. It is, in fact, a question that many metaphysicians, and even more defenders of metaphysics, ignore. But any decent defence and justification of metaphysics must face the task of explicating the concept of existence, must help us to understand what it means to say that these strange items *are* part of the world. We need no longer point out that what there is in the world need not, even by careful philosophical standards, be restricted to items in space, to physical objects and processes, to what can be verified through scientific procedures. It should not require any peculiar philosophical techniques of essential analysis to convince us that the world is inhabited by a number of different kinds of items: solids, gases, waves, colours, sounds, relations, pains, emotions, images, concepts, behaviour, action, consciousness, intentions—just to mention some items that come readily to mind. Much careful analysis of these items is necessary before we need invoke the metaphysician's strange, transcendent items. The recognition of a plurality of items independent of justificatory and essentialist considerations is salutary for freeing philosophical analysis from the narrow use of "exist" frequently found among empiricist and scientifically oriented philosophers. But we have no guaranty that the explication of the existence of the items I have just listed will aid in clarifying the transcendent metaphysician's use of "exist."

The division of the metaphysician's inventory into empirical and non-empirical items points up the problems confronting the one who uses the latter. One main difference between the two sorts of items is that those on the transcendent, non-empirical list are not available in either the "observation" way or in the "having" way. Many philosophers would argue that while we can and do experience rocks, trees, gases, behaviour, even perhaps atoms and electrons, we do not experience thoughts, pains, emotions, intentions—at least not in anything like the same way. And to claim that from an awareness of our intentions we can conclude that there *are* intentions, sounds to many as if we are multiplying entities. Furthermore, while we can obtain evidence for the existence of rocks, trees, behaviour, even atoms, the notion of evidence for my pains, thoughts, and intentions may be inappropriate. The only connection between experience and the items on the transcendent, dualist list is a causal one. Given an experience of such and such a sort, we can say that it was caused by items A, B, or C. But to be able to make such a causal ascription, we must be told what experience, or what features of the appearance world, are linked to what items in the transcendent-reality world. This connection is a function of the particular metaphysical theory; we do not discover that connection through experience. Since the connection between experience and transcendent world is constructed, not discovered, the ascription of truth to the transcendent list or to that connection is difficult if not out of order. Normally, when we say some judgment or proposition is true, we mean that that judgment or proposition stands in a special relation to what there is, such that the judgment or proposition says what is the case in the world or in my experience. If there were some vantage point from which both the appearance and transcendent worlds could be "viewed," I suppose this sort of truth relation between proposition and what there is might be said to hold. But man—even the metaphysician—does not seem to be in such a favoured position. He is in a less than favoured position for making transcendent-truth claims. Some critics of metaphysics have charged that the connection between transcendent items and experience is deductive; that the transcendent items have been offered as explanatory of experience, but that what features of experience those items explain are deduced from the transcendent theory. Kant called this a *transcendental deduction*. Such a deduction seems to characterize all transcendent hypotheses, whether in metaphysics or in science.

Confirmation or verification of an hypothesis always occurs within the context of theory and hypothesis. We cannot, even in science, just look out upon the world; we must look with some purpose. The data of our experience can function as evidence only when we have some hypothesis which specifies the sort of data which would confirm that hypothesis. In this respect, transcendent hypotheses do not differ from experiential ones. The difference lies in a curious feature of transcendent hypotheses, namely, that the data said to confirm such hypotheses do not disclose the items referred to in those hypotheses. To take a simple instance of an experiential hypothesis, we might conjecture that there are mountains on the other side of the moon, or life on Mars. The data which would confirm that conjecture would be experiences of mountains on the other side of the moon, or life on Mars. Such data would be obtained either by photographic or other instrumented means, or by actual looking. In either case, the items talked about in the hypothesis are, when the hypothesis is confirmed, the very items experienced in the verification process. Not all hypotheses in science are of this simple form; many of them seem to talk about items which are not the confirming data. In other instances, the indirect verification of an hypothesis in terms of data different from the items referred to in the hypothesis is subsequently reinforced by a more direct confrontation of the items in the hypothesis.

Indirect verification is an accepted practice in science, but it functions as verification only because the data which can function in such a verificatory way are specified somewhere in the hypotheses or theories of science. If we enquire whether the world is composed of the items cited in the transcendent hypotheses of science, the answer would seem to depend upon our readiness to accept the specifications of the hypotheses as to what items will indirectly confirm those transcendent hypotheses. It may be that we should interpret the transcendent metaphysician's talk about the world in a similar way; he offers accounts of the world in terms of items in our experience. The fact that the metaphysician seems more concerned with intelligibility than with verification need not prevent us from interpreting his accounts in terms of indirect verification. Someone might urge, however, that the items in the metaphysician's accounts are so strange—much more odd than the items in transcendent scientific accounts—that acceptance of certain experiential items as confirmation of the truth of the metaphysical hypotheses is difficult indeed. Moreover, the metaphysician does not talk in the language of verification; he does not specify that if we experience such and such items, such experience will confirm his transcendent statements.

The transcendent metaphysician is frequently concerned to ascribe a causal connection between experiential and transcendent items. Indirect verification in science frequently involves causal connections. Even the detective seeks to find the causal agent of the crime by discovering data which indirectly link suspect with crime. But the indirect or circumstantial verification of the detective and the judge rests upon observed correlations between items in the cause and items in the effect. We do not have such a favoured occurrence in science, metaphysics, or theology. How then do we decide what experience-events can serve to support our transcendent hypotheses or beliefs? The transcendent theorist believes that his theory does relate to the world as experienced. He offers it to us only because he sees ways in which the two are related. At the same time, we all know the tendency such theorists have to protect their theories by rendering them unfalsifiable, by accepting no data as disconfirming their theories. I would not wish to say whether anything at all like the refusal to recognize negative evidence characterizes the use of transcendent hypotheses in science. Some philosophers of science must have had a guilty conscience, else we would not have had operationalism and the substitution of talk of theoretical constructs and intervening variables for talk of real items in the world. But clearly, theories and hypotheses are disconfirmed in science. There is no body of beliefs, no account of the world, which is defended no matter what negative data are discovered. The parallels between science and metaphysics stop at the point of negative instances. The significant parallel is the way transcendent statements determine the sorts of experiences to which those statements refer, causally or explanatorily. If truth can be ascribed to transcendent statements, such ascription is possible because the experiences specified by the transcendent statements as having relevant data have occurred. But we must note that the relation between experience and the transcendent statements is specified by the transcendent statements. This fact makes the verification of such statements not only indirect, but circular. Transcendent statements specify their own truth conditions.

11

Truth and Metaphysics

BEHIND MOST PHILOSOPHICAL TALK about the nature of truth lie two basic confusions. The one is failing to distinguish between the ontological and the epistemological features of truth, the other is mistaking a difference in emphasis for a difference in theory. The former confusion finds its manifestation in all idealist discussions of truth, while the latter is found in the defenders of correspondence and coherence theories alike. Coherence is contrasted with correspondence between idea and fact, truth-claim and existence. Some idealist philosophers talk about states of affairs being true although it is improper to speak of them being false: the "metaphysical verity" of things. Other idealist philosophers speak of truth in capital letters as in the triumvirate Truth, Goodness, and Beauty. Both such usages require the assumption of some broad ontological position about the nature of reality. Plato argued that the world of sense perception is less real and less true than the world of forms or essences, meaning that the world of forms is causally basic as well as epistemologically primitive. A correct understanding of any aspect of existence is obtained only by apprehension of the forms. Knowledge of the forms has instrumental value in that, for example, to be a good statesman one has to rule in harmony with the dictates of the forms. Moreover, in the causal series of creation depicted in the *Timaeus*, the forms play a basic determinative role in the hands of the demiurge. Truth is comprehensive, deductive, and instrumental. Truth is not man-made, but is in some sense waiting to be discovered.

In this sense of "true," the term "correspondence" has no meaning or application, unless we speak about our knowledge as being in correspondence with the forms; a relation of knowledge to an essential, not an existential, realm. It was clearly against a truth of this ontological nature that James and the pragmatists were reacting. James referred to this kind of truth as "essential" truth, the truth of the intellectualists, the truth with no one thinking it: the coat that fits but has never been tried on. The pragmatists combine logic with voluntarism to derive the conclusion that "man makes truth." The absolute idealists like Bradley had mixed together the ontological features of truth with the truth of judgment. On both ontological and epistemological levels the idealists have defended a coherence theory: reality is interrelated, knowledge of any part is implicated in a knowledge of the whole. Certain linguistic philosophers of the present century are inclined to defend the epistemological side of this coherence theory. They have been concerned to develop a deductive system within which the concept of truth can be defined to exclude any references outside the system. The logical truth of a sentence must be determined with reference to the semantical rules of its system alone, without reference to extra-linguistic facts.[1] Similarly, the idealists have been dedicated to a metaphysical point of view patterned after a deductive system, where all the elements of the world are interrelated. In both systems, knowledge of any particular involves a knowledge of many other particulars. In the case of the idealists, truth has been taken in an ontological sense such that we can say "truth is the whole," meaning that we do not have a full and adequate understanding of reality until we view it from the point of view of the whole of the universe: the divine perspective. Individual judgments similarly rest for their meaning and truth upon inclusive relations to all other judgments. The ideal of truth is the *sub specie aeternitatis* perspective. The language of correspondence has no meaning in an idealistic or rigidly linguistic system, since the concepts of inner and outer, of truth and reality, have been replaced by those of *ideae* and *ideatum*.

In Spinoza's system, the denial of the inner-outer language means that the realm of ideas is adequate to itself: all that is characteristic or "true" of reality can be found in any segment of the real. The relation between *ideae* and *ideatum* is not one of identity, since the idea has an essence, a nature of its own, and can be understood and known independently of its *ideatum* or objective essence. But no idea or subjective essence can be known directly; like Locke, Spinoza would seem to require mediation. Thus, the idea serves in two capacities: as means of knowledge for its *ideatum* and as object known through another idea. This means that the *ideatum* can never be known directly. Representation characterizes the relation between the idea and its object; but no problem of transcendence arises since knowledge of the

[1]Cf. Carnap's *Meaning and Necessity*.

object is adequately obtained through the subjective essence alone. True knowledge consists in having a true idea, and false ideas are distinguished internally, solely, by reference to the impossibility, possibility, or necessity of the ideas. A true idea never requires to have its truth certified by external reality. Falsity consists in affirming of something that which is not in the idea. External sensation does not precede internal ideation: both processes go on simultaneously, since they are both modifications of the same substance. Ideas are not dependent upon sensation, mind is not dependent upon body. Both realms depict the same panorama of events. To avoid error and attain truth, we need to concentrate upon our conceptions, to learn what is contained there.

In the same manner but with voluntarist language, Royce sought to assimilate correspondence to intention. The object possesses a set of "ideally definable" properties which it shares in common with the idea. The object and its idea stand in a purposive relation: a true idea becomes one which has the kind of correspondence with its object which the idea "wants" to have.[2] Not just agreement, but *intended* agreement constitutes the mark of truth. For Royce, as for Spinoza, there is no external criterion of truth. One has to examine the internal meaning of ideas in order to determine their truth value in terms of their external meaning. In other words, it is not the object which plays the determining role in the likeness of idea and object: it is the idea, the intention, which decides its own meaning. The very fact that an idea has an object rests upon the selective activity of the idea itself. But the idea, while predetermining what object it means or intends and what sort of correspondence it intends to have with its object, cannot determine whether the idea will fully agree with its object. Royce thinks that if the object could determine the full agreement between idea and object, truth would be tautological. Thus, the object, which is part of the very intention of every idea, is nothing else than the idea's own further determination. Complete determination is, for Royce, impossible for finite ideas, but any determination which an idea undergoes consists of making explicit what is already contained in the idea. The external meaning of ideas is the expression of the internal meaning, the referent is specified by the reference.

Any given statement involves, for its meaning and its truth, certain other statements and conditions. But it is only the idealist metaphysics of monistic interrelation which leads these philosophers to claim that the meaning and truth of any statement involve all other statements

[2]Cf. Royce, *The World and the Individual,* chapter VII, and *Logical Essays,* chapters III, IV.

about the real. Ontology has clearly determined the analysis of judgment. The idealist analysis of judgment, however, may prove to be independent of its particular ontology. What the idealists were saying is that every assertion involves, as part of the assertion, the conditions for its verification. It is this claim which marks the more important aspect of the idealist-coherence theories of truth. When James talks about truth involving satisfaction, he does not mean personal satisfaction, but the fulfillment of the conditions prescribed by the asserted truth-statement. Mere satisfaction of the psychological sort is not the criterion of truth: it has to be a satisfaction in terms of the intended objective and must lead one to the reality or experience desired. Whereas Royce spoke of the relation of agreement between ideas and things as being defined in terms of the intention of the ideas, James and the pragmatists define truth in terms of what we as individuals intend to do with it. What both Royce and James contend is that in seeking the conditions of truth in the world for any statement, we are actually seeking and finding (or failing to find) conditions which have already been specified by the original statement. It makes no difference whether we know from the start what these conditions are, since whatever they are they are prescribed by the original statement. To ask a question, to form an hypothesis, to assert a truth, draws a line around the area of relevant confirmation-material. If the scope of relevancy were not already dictated by the question, the hypothesis, or the assertion, we could never confirm the query, check the hypothesis, or validate the truth. If we did not know what sort of objects were being talked about, we could not understand the statement. In the cases of scientific hypotheses, we follow precisely this pattern, prescribing the conditions which should prevail if our hypothesis is correct. The hypothesis prescribes its own confirmation. We do not merely go to look, we look from a definite point of view, with specific questions in mind, and if we are clever enough, we can outline the necessary conditions for the verification of our lookings. We cannot begin to look until we know what to look for: observation is theory-laden, and must be controlled by hypotheses.[3] Historical relativists in meta-history have argued in the same fashion, seeking to show that understanding of the significance of the past rests upon the categories of meaning embedded in the present.

Hypotheses entail confirming conditions, truth assertions contain their own truth conditions. But the prescription of the conditions for

[3]Cf. Hanson, *Patterns of Discovery*, chapter I, and Toulmin, *The Philosophy of Science*, chapter II.

truth does not itself bring into being the existence of those conditions. The asserted truth plays no causative role in generating the existence of its own conditions. Existential determinations must transcend the coherence realm, unless we make the assumption that whatever is conceived as possible must also exist in actuality. The establishment of truth depends upon two factors: the delineation of the conditions which would verify or confirm our assertions and the discernment that these conditions really do exist. We are not, in this process, establishing a correspondence between existence and assertion in any other sense than seeking to determine whether the conditions which would make the assertion true do in fact find their exemplification in reality. Even if we allow the language of correspondence, it is not the assertion which corresponds with existence, but the conditions prescribed by the assertion. Every truth situation involves three factors: the truth claim, the confirming conditions, and the existential actualization of the confirming conditions. Interpreted in this way, no assertion can ever be shown to be false by discovering that the conditions do not correspond with the assertion, since conditions and claim have been found to be united and inseparable. Falsity arises through the existential failure of the conditions being realized in whole or part. It seems clear that the correspondence philosophers have been essentially concerned with the existential situation (being empiricists) while the coherence philosophers have directed their attention upon the relation between *ideae* and *ideatum*, between assertion and conditions.

James and the pragmatists are special types of coherence philosophers. They have called attention to the fact that correspondence philosophers view truth as a static thing, since they have been inclined to say that it is the existential actualization which "makes" any assertion true or false. The existential situation becomes the "truth" which confirms the assertion. The pragmatists have preferred to emphasize the coherence side of the truth process, pointing out that since the conditions for truth are laid down in the very act of assertion, man actively "makes" truth himself in making assertions. But at the same time, the pragmatists were empiricists enough to recognize that the mere conditions for truth would be useless in action. Thus, the activity of the truth process continues over into the process of realizing the conditions for truth. Assertion and actualization are taken as two phases of the same process, but the marks of the assertive stage are taken as characteristic of the entire process. If we view truth from the point of view of the relation between assertion and confirming conditions, truth is immanent within the realm of assertion or truth claim. If we view truth from the point of view of the existence of the confirming conditions for the assertion, truth transcends the assertion. The pragmatic test of workability becomes a test for the existential reality of the conditions prescribed by the truth claim.

This much of the account of truth expresses the fundamental features of the truth relation, no matter what ontology we wish to defend. Ideas and judgments are true only to the extent that they reveal something about the nature of reality, no matter how we characterize "reality." The phenomenalist has to recognize the representative and correspondence features of truth as well as the realist does; but just as there are two senses of "transcendence" (the phenomenalist's temporal transcendence and the dualist's experiential transcendence), so the notions of "representation" and "correspondence" become defined in accordance with the ontological rules of each system. Within the phenomenalist's dictum that "seeming is being," "X is true" means that some future bit of experience has confirmed the expectation of some past or present experience.[4] Since "the world" for a phenomenalist is just his self and its conscious contents, it might look as if falsity was impossible in such an ontology. Whatever is, is *and is for* that self. But this sense of "true" holds for any theory of reality. Truth as coextensive with existence has no special application within this or that ontology. It is truth in the epistemic sense, the sense of judgment, that is the significant notion. This notion differs with differing ontologies. Ontology determines truth.

Protagoras offers an interesting example (one cited by the pragmatists) of a phenomenalist definition of truth. For him the term "true" is equivalent to "is"; since "is" is defined in relation to awareness, "X is true" is equivalent to "it seems to me that X is true."[5] Protagoras' ontological position prevents him from saying simply, "X is true," since this statement sounds as if it asserts something about the world independent of experience. But "true for me," or "it seems that X is true," translates into a familiar form: the basis of present experience and the usual laws of verification enable me to say, "X is true." Verification is always a process within experience. Predictions are made within my experience. If I say, "I think that X will occur in five minutes," this is a claim and an expectation about my future experience. It may or may not be fulfilled. But when the results are in, they must always be construed as true or false of my experience, never of a world

[4]Cf. Husserl's account of evidence in *Cartesian Meditations*, I and III.
[5]Vide *Protagoras*, 167 A, B.

outside my experience, or of your experience. Within my experience, I can still retain the distinctions of true and false as well as those of illusion and error. These distinctions are drawn in exactly the same way as usual. All that is denied is that the distinctions apply to your experience or to an independent real.

To ask Protagoras whether his statement "X is true for me" is itself true, is only to ask him whether he has made a correct report of how things seem to him. No infinite regress is involved unless we make Protagoras say—what he cannot say—that "X is true for me" is true; although there is a sense in which this is correct: it asks for a report on the state of Protagoras' world. An answer can always be given to this request. Neither is Protagoras' use of "true" self-refuting, as Passmore charges in *Philosophical Reasoning*. Passmore argues that "p is true for X" means that "X thinks p is true" (p. 67), and this latter proposition raises the question of the truth of p. Passmore's reading of Protagoras is based upon a view about the formal requirements of all discourse. To talk at all, he claims, presupposes some true propositions. "We cannot in discourse renounce the claim to be able to make true statements." (p. 68) But Protagoras has not renounced this claim; he has only said that "true" has for him a meaning different from what it has for a realist. Passmore does not recognize the double point of view in metaphysics. He talks as if everything said *in* a philosophical theory must be justified *by* that theory. (pp. 38, 42–43) Such a demand would make it impossible for the philosopher to tell us what he is doing, to explain his fundamental concepts. We might still be able to understand what he is doing by watching him work and talk. But whenever he is challenged, confronted by critics, he must step out of the language of his theory and engage in talk mutually intelligible to his critics and himself. Protagoras was in precisely that position, as Plato depicts him. The dicta, "man is the measure of all things," and its corollary, "true always means true for me," are offered for foreign consumption. They mark out the bounds of his ontology and show us how his conception of truth follows from his ontology: "real" and "true" apply only to each man's experience.

Since Protagoras includes in his position other persons, all that he says about his experience holds for others' experiences, but never between experiences. On the intersubjective level, there are no physical objects common to all experiences, since physical objects are appearances to some self. There are no truths pertaining to all experiences, since there is no common world to be referred to by our individual truth claims. There may be an overlap in our truth claims but this is coincidental. This coincidence may, however, be the basis for inter-subjective discourse. It makes no practical difference that we never know whether our terms refer to the same experiential content. For the realist, we can never *know* this; for the phenomenalist, this could never *be* the case. If language functions as if it had something in common, that is sufficient for discourse. From an external point of view, inter-subjective discourse may just be a bit of pre-established harmony.

Truth, like knowledge, must be *about* something. Knowledge claim and truth claim are both intentional. Hence, there has to be a distinction between the claim and the referent of that claim. Coherence, even for the phenomenalist, is insufficient to decide truth claims, since his claims are, like those of the realist, about his world. It may be the case that idealist philosophers, in constructing their metaphysics, use coherence and consistency as a test for permissible (and hence "true") statements. But we must distinguish between two points of view again. The metaphysician must, as I have suggested before, stand on the outside of his system in elaborating it as a system, as a world view. Once launched, he can then ask for or indicate the truth conditions *within* that system. A metaphysical account of the world hopes to make sense of experience; but the level of metaphysical explanation differs from the level of one who lives within that system. Within the system, coherence is inadequate as a test for or account of the truth of judgments. Claim must be checked with claimee, present experience must be compared with future experience. Idealist philosophers in particular, but all metaphysicians who talk of truth, tend to overlook this consideration of what it is like to live inside the world depicted by their metaphysics. This oversight explains why the idealists have favoured coherence as either the test for or the account of the nature of truth. For they have thought of "the world" as coinciding with their system. To make a true statement was not to advance a claim about some feature of a world outside their linguistic and conceptual system. If true, any statement has only to be consistent with all the other statements in that system. The idealist was, in talking of truth, standing on the outside of his system, trying to predicate truth of the system as a whole. A self-consistent system was a true system. The truth of particular statements or judgments was a function of the truth of the totality. If the idealist denies that his linguistic and conceptual system is identified by him with the world, then he must recognize a correspondence relation between his system and the world. His reply is, of course, that the correspondence of his system to the world (to some

Absolute, say) is fully attested if his system is consistent throughout. Consistency of statement or judgment is taken as the criterion of correspondence with reality. We are given little help in understanding why *this* particular consistent system, rather than any number of other possible ones, is true of the world. The answer, I am sure, lies in the contents of his system: the particular propositions of *this* system express the way the world is, even if we must take them all together and not singly.

Correspondence appears in another, more important, place in every metaphysical system which distinguishes between appearance and reality. When what the metaphysician says the world is like stands in contrast to the way it appears to be, this difference must be explained. The appearances must be shown to be well founded. In showing this, a correspondence relation has to be found between appearance statements and reality statements. Leibnitz was explicitly concerned with establishing the appearances as well founded; we can accordingly find some clear-cut instances of the correspondence between the one and the other kind of statement in his metaphysics. The dualism of appearance and reality is also found at the heart of Spinoza's attempt to articulate a totalistic monism. The gap there is not bridged. Instead, we are invited to ignore the world of appearance for the benefits of the totalistic perspective.

I have already mentioned this dualism in Spinoza by way of showing that the metaphysician does not claim to deduce existence from his concepts. In that proposition (#28 of part I), Spinoza says that finite modes are not determined to existence immediately by God, but by a series of causes, finite like themselves, of infinite number. It would seem, then, that we could never work from finite things back to substance via a causal series, since the causal series of finite modes will only lead us indefinitely along one infinite series of such things. We cannot deduce finite modes from God's nature since they do not follow necessarily. Finite things are contingent (water, tables, Jones's mind, this thought of the moment): we must look to empirical observation in order to determine what finite modes there are, what forms individual things take in the world. The relation between God and the world is twofold. On the one hand, it is a necessary, logical relation. Here we can view the world either as the whole unified substance (*natura naturans*), or as the system of logically necessary properties which follow from God's nature (*natura naturata*). On the other hand, the world can be viewed as a collection of contingent facts, none of which can be deduced or inferred from God. According to proposition

#28, contingency seems to be an ontological necessity, but then the unity of substance is disrupted. Not even the highest form of knowledge seems likely to fit finite modes into the structure of the one substance. Viewed from the point of view of the whole, substance is eternal, the cause of itself (in that the whole is uncaused), possessed of infinite attributes. Viewed from the point of view of individual parts of the totality of the world, we might be able to understand how the parts require the whole. But contingency arises on a level of causation so different from that of the causation of the necessary parts by the whole that Cartesian dualism reappears. The causation of particular bodies follows the accepted laws of motion and dynamics. Spinoza wants to talk of the universal, the whole, causing the particular. One particular object which causes another object to move has God as its cause in so far as the order of objects forms a causal series which is part of the totality of the world. Causation on the universal level means logical entailment and deduction. The attempt to relate universal with particular causal order would thus seem to involve relating a logical with an empirical order. This cannot be done, or it can be done only in the sense that the logical order (substance, attribute, and infinite modes) encompasses the *a priori* categories of the totality of which the empirical order is a member. But we have no rules instructing us in how to move from logical to empirical orders.

Spinoza enjoins us to understand the world as viewed through the logic of totality, a logic which discovers some universal logical relations in the world. The logical relations, however, only apply to the world when taken in its totality and as a totality. Leibnitz's monads are an enactment of the Spinozistic logic but in a pluralistic world. It could be argued that there is no metaphysics in Spinoza's *Ethics*, that there is only a theory of knowledge urged as a prolegomenon to ethical attitudes. The theory of knowledge instructs us in the proper way to understand the world; it does not offer an ontology. Such a reading of Spinoza may be too one-sided but it does bring out the differences between Spinoza and Leibnitz's doctrine of monads. Of course, the *Monadology* was written for more general readers. Leibnitz was also concerned with logical relations in the world, with ways of understanding what there is. But the doctrine of monads does illustrate many important features of metaphysical systems, including the correspondence which holds between the way the world appears to us and the way the world is said to be by the metaphysician. Monads may have been Leibnitz's way of picturing the logical structure of the world. He was nevertheless concerned to show the appearances to be well founded, to be intelligibly related to the logical structure. We can best understand this relation of appearance to reality by picturing a spectator (the philosophical observer) among the monads.

For such a spectator, the monads are invisible. In their place, he sees and experiences interaction on various levels up to that of language and communication. The monads do not in reality interact, but their function on the composite level of large-scale objects results in the appearance of interactions to the spectator. From the point of view of each monad, we have a rigid solipsism. From the point of view of the philosophical observer, we have realism and causal interaction. If our spectator were God, he would know, since he has arranged it all, that the apparent interaction of the monads is deceptive although well founded: just the sort of appearances this sort of reality should have. But our human spectator is in the peculiar position of being aware of the appearances and not of the reality, although he himself is one of the real monads ultimately made by God. Man is a spectator without the insight into reality. When he becomes a metaphysician, he becomes like God: aware of the appearance but understanding the reality. The dualist challenge asks whether man can achieve understanding of reality while only aware of the appearances.

We find in this situation the typical double level of metaphysics: the level of exposition, which is always external to the system being developed, and the level of participation in the system. What can be said inside the system differs from and is much less than can be said outside that system. Inside Leibnitz's system, all that can be said, expressed, or done is whatever constitutes the totality of states of any particular monad. If the spectator of this system were able to go behind the appearance and record all that every monad says, expresses, or does, he would record the total history of the world: the book of the recording angel. If this same spectator were to study the completed history of this world, he would discover correlations between the individual recordings of each monad. These correlations would be of the nature of reciprocal expressions, statements, and doings. If this recording angel is clever enough, he would soon learn that he could make retrospective predictions from one part of this world to another. Ideally, that is omnisciently and divinely, the whole history of the world could be read off (predicted) from any single statement in the book of the recording angel. Less ideally, the recording angel would be able to perform like any ordinary historian in our world:

he could anticipate that certain parts would be related in certain ways, that a move recorded here will preclude a certain sort of move from being recorded elsewhere in that history.

The recording angel we have introduced into our analysis records the events in reality, not the events in appearance. The events in appearance are recorded by man when he acts as historian. His account is familiar; it is the chronology of the past. Let us suppose that our human historian is allowed to consult the book of the recording angel, the book which chronicles the doings and states of monads. Let us also assume some temporal scale which would enable the human historian to synchronize his records with those in the great book of the recording angel. He would discover the kind of isomorphism between events in his records and events in the records of the angel that we have just noted. But the events would be different, of a different order and category. Where he had recorded the impact of armies, the upheavals of geological strata, the movements of physical bodies, the angel would have noted down the timeless presence of immaterial entities, grouped or single, perceiving and striving and achieving in isolation from all other such entities. From the account of monads, that is, from the ontological rules—we can see what the specific translations from appearance to reality would look like.

Our human historian would discover that where he records the movement through space and time of extended bodies, the angel records the non-spatial ordering of the states of monads. All monads and every state of every monad has a place in the ordered set of relations laid out for it by God. The space of monads just is this ordered relation, ultimately the ordered set which includes the totality of monads. Space is the co-existence of compatibles. Since every monad reflects the nature of every other monad, clearly or confusedly, and since each state of every monad reflects the corresponding ordered states of every other monad, clearly or confusedly, what appears to our spectator historian as the movement of bodies closer to or farther away from each other finds its counterpart in the real history of the invisible monads as the clarity or confusion of the reflection of one monad by another. All spatial relations are in fact non-spatial relations of reflection or adaptation of all by each.

Time, too, is unreal. Time is defined as the order of possible states of affairs which are mutually incompatible. The definition of space as the co-existence of compatibles suggests that space is the whole universe at an instant; that is, at what our human observer would take to be an instant. But space is really the totality of the states of all monads, which means that all the states of all monads are co-present to each other at an instant: or, that time is unreal, is irrelevant to monads. This definition of time must mean, then, that if two events appear in temporal succession, they are incompatible, could not co-exist at the same time. This is another way of saying that the events perceived by our human historian are unreal. There is no special counterpart in the real history to these perceptions of these unreal events; the same ordered relations which are the spatial counterpart will be seen as the angel's entry for both spatial and temporal appearances.[6]

What appears to the human chronicler of events in the world as interaction and communication will emerge in the real history as the co-ordinated states of all monads. One thing expresses another when there is a constant and regular relation between what can be said of one and of the other. Thus, where we see one billiard ball strike another, then see the second move off in a certain direction, no causal interaction has taken place at all on the level of reality, since the monads do not interact: they are all little solipsistic worlds. What Hume declared of man's knowledge—that we have no basis for asserting any causal connection between bodies (as necessary connection)—is given ontological expression by Leibnitz. Our human historian will find only phenomenalist statements in the book of the recording angel: no statement, expression, or action of any monad has any external reference. But in a pluralistic system, unless there is some way of relating the members of that system, we shall have no more than a set of discontinuous entities. Externally referring statements and gestures are the ways in which we normally relate. For Leibnitz, there is no need for such external reference: the external references have become internal. Like Spinoza, he feels no need to raise the question of the existence of the external world since the question of its existence has been ruled out of order. It is out of order for Spinoza, because he declares all things to be the expression of one thing. Moreover, all the different ways of expressing this one thing are co-ordinated. The question of external existence is out of order for Leibnitz because of the application of Spinoza's postulate of parallelism to each and every monad: the total state of the world, that is, the totality of monads, is reflected in the internal states of each monad. The mirroring relation, in other words, cancels out the solipsism; it annuls it, for those who can read off from any given individual state the state of the rest of the universe. Our human historian can only report the protocol statements noted down by the angel: he is unable to see all the rest of the history

[6]Cf. R. L. Saw's *Leibniz*, chapter 4.

book in any one such statement. Only God has that sort of insight into the totality of his creation.

The function of the mirroring relation is such that we must alter our original analysis of the recorded statements and actions of monads. For though in reality they do not have external reference, in effect and in verbal form they do. The notion of other people is built into the composite monad, so that even for the recording angel the speech and thoughts of men are as they appear to our spectator historian. Spirits, as they function in composites called men, are the self-aware, reflective, language-using monads. What appears to our spectator historian as the physical world is misperceived by spirit monads just as it is by the spectator. Spirit monads are both spectators of and participators in reality: exactly the role of the metaphysician. Were our spectator historian to discover his own verbal utterances in the book of the recording angel, were he to discover, that is, that he too is part of the real world whose appearances he witnesses, he would be on the threshold of becoming a metaphysician too. Where he records or notices his perceptions of his own body, he finds that the angel has recorded the translations we have noticed above. The statements recording his spectator-perceptions do not appear in the book of the recording angel, but the verbal formulation of those perceptions which he has made as a participator in reality *are* recorded. His perceptions are unreal, are misperceptions as McTaggart would say, but his thoughts and speech are real. The misperceptions which constitute appearance are a function of the spectator and of the spirit monads in the spectator role.

The correspondence between appearance and reality statements in a system like that of Leibnitz resembles the correspondence within material-substance theories. In both, there is some systematic correlation between the phenomenal and real worlds which makes possible epistemic and linguistic moves from one to the other. But while material-substance theories take some phenomenal experiences as evidence for the truth of physical-object statements, the correlations we have examined in Leibnitz do not stand in an evidential relation. I do not think that Leibnitz claimed a logical relation between statements of appearance and of reality either. There is no deduction of existence from the ontological concepts. His notion of well-founded appearances is an appeal to intelligibility: given the sort of world he depicts, we can see some reason for that world appearing as it does. The correspondence in this case does not generate a truth relation; such a relation arises only where appearance statements are taken as the basis for some reality claims. Where, then, is the truth relation in idealism? I fail to see much point in saying of the idealist's position itself that it gives a true account of the nature of reality. Either such a claim only means that that account is consistent, a trait it would share with any system, or the claim plays upon the concept of correspondence, suggesting that "in some sense" the whole metaphysical account is true of the world. The first alternative seems insignificant as a truth claim. The second is impossible of confirmation.

The dualists have tried to devise methods for allowing the notion of confirmation to apply between phenomenal- and reality-statements; they try to introduce elements or principles into their theories which will bridge the gulf between the two worlds. Physical-object statements do not pretend to be about experience. Conceptual statements of the dualist sort may reveal something about the phenomenal world not noticed before, but for the most part they attempt to deal with the undigested remainder in phenomenalism—the environment of the phenomenalist self. If these statements about the environment of the phenomenalist self can be said to be true, it can only be in the sense that, according to the rules of that ontology, what these statements say is correct. The dualist is confronted by a curious difficulty. Reality, as opposed to appearance, is by definition beyond reach of confirmation, yet he wants to make truth claims about that reality. Scientists speak of indirect confirmation, but what passes for confirmation indirectly is a direct result of theory: if our theory is accepted, then these signs are confirmation of the assertion which is interpreted in terms of the theory. If the isomorphous relation between sensible and physical worlds which Broad and Russell suggest does in fact hold, then certain sensory solids can be taken in evidence for certain physical objects. Confirmation is built into the system. The ontological rules become rules of truth. The isomorphism involves the geometrical properties of sensory and physical objects. Thus, as the Aristotelians said that the form of the object exists in the understanding at the time of cognition, so these dualist philosophers are saying that the entire world of appearance contains the form—the geometrical structure—of the physical world. Confirmation that there is a physical object and that it has certain properties results not from observation but from the ontological rules laid down in advance.

In those metaphysical systems where the appearances do not stand in an evidential relation to reality, the appearances are either overlooked for the greater value of understanding reality (Spinoza) or they become explained in terms of reality (Leibnitz). In both these instances, the truth relation is within the reality part of the metaphysics. Coherence and consistency of course play their role, for the truth claims made within the ontology must be in harmony with the basic ontological rules. But the statements on the metaphysical level are *intelligibility claims*, not truth claims. The truth relation proper, whether in phenomenalism or dualism, is between components of the world as depicted by each ontology. For phenomenalism, this relation is between experiences. For the dualist (whether of the material or spiritual sort), it is between experience and entities which cannot be experienced, or between the statements said to characterize reality. It is improper to apply the concept of truth to the ontology as a whole since truth is consequent upon ontology, upon the rules which specify where the truth relation occurs. If the ontological rules are seen as meaning-rules, truth and meaning are after all closely bound together, not so closely as to make any meaningful statement true, but close enough to specify that certain statements are true because their meaning (their sense *and* their reference) is delineated by the ontological rules. If we know what the dualist statements about physical objects mean, if we know what the statements about monads and their states mean, we see that and in what way they are true. Metaphysical truth, the truth of metaphysical statements, incorporates in an ontology the feature of all judgments, namely, that what would confirm or disconfirm the judgment is contained in the judgment itself, in its meaning. A metaphysical system simply ontologizes this internal relation.

CONCLUSION

Philosophical Languages

IN THE COURSE of these metaphysical analyses we have made several distinctions which have helped to illuminate the theories discussed. Epistemologically, the decisive distinction is that between perceptual and conceptual responses to the world; this distinction is at the root of the difference between phenomenalism and dualism. Methodologically, the basic distinction has been between empirical and nonempirical construction of theories. Linguistically, the distinctions have been diverse and multiple: we have found our meta-philosophical point of view requiring us to talk of various languages as reflections of diverse ways of looking at the world. This linguistic and conceptual pluralism has, despite the monism of the conceptual analysts, been recognized by a number of recent philosophers. We find, for example, Cassirer speaking of language itself as one among a number of symbolic forms employed in organizing the data of experience. Art, history, science, myth are other examples of symbolic forms. Cassirer's notion of the organizing forms of thought is itself a variant of Kantian phenomenalism; there may be a world apart from our forms of organization but all we have to work with is the world as organized. The important aspect of Cassirer's notion is not this Kantian emphasis but his recognition of a plurality of conceptual schemes, each of which must be analyzed on its own merits, its internal structure revealed. Phenomenology has also been stressing the need for a careful examination and analysis of any kind of phenomenon. The phenomena are taken on their own ground, analyzed from a neutral point of view. The method used is that of "same-level analysis," the analysis of each mode of awareness, of each linguistic form in terms of itself, not by means of some external criteria or language.[1]

Wittgenstein has become well known for, among other things, his

[1] *Vide*, John Wisdom, "Ostentation," and "Is Analysis a Useful Method in Philosophy," in *Philosophy and Psychoanalysis*.

notion of language games, of different modes of talk defined in terms of their context in different modes of activity. From this notion, and related to it, are Ryle's notion of *categories* (and the corresponding "category mistake"—the mistake of crossing type-boundaries in our talk and language); Waismann's notion of language *strata*, where truth, verification, and even meaningfulness have different senses; and the talk of the different languages of morals, art, science, and religion with its recognition of the inappropriateness of applying criteria of meaning in one language which are taken from those of another.

More recently, Michael Oakeshott, in an important but generally overlooked little book, has put these notions in terms of the conversation of mankind and the plurality of its voices.[2] Oakeshott views philosophy as a neutral stance from which the plurality of voices is surveyed. "Philosophy, the impulse to study the quality and style of each voice, and to reflect upon the relationship of one voice to another, must be counted a parasitic activity; it springs from the conversation, because this is what the philosopher reflects upon, but it makes no specific contribution to it." (p. 12) Philosophers *have* engaged in this sort of activity, charting the structure of the various voices or languages. But these metaphysical analyses suggest that philosophy is also, in another aspect of its activity, its metaphysical aspect, one of the voices, that it has a language of its own. In fact, there is not one language of philosophy but many: there is a pluralism of voices within philosophy. Many contemporary philosophers tend to overlook the fact of a philosophical domain distinct from the meta-activity of surveying the different voices of mankind (some have denied it outright); few have been prepared to recognize a pluralism of languages within philosophy. Philosophy as an autonomous discipline of its own, with its own genuine set of problems and solutions, its own way of looking at the world, is no longer popular among practising philosophers. A phenomenology of modes of philosophizing has hardly been practiced since Hegel's *Phenomenology*. The rejection of metaphysics in contemporary philosophy has arisen from various causes, prime among them being a theory of meaning which, while recognizing the contextual nature of the meaning of non-philosophical languages, has failed to apply this recognition to philosophy itself. The concern with the philosophy of language has obstructed the analysis of the language of philosophy.

There has been a recognition of linguistic pluralism in the non-

[2]*The Voice of Poetry in the Conversation of Mankind.*

philosophical area. But the contrary tendency towards linguistic monism has tended to predominate. Philosophers talk as if there is only one "authentic voice." "There are," Oakeshott reminds us, "philosophers who assure us that all human utterance is in one mode. They recognize a certain variety of expression, they are able to distinguish different tones of utterance, but they hear only one authentic voice." (p. 9) Such linguistic monism appears primarily in the analysis of and pronouncements upon philosophy. Any recognition of the authenticity of the language of philosophy can occur only after we have rid ourselves of this normative notion of linguistic or conceptual monism. We must reject two meta-philosophical conceits, those of the formalists and the informalists. The analysis of ordinary language as well as the construction of formal languages has very little to do with philosophy. The pretension that philosophical problems are resolved by taking philosophical terms and revealing their meaning in ordinary or in constructed languages is after all only a pretense, is in fact a deception. As Oakeshott remarks again: "What I have called the conversation of mankind is, then, the meeting-place of various modes of imagining; and in this conversation there is, therefore, no voice without an idiom of its own: the voices are not divergencies from some ideal, non-idiomatic manner of speaking, they diverge only from one another." (p. 19) There is, as Paul Ziff recognizes, "no privileged context of utterance."[3] The normative conceits can only be fostered by denying that philosophers have used terms in an extra-ordinary way. If we are concerned "to explicate technical terms of philosophy, or of sailing, or of chemistry, it is useless to consider everyday discourse since such terms are hardly likely to occur in such discourses."[4]

That there are technical terms characteristic of different areas of activity, such as those of sailing, chemistry, diplomacy, even philosophy, seems beyond doubt. What warrant is there, however, for speaking of these terms as incorporated into different *languages?* All of these so-called languages take place within *a* language. We must have a language, a tongue, before we can have special or technical variants. The variants of science, art, or philosophy may only be special vocabularies. After all, they have to be grammatical, the syntactic structure must follow the same rules whether we are talking philosophy or art, science or sailing. If you and I talk philosophy we do so in our native tongue. Philosophical talk is not another species of language in the obvious sense. To treat philosophical talk as a kind of language is in

[3]*Semantic Analysis*, p. 74.
[4]*Ibid.*, p. 73; cf. pp. 196–97.

part simply a device for bringing out some important features of philosophical systems which contemporary philosophers tend to overlook. However, there are a number of similarities between philosophical talk and language which justify the notion of philosophical languages as being more than just a device.

Langer suggests that the motive behind language is the transformation of experience into concepts.[5] Cassirer contrasts language as "an aggregate of sounds and words" with language as a system of *significant* sounds.[6] Significance or meaning is surely varied, so much so that any attempt to render poetic meaning, say, in non-poetic terms, or scientific meaning in layman's terms runs a dangerous risk of losing some of the original meaning. Significance in these different contexts acquires some idiomatic qualities which defy translation. The autonomy of significance within diverse contexts is more striking still when we read metaphysics. A good command of the English language is insufficient for understanding Bradley, McTaggart, or Whitehead. In addition, we must pay close attention to their own special vocabulary and acquaint ourselves in depth with the philosophical tradition. The meanings of the terms in these special vocabularies are partially revealed by attending to their use in their context. The role of any of the special languages is to alter the usual meaning of words so as to catch significances otherwise passed over. The philosopher may be more inclined towards this sort of transfer of familiar words into unfamiliar contexts than are other language users. There has been a misconception of the philosopher's task, that it is that of discovering, disclosing, and rendering clear the meanings of words in the language. In most instances, the reverse is the case: the users of language, especially the special users, try to manipulate words to mean what they wish. The notion of the philosopher naïvely misled by grammar should be replaced by that of the philosopher purposefully trying to mould language to his uses.

Each of the special sets of vocabulary I am suggesting calling "languages," has a specific task to perform, each refers to a special and definite subject-matter, and they all require time and understanding to acquire the proficiency and fluency to speak them. As with language in the usual sense, these special languages raise problems of *understanding* and *translation*. Metaphysical systems usually contain expressions which cannot be translated into other metaphysical systems. What John Wisdom calls the "Idiosyncrasy Platitude" stresses this

[5] *Philosophy in a New Key*, p. 103.
[6] *Essay on Man*, pp. 160–61.

point, insisting even that each metaphysics is closed to all others, that no analysis is possible save same-level analysis. I want to examine these two questions of understanding and translation as a terminus to these metaphysical analyses. But one other feature of philosophical languages, one which has played a prominent role in this study, needs to be noticed first.

This feature *may* be shared with language, but I am inclined to think that it is especially characteristic of philosophical languages, may even constitute a differentia. I refer to *conceptual frameworks* of philosophical languages. There have been philosophers of language who have insisted that language itself contains ontological commitments. The Sapir-Whorf hypothesis sees such commitments in all standard European languages, for instance.[7] Similarly, it is the fashion in some places to talk of the conceptual necessities of our language. It may be the case that we all do acquire from our society, perhaps even from learning the language, a certain rough-and-ready metaphysics. This metaphysics always turns out, in the hands of the conceptual analysts, to be some version of direct realism. Frequently this claim that direct realism is embedded in our language is used in a normative way to argue for the impossibility of any other conceptual orientation. Metaphysicians *have* defended alternative ontologies; their defence has also been a function of the special language with which they worked. I cannot find anything about language itself which draws the limits to what can be thought at the edge of realism. What is striking is the way in which the special philosophical languages are expressions of ways of looking at things, of what Hodges calls "standpoints." The language in these instances is integral to the standpoint. "No standpoint can be understood by those who have not learned something of the appropriate language; and no statement can be properly understood except by entering into the standpoint from which it is made."[8] David Pole's way of putting Wisdom's Idiosyncrasy Platitude is that linguistic categories define ontological ones.[9] Conceptual orientations are correlates of linguistic systems. For each language, there corresponds a different conceptual point of view. Languages express something believed in or accepted by the language user. To change our special language—especially our philosophical language—

---

[7] *Vide*, Benjamin L. Whorf, *Collected Papers on Metalinguistics*, and Edward Sapir, *Language, An Introduction to the Study of Speech*. For a careful discussion of the Sapir-Whorf hypothesis, see Max Black, "Linguistic Relativity: The Views of Benjamin Lee Whorf," *The Philosophical Review*, LXVIII (1959), pp. 228–39.

[8] H. A. Hodges, *Languages, Standpoints and Attitudes*, p. 17.

[9] *The Later Philosophy of Wittgenstein*, pp. 122–23.

requires an alteration in our conceptual framework, an alteration in our beliefs. If we talk about the world in phenomenalist terms, we think about the world differently from when we talk about it in physicalist terms. A pantheist language requires a different conceptualization than does a theistic language. Human action and the world can be talked about and understood in many ways, each of which depends upon a context of situation, problem, attitude, concepts, and a language for formulating this context and this mode of understanding.

A reductive analysis of these various conceptual frameworks can only violate the position being analyzed. To understand a conceptual orientation different from our own, to learn to talk meaningfully in that language, requires an internal understanding; we must put ourselves in that frame of mind which characterizes the believer in each of these ontologies. Anthropologists have made us acutely aware of the difference between such an internal approach and the external, reductive analysis. The anthropologist finds it insufficient for understanding the culture he studies merely to live with a society and observe the actions of its people. He has to penetrate the culture, place himself on the inside of the society he wishes to understand, seek to grasp the observable actions of the tribe in the tribe's own perspective, plumb the meaning of the events as they are felt and lived by the society under consideration.

How does one go about acquiring an internal understanding of some conceptual orientation foreign to our own? The task for the anthropologist and historian is to increase the analogies and sympathies between himself, his thoughts and feelings, his society, and those people he studies. But the anthropologist who takes this directive seriously may end by becoming a native and shunning or losing his own culture. What the anthropologist must try to do is to operate in two cultures at once. Does the anthropologist, then, have to understand both his own and the foreign culture at the same time, always ready to slide from one to the other? Or is it the case that understanding, as opposed to feeling and acting, can really only be done from the outside? Only to the extent that I free myself from the feelings and actions of my own society and succeed in stepping outside that society, am I able to grasp the characteristics of that society. Social introspection, like self-introspection, requires a distinction between observer and observed. However, such introspection does not include forgetting the feelings and biases which motivate us in action; we only succeed in introspecting to the extent that we measure our intellectual analysis by our feelings. In the same way, a sympathetic inspection of other societies and cultures must strive for an approximation to the emotional life of the people we are studying in order that our cognitive understanding may have some basis in fact.

Ontologies are not marked by intense feelings on the part of the believer, although the history of philosophy has produced some emotional wars between conflicting ontological perspectives. But although philosophical systems may be markedly different from cultures and societies, the structure of understanding is similar. That is, the same sort of internal and external perspective is required for properly understanding any philosophical system: we must allow our understanding to make a sympathetic intrusion into the system being studied, while not forsaking our own point of view. The phenomenalist and dualist cannot really communicate with each other without each of them abandoning his position, at least to the extent of accepting some new rules of meaning, translation rules between their two worlds. But to understand across differing ontologies requires a special technique or standpoint of its own. To talk about the nature of philosophy, of philosophical reasoning, to understand different metaphysics, can be done only to the extent that we get outside our own provincial perspective. But if we are to avoid simply replacing our old ontology by a new one, our understanding will have to arise on a meta-philosophical level. Many apparent meta-philosophical standpoints hide a metaphysics of their own.

Hegel made frequent appeals, in his *Phenomenology*, to this double perspective of the self engaged in the reflection depicted in that book and the philosophic self watching the antics and contortions of that reflecting self. But Hegel was not always as clear as he should have been about the difference between the externality of one position towards another, and the externality of the meta-level. The meta-level may itself be turned into just another ontology; it may, that is, cease to be a meta-level. The anthropologist may view the foreign culture only through the values and concepts of his own society. The externality of the meta-level must be differentiated from the externality of another position. Hegel seems to have offered his phenomenological analysis as made from a meta-level, but close attention to his Absolute reveals it to be another, albeit a comprehensive, point of view. The dialectical method was for him the successive enactment of points of view: empiricism, rationalism, idealism, and many other positions explored internally. What emerges from this application of internal understanding is at once an understanding of each perspective and the recognition of the absurdity of each if taken as complete and self-sufficient in itself. But the criticism against self-sufficiency which Hegel makes remains open to him within the dialectic only because he has implicit in his point of view that which becomes explicit once he has explored intrinsically all possible points of view: the absoluteness of a totalistic perspective. In the endeavour to comprehend the claims of sense-certainty, of reason, and of spirit, understanding gives way to criticism only because there is a direction and a significance to the passage from one to another. We begin by the enlightened conviction that there is truth in every position, if we can only penetrate inside it. But this effort results in the insight that every position but one is incomplete. The invulnerable position is the totalistic perspective from which we see the necessity of the combination of part and whole, of particular and universal: subject and object, thought and being must be taken conjunctively. The partial views examined sympathetically have been absorbed into a totalistic metaphysic.

In order to think and understand reality from this totalistic level of knowledge, we must forge a new set of logical and metaphysical categories. The enactment of this perspective yields a sympathetic understanding and a recognition of the truth of its claims. From the perspective of the absolute knower, reality may be self-contradictory, identity may involve difference. But though this perspective has the appearance of being inclusive, comprehensive, and the natural and inevitable product of the attempt to take each prior position seriously and sympathetically, it swallows too much. If we try to impersonate the point of view of the absolute perspective, to re-enact its claims, to grasp the intrinsic truth which it offers, the pretentiousness of this totalistic perspective, taken as definitive and final, becomes clear. The logical categories of the absolute are intelligible and understandable when viewed internally from within that perspective, for they are the categories of phenomenalism; they fail to apply to reality from other orientations. The phenomenalism of Hegel's absolute differs from that of a simple sensory phenomenalism only, as we saw in Part I, in that it is larger, more comprehensive. Even Hegel recognized the many parallels between the logic of spirit and that of sense, reason, and understanding. The metaphysic of the absolute is that of a divine phenomenalism.

Each ontology arises under the conviction that it is *the* way to look at the world, the way the world is. Just as each of the partial positions taken up and examined by Hegel sheds light upon some aspect of reality, makes sense when viewed internally, so the final perspective bequeathed by the dialectical method also helps us to understand other facets of reality. But to say that the claims of empiricism are in part true means no more than that the claims of rationalism and idealism are also partly true. To urge such partial truth is only saying that, when viewed from within, the claims of each position are valid. The same claim can be made for Hegel's Absolute.

The genuine meta-level is a means of describing and characterizing different ontologies; it proceeds without any ontological biases. Hegel's Absolute errs just here: it pretends to be "meta" while only being a comprehensive perspective with its own ontology to defend. The genuine meta-level must be able to get inside different points of view without succumbing to those points of view. It can only do this by taking the inner-outer contrast as its focal point: it must ask of each position how it looks from inside—how one talks in that language— as well as how it looks from the outside. There is no special language for the meta-level. There is only language which is examined in its special uses. In order to talk the special language of any particular ontology, we have to understand the conceptual attitudes which are being formulated in that language. For this sort of internal understanding, we have to shed all external prejudices.

One of the very first prejudices the meta-level requires us to reject is the prejudice against reification: turning qualities and relations into things. There is a prevailing belief that when we depart from ordinary uses of terms—to take a poetic or a metaphysical use—we have replaced literal with metaphorical meaning. The fear of reification hovers about these extensions of language. Leibnitz's talk of monads, Whitehead's of actual occasions are felt to be just ways of talking about our world; but if taken to mean that there are entities corresponding to these terms, the prejudice argues that an error has been committed. The world does not consist of men, trees, events, *and* monads or actual occasions. The empiricists have taken the term "object" in only one sense and then argued that any other use of that term is analogical. The pure empiricist might be thought of as working with a sensory or ostensive language: the sort of language Russell tried to construct with statements like "redness here now." The extreme opposite of this ostensive language is a purely conceptual language, for example, those statements of scientific theory which deal with theoretical constructs. Most of our talk consists of various kinds of combinations of sensory and conceptual statements. The philosopher may be trying, when talking ontology, to give to his conceptual terms the same kind of reference as ostensive, sensory terms have. He most certainly is not saying that the objects referred to have one kind of existence. It is wrong to think of the philosopher as supposing that gods, universals, forms, sense-data, or monads exist in the same way that coloured, extended tables and chairs exist. Philosophical languages are conceptual languages which cannot be reduced to or translated into an ostensive, sensory vocabulary. To assume that either the ontologist's "existence" can be translated into a sensory language or it must be a mistake, is to commit ourselves to the empiricist bias of thinking that there is only one fundamental language, with all others metaphorical or mistaken extensions of it. The task for the user of an ontological language is to explicate what it means in his language to say "X exists" or "X is real." To insist that the explication must be made in ordinary or some other constructed language is to impose impossible conditions upon the explication.

Can we, then, make no translations from one philosophical language to another, or from any philosophical language into some non-philosophical language? Some of the things a realist says can be translated into the phenomenalist's language, but not all. Some of the terms in Whitehead's terminology find their counterparts in Bergson's or Santayana's language. Moreover, there is probably no philosophical language which cannot partially be translated into other philosophical languages. But we must be very cautious about our translations; the fallacy of translatability hovers over all attempts at philosophical translation. The task of exegesis is just this: to determine how much of some particular language can be and what parts cannot be translated into some other philosophical language. Exegesis may even be possible in some cases in terms of a formal or constructed language, although the possibility of distortion is very great. The translatability into ordinary language seems much less sure and more open to mistranslation. The relation between ordinary language and philosophical language is largely idiomatic. Translation must always be a function of understanding made from the external, meta-level. But the attempt to formulate in language the fruits of internal understanding appears to hover between redundancy and superficiality. Language learning is not without its ambivalence: the child learns to operate with imaginative, make-believe as well as with literal meanings, or he learns to use two different languages. Although the translation from, for example, French to English can usually be made without any serious loss of meaning, the translation from make-believe to literal language suffers from an idiomatic remainder. The difficulties of translation within one cultural language, from one ideational construction to another— for example, from a physicalist to a sense-datum ontology, or from a Hegelian to an empiricist metaphysic—raises more problems. Assuming that understanding has occurred, how can we place the Hegelian analysis in empiricist language, or how can an eastern religious philosophy be presented to the western mind? One point seems evident: the verbal translation of one philosophical system into the language of another will be fruitful only to the extent that understanding of the translated system follows upon the translation. In general, the translation from one ontology to another is possible, if at all, only where there are rules of translation imposed upon the ordinary rules employed in the language into which one is translating. But to introduce translation rules external to the language used in the translation, appears to render the translation impotent. Just as an adequate understanding must be internal, so an adequate linguistic formulation would appear forced to be internal, that is, redundant: a commentary or gloss is adequate to the glossed material only where it employs no terms not appearing in the work which is glossed. A commentary which ignores this injunction ends, it would seem, by being superficial and irrelevant.

A verbal translation from one point of view to another contrasting one never is fully possible, although many apparent contrasts yield some basic similarities upon close attention and careful glossing. There may, in fact, be few philosophical positions which stand so radically opposed that there are no similarities and hence no verbal transitions; the radical empiricism of the present century and the previous century's metaphysics may be cases in point. But even where the contrasts are striking and pervasive, the semantic difficulty is clearly circumvented by the role which internal understanding plays in the entire process. Without such understanding, no formulation yields any fruits. But once such understanding begins to emerge, the commentary becomes effective, despite its semantic inadequacy. Formulation and understanding work together. The most effective and difficult gloss is precisely the one which does use an external language while nevertheless aiding in the achievement of internal understanding. In such a process, it is the understanding which is fundamental and prior. It is only understanding which can penetrate inside another thought system—philosophical, historical, or anthropological. It is one of the characteristics of our understanding that it can escape our emotions and biases. We are not always tied down to our own context or value-orientation. In arguing that we are so constricted, the historicists and sociologists of knowledge have over-played their hand. An internal understanding is possible for the "meta" point of view.

Such internal understanding may be bought for a rather high price, the loss of originality. The perspective requisite for understanding and exegesis entails the severance of all allegiances. The meta-philosopher must be *of* the world but not *in* the world. Again the parallels with anthropology are illuminating. "The dilemma is inescapable: either the anthropologist clings to the norms of his own group, in which case the others can only inspire in him an ephemeral curiosity in which there is always an element of disapproval; or he makes himself over completely to the objects of his studies, in which case he can never be perfectly objective, because in giving himself to all societies he cannot but refuse himself, wittingly or not, to one among them."[10] If the anthropologist tries to avoid these two dangers in his quest for objective understanding, he is threatened by another: "If, in the first instance, we are threatened by obscurantism, in the form of a blind rejection of anything that is not our own, there is also an alternative danger: that of an eclecticism which bids us reject nothing at all, when faced with an alien culture." Moreover, action whether at home or in the foreign culture, is stopped: "The man who takes action in his own country cannot hope to understand the world outside: the man who takes all knowledge for his ambition must give up the idea of ever changing anything at home."[11]

The case may be somewhat different for the meta-philosopher: he may always be more detached from action than the anthropologist. But if commitment to a philosophical point of view requires conviction in the values and meanings of that position, the meta-philosopher may never be able to reach the full extent of the systems he studies. The philosopher may be able to combine in one person, though at different times, both metaphysician and meta-philosopher; but I am rather inclined to think that Lévi-Strauss is correct: the man who is genuinely committed at home cannot rise to the meta-level, and those who operate successfully on the meta-level may be forced to abandon all commitments.

Philosophical systems, especially ontologies, are written in the language of the philosophers who originate them. They follow the syntactic rules of that language and share most of their words with other language users. It is the presence of special words, a technical vocabu-

[10]C. Levi-Strauss, "Tristes Tropiques," *Encounter*, p. 35.
[11]*Ibid.*, p. 36.

lary which can be made the subject for a special dictionary, which indicates that language is being used for a special purpose. Philosophical languages, however, are not entirely characterized by reference to their technical vocabulary: the vocabulary is merely an indication of the special language. It is the conceptual orientation accompanying this technical vocabulary which transforms the vocabulary into a language. In fact, it is the demands of the conceptualization of the philosopher which give rise to the special vocabulary. What he feels is necessary to say cannot be expressed in the normal mode or with the usual words of language. To think in a foreign language requires both the facility of speech in that language and the cognitive understanding of the meaning of the words and expressions of that language. The systems of the traditional metaphysicians are foreign languages whose idioms must be mastered, whose syntactical modifications must be noticed, whose technical vocabulary must be learned. To learn to speak these special philosophical languages with understanding, discernment, and appreciation can only be achieved through prolonged and intimate contact with the internal structure of the thought being expressed by those languages.

Bibliography

THE ENTRIES on this list are for the most part the more recent books and articles relevant to the various parts of this study. I have not listed the obvious references to historical philosophers except in a few instances.

ANSCOMBE, G. E. M. *An Introduction to Wittgenstein's Tractatus*, London: Hutchinson, 1959.

ARMSTRONG, D. M. *Perception and the Physical World*, London: Routledge and Kegan Paul, 1961.

AUSTIN, J. *Sense and Sensibilia*, Oxford: Clarendon Press, 1962.

—— "Other Minds," in *Logic and Language*, 2nd series, edited by Anthony Flew, Oxford: Blackwell, 1953.

AYER, A. J. *The Foundations of Empirical Knowledge*, New York: Macmillan, 1940.

BASSON, A. H. *David Hume*, London: Penguin, 1958.

BEARE, JOHN. *Greek Theories of Elementary Cognition*, Oxford: Clarendon Press, 1906.

BERLIN, I. "Empirical Propositions and Hypothetical Statements," *Mind*, LIX (1950).

BLACK, MAX. "Linguistic Relativity: The Views of Benjamin Lee Whorf," in *The Philosophical Review*, LXVIII, 2 (1959), pp. 228–239.

BROAD, C. D. *Examination of McTaggart's Philosophy*, I, Cambridge: Cambridge University Press, 1933.

—— "Some Elementary Reflections on Sense-Perception," *Philosophy*, 27 (1952).

—— "What do we Mean by the Question: Is our Space Euclidean," *Mind*, XXIV (1915).

—— *Physics, Perception, and Reality*, Cambridge: Cambridge University Press, 1914.

—— *Scientific Thought*, London: Kegan Paul, Trench, Trubner, 1923.

—— "Phenomenalism," *Proceedings of the Aristotelian Society*, XV (1914–15).

—— "The External World," *Mind*, XXX (1921).

—— *The Mind and its Place in Nature*, London: Kegan Paul, Trench, Trubner, 1923.

BROCHARD, V. *Etudes de philosophie ancienne et de philosophie moderne*, Paris: Alcan, 1912.

BURLOUD, ALBERT. *De la psychologie à la philosophie*, Paris: Hachette, 1950.

BURNET, J. *Greek Philosophy*, London: Macmillan, 1914.

CARNAP, R. *Meaning and Necessity*, Chicago: University of Chicago Press, 1947.

CASSIRER, E. *An Essay on Man*, New York: Doubleday, 1953.

CHISHOLM, R. *Realism and the Background of Phenomenology*, London: Allen and Unwin, 1960.

—— *Perceiving: A Philosophical Study*, Ithaca: Cornell University Press, 1957.

—— *Theory of Knowledge*, Englewood Cliffs, New Jersey: Prentice Hall, 1966.

DEMOS, R. *The Philosophy of Plato*, New York: Scribner's, 1939.

DIÈS, A. *Autour de Platon*, Paris: Beauchesne, 1926.

FIRTH, R. Review of Warnock's *Berkeley, The Philosophical Review* (1955).

FREGE, G. "On Sense and Reference," in *Philosophical Writings of G. Frege*, edited and translated by P. T. Geach and M. Black, New York: Philosophical Library, 1952.

GEACH, P. T. *Mental Acts*, London: Routledge and Kegan Paul, 1957.

—— *Reference and Generality*, Ithaca, Cornell University Press, 1962.

HAMPSHIRE, S. *Thought and Action*, London: Chatto and Windus, 1959.

HANSON, N. R. *Patterns of Discovery*, Cambridge: Cambridge University Press, 1958.

HODGES, H. A. *Languages, Standpoints and Attitudes*, London: Oxford University Press, 1953.

HUSSERL, E. *Cartesian Meditations*, translated by D. Cairns, The Hague: Nijhoff, 1960.

—— *Erfahrung und Urteil*, Hamburg: Claassen und Goverts, 1948.

JAMES, W. *Essays in Radical Empiricism and a Pluralistic Universe*, New York: Longmans, Green, 1947.

JARVIS, J. "Definition by Internal Relations," *Australasian Journal of Philosophy*, 39 (1961).

—— *"Ethics* and Ethics and the Moral Life," *Journal of Philosophy*, 58, No. 3 (1961).

KLEIN, M., PAULA HERMAN, R. E. MONEY-KYRLE. *New Directions in Psycho-Analysis*, London: Tavistock, 1955.

KNEALE, W. *The Development of Logic*, Oxford: Clarendon Press, 1962.

KREMER, THOMAS. "The Significance of Solipsism," *Proceedings of the Aristotelian Society*, LX (1960).

LANGER, S. *Philosophy in a New Key*, New York: Penguin, 1948.

LEAN, M. *Sense Perception and Matter*, New York: Humanities, 1953.

LEVI-STRAUSS, C. "Tristes Tropiques," *Encounter*, April 1961.

LEWIS, C. I. "Realism or Phenomenalism," *The Philosophical Review*, LXIV (1955).

—— *An Analysis of Knowledge and Valuation* (Seventh Paul Carus Lectures), La Salle, Illinois: Open Court Publishing Co., 1947.

MILL, J. *A System of Logic*, New York: Harper and Brothers, 1846.

MINKUS, P. *Philosophy of the Person*, Oxford: Blackwell, 1960.

MONEY-KYRLE, R. E. *Man's Picture of his World*, London: Duckworth, 1961.

MOORE, G. E. "The Nature of Judgment," *Mind*, n.s. 8 (1889).

NAKHNIKIAN, G. "Plato's Theory of Sensation," *The Review of Metaphysics*, IX (1955).

OAKESHOTT, MICHAEL. *The Voice of Poetry in the Conversation of Mankind*, London: Bowes and Bowes, 1959. (Reprinted in *Rationalism in Politics and Other Essays*, London: Methuen, 1962.)

PASSMORE, J. *Philosophical Reasoning*, London: Duckworth, 1961.

PLATO. *Theaetetus*, in Cornford's *Plato's Theory of Knowledge*, London: Routledge and Kegan Paul, 1960.

—— *Timaeus*, in Cornford's *Plato's Cosmology*, London: Routledge and Kegan Paul, 1937.

—— *Timaeus*, in *Œuvres complètes*, t. X, *Timée—Critias*, edited and translated by A. Rivaur, Paris: Société d'édition "Les Belles Lettres," 1949. (Publiée sous le patronage de l'Association Guillaume Budé)

POLE, D. *The Later Philosophy of Wittgenstein*, London: Athlone Press, 1958.

PRICE, H. H. *Perception*, London: Methuen, 1932.

—— *Thinking and Experience*, London: Hutchinson, 1953.

QUINE, W. V. O. *From a Logical Point of View*, Cambridge, Mass.: Harvard University Press, 1953.

QUINTON, A. "The Problem of Perception," *Mind*, LXIV (1955).

RIVAUD, A. *Le Problème du devenir et la notion de la matière dans la philosophie grecque depuis les origines jusqu'à Théophraste*, Paris: Alcan, 1905.

RIVIERE, JOAN (editor) *Development in Psycho-Analysis*, London: Hogarth Press, 1952.

ROBIN, L. *Platon*, Paris: Alcan, 1935.

ROYCE, J. *The World and the Individual* (Gifford Lectures, Second Series), New York: Macmillan, 1901.

—— *Logical Essays*, edited by D. S. Robinson, Dubuque, Iowa: W. C. Brown, 1951.

RUNCIMAN, W. G. *Plato's Later Epistemology*, Cambridge: Cambridge University Press, 1962.

RUSSELL, B. *Inquiry into Meaning and Truth*, London: Methuen, 1940.

—— "The Limits of Empiricism," *Proceedings of the Aristotelian Society*, 36 (1935–36).

—— *The Problems of Philosophy*, London: Oxford, 1912.

—— *Mysticism and Logic*, New York: Longmans, Green, 1918.

—— *Introduction to Mathematical Philosophy*, London: Allen and Unwin, 1919.

—— *The Principles of Mathematics*, Cambridge: University Press, 1903.

—— *Human Knowledge, Its Scope and Limits*, New York: Simon & Schuster, 1948.

—— *Logic and Knowledge*, edited by R. C. Marsh, New York: Macmillan, 1956.

RYLE, G. "The Theory of Meaning," *British Philosophy in the Mid-Century*, edited by C. A. Mace, New York: Macmillan, 1957.

SANTAYANA, GEORGE. *Reason in Common Sense*, New York: Scribner's, 1936 (one volume edition, *The Life of Reason, or, The Phases of Human Progress*, New York: Scribner's, 1954.)

SAPIR, EDWARD. *Language: An Introduction to the Study of Speech*, New York: Harcourt, Brace and World, Inc., 1921.

SAW, R. L. *Leibniz*, London: Penguin, 1954.

SCHILPP, P. A. (editor) *The Philosophy of C. D. Broad*, New York: Tudor Publishing Co., 1959.

SEARLE, JOHN. "Meaning and Speech Acts," *The Philosophical Review*, 71 (1962).

SHWAYDER, D. S. *Modes of Referring and the Problem of Universals: An Essay in Metaphysics*, Berkeley: University of California Press, 1961.

SHOREY, P. *What Plato Said*, Chicago: University of Chicago Press, 1933.

SLUGA, H. D. "On Sense," *Proceedings of the Aristotelian Society*, LXV (1965).

STRAWSON, P. *Individuals, An Essay in Descriptive Metaphysics*, London: Methuen, 1959.

—— "On Referring," *Essays in Conceptual Analysis*, edited by Anthony Flew, London: Macmillan, 1956.

—— *Introduction to Logical Theory*, London: Methuen, 1952.

—— Review of Wittgenstein's *Philosophical Investigations*, *Mind*, 63 (1954).

TOMS, E. *Being, Negation and Logic*, Oxford: Blackwell, 1962.

TOULMIN, S. *The Philosophy of Science*, London: Hutchinson, 1953.

URMSON, J. O. *Philosophical Analysis: Its Development Between the Two World Wars*, Oxford: Clarendon Press, 1956.

VAN PEURSEN, C. A. "Phénoménologie et ontologie," *Rencontre, Encounter, Begegnung: Contributions à une psychologie humaine, dédiées au Prof. F. J. J. Buytendijk*, Utrecht/Antwerpen: Spectrum, 1957.

DEWAELHENS, A. "Sciences humaines, horizon ontologique et rencontre," in *Rencontre, Encounter, Begegnung*.

WARNOCK, G. *Berkeley*, London: Penguin, 1953.

WHITEHEAD, A. N. *The Concept of Nature*, Cambridge: Cambridge University Press, 1926.

WHORF, BENJAMIN L. *Collected Papers on Metalinguistics*, Washington, D.C.: Foreign Service Institute, Department of State, 1952.

WISDOM, JOHN. *Philosophy and Psychoanalysis*, Oxford: Blackwell, 1953.

WITTGENSTEIN, L. *Philosophical Investigations*, Oxford: Blackwell, 1953.

YOLTON, J. W. "Act and Circumstance," *The Journal of Philosophy*, LIX (1962).

—— *Thinking and Perceiving: A Study in the Philosophy of Mind*, La Salle, Illinois: Open Court, 1962.

ZIFF, P. *Semantic Analysis*, Ithaca: Cornell University Press, 1960.

Index

THE TRUTH ABOUT THE FOOD SUPPLY™

FRUITS AND VEGETABLES

FROM THE GARDEN TO YOUR TABLE

ANN BYERS

rosen publishing's
rosen central®
New York

Published in 2013 by The Rosen Publishing Group, Inc.
29 East 21st Street, New York, NY 10010

Copyright © 2013 by The Rosen Publishing Group, Inc.

First Edition

Library of Congress Cataloging-in-Publication Data

Byers, Ann.
Fruits and vegetables: from the garden to your table/Ann
Byers.—1st ed.
    p. cm.—(The truth about the food supply)
Includes bibliographical references and index.
ISBN 978-1-4488-6799-8 (library binding)
1. Fruit—Juvenile literature. 2. Vegetables—Juvenile literature.
3. Food—Safety measures—Juvenile literature. I. Title.
TX397.B94 2013
363.19'2—dc23

                                        2011039423

Manufactured in the United States of America

CPSIA Compliance Information: Batch #S12YA: For further information, contact Rosen Publishing, New York, New York,
at 1-800-237-9932.

CONTENTS

Jillian Kohl knew how to keep healthy. She was in training for her third marathon. She ate plenty of vegetables, and she preferred them raw. On August 30, 2006, she fixed herself a big salad from a bag of prewashed spinach.

The next day, when she felt worn out, she assumed her schedule was too busy. The twenty-four-year-old was in graduate school, working two jobs, and running three or four days every week. Why wouldn't she be tired? But two days later she developed stomach cramps,

Raw spinach in bags like this one is usually safe and healthy, but in 2006 some was contaminated with *E coli*. The information on the bag helped people find the source of the contamination.

felt nauseous, and had a fever. In another two days she was passing blood when she went to the bathroom and she could barely stand up.

Before the doctors could figure out what was wrong, Kohl's body went into spasms. She was hallucinating and her organs were failing. The young woman who had been the picture of perfect health less than a week earlier spent seventeen days in the hospital and nearly died.

Kohl was diagnosed with *E. coli* O157:H7, which came from the salad she ate. She was one of more than two hundred people in twenty-six states to contract the deadly disease from the spinach. Five of them died. Kohl got well, but the disease permanently weakened her kidneys. She is now part of an organization called STOP Foodborne Illness (formerly Safe Tables Our Priority), which makes people aware of what foods are safe and what foods are unsafe. As she told her story to STOP Foodborne Illness, she said, "I'm extremely lucky to have recovered … I think of how innocent I used to be when I would buy bagged spinach at the grocery store and not think twice about it. Now … I shop through the produce section with more skepticism. I no longer assume food is safe."

HOW CAN GOOD FOOD EVER BE BAD?

Was Jillian Kohl right to think that a spinach salad would be a healthy meal? Absolutely! Fresh vegetables and fruits are among the best foods a person can eat. They contain vitamins, minerals, and fiber. They are low in calories, low in sodium, and have no cholesterol. But according to the Center for Science in the Public Interest (CSPI), produce accounted for twice as many cases of sickness between 1990 and 2005—more than thirty-four thousand—than any other type of food. How can something so good make people ill?

What causes illness is germs. Germs are microorganisms—tiny (micro) living things (organisms)—also called microbes. Four kinds of microbes affect food: bacteria, fungi, parasites, and viruses.

All microbes are not bad. In fact, without bacteria and fungi people would not have many of the foods they enjoy. To make cheese and yogurt, bacteria are added to milk. Bread would be flat without yeast, which is a fungus. Yeast creates the fizz in root beer. Chocolate comes from cacao beans, but the beans have to be

Unlike bacteria and viruses, fungi are easy to spot. Mold, like that growing on these oranges, is a fungus.

fermented with both yeasts and bacteria.

Some microbes cause food to decay. Spoilage microbes eat the nutrients in fruits and vegetables and deposit their waste in or on the produce. This activity makes foods soft and mushy. It makes fruits and vegetables look, smell, and taste bad, but it usually does not make people sick.

PATHOGENS

The microbes that make people sick are called pathogens. Unlike spoilage microbes, pathogens do not affect the appearance, smell, or taste of foods. A plate of mixed salad greens can look perfectly fine but be covered in pathogens. And a few days may go by before the microbes make their victim feel bad. Symptoms may appear in a few hours or not for several weeks. So people can become sick and not know why. They may think they have the flu. What they have is a foodborne illness—a disease carried (borne) by food.

Harmful bacteria can cause illness in two ways. One is by infection. When someone consumes the bacteria that produce listeria, salmonella, shigella, or *E. coli* O157:H7, the bacteria continue to multiply in the intestines. The human body produces antibodies that kill the bacteria, but if a large number of bacteria are taken in, the body cannot make enough antibodies to destroy the pathogens. The result is a foodborne infection.

Some bacteria do not harm people directly, but they make toxins, or poisons, that can make people very sick. Even if the bacteria are killed before the food is eaten, the toxins are still present. Botulism is one serious illness that is actually food poisoning.

In addition to bacteria, fungi and viruses can cause foodborne illness. The great potato famines in Ireland in the 1800s were caused by a fungus. Before a vaccine was developed against it, the hepatitis A in frozen strawberries, fresh green onions, blueberries, and lettuce sickened many people. Noroviruses cause more foodborne illnesses than any other pathogen.

PATHOGENS AND PRODUCE

Microbes are everywhere: in soil, in water, in air. The bacteria responsible for botulism and listeria live in many soils. The listeria bacterium lives in soil, water, damp environments, humans, and animals. The bacterium that causes botulism can be present on almost any food of animal or vegetable origin, in soil, and in water. The pathogens that cause salmonella, shigella, and *E. coli* live in the intestines of healthy animals, and some live in small amounts in the intestines of humans. These organisms can get on fruits and vegetables if the produce touches soil or water that is contaminated with the pathogens.

Once a fruit or vegetable is contaminated, the pathogens begin to multiply. Foodborne pathogens need six conditions to grow: food, acidity, time, temperature, oxygen, and moisture. (The words "FAT TOM" can help you remember these conditions.) Fruits and vegetables are great places for microbes to grow. They are rich in nutrients, so they supply plenty of food. The average fruit or vegetable is at least 85 percent water, more than adequate for bacterial growth. Pathogens grow best at temperatures between 40° and 140° F (4.4° and 60° C), which is a wide enough range for nearly all produce. Under the right

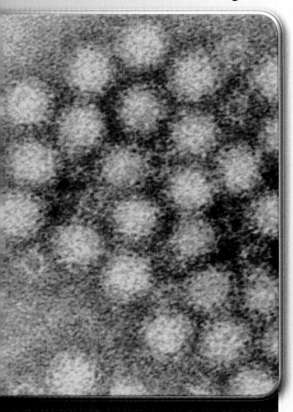

This image taken by a special electron microscope shows norovirus virions. Virions are the particles of the virus that infect people.

conditions, some bacteria can double in number every twenty minutes.

CHEMICALS

In addition to microbes, the chemicals used in growing and preparing produce sometimes cause foodborne illness. Many farmers use pesticides to keep rodents and other pests from harming their crops in the field. The pesticides may contain herbicides, insecticides, fungicides, and germicides to kill weeds, insects, and microbes ("-cide" means "kill"). If these poisons are not thoroughly washed off the plants, they can make people who eat the produce quite sick.

Many growers clean their harvested crops with a chemical wash. The chemicals kill pathogens that might be on the plants. Some bags of packaged lettuce you see in stores say the product

FINDING THE SOURCE

In a nationwide epidemic of food-borne illness, how do medical sleuths track down the culprits? For the 2006 spinach E. coli outbreak, the detective work began in Wisconsin. Someone noticed five cases in one county—a cluster. Then he learned of other cases in other parts of the state, all the same strain of E. coli. He alerted the national Centers for Disease Control and Prevention (CDC). The CDC began getting reports from other states. Eighty percent of the sick people remembered eating prepackaged spinach. Health officials examined bags from victims' refrigerators and garbage cans. From a code on the packages, investigators traced the tainted food to a 2.8-acre (11,331-square-meter) field in California. One thousand pounds (454 kilograms) of spinach had become contaminated during one shift on one day. Case solved.

The arms on both sides of this tractor spray pesticide on the tomato plants in a commercial field.

is "triple washed." However, if the packagers are not careful to remove not just the pathogens, but also the chemicals they used to clean the product, they leave the risk of chemical foodborne illness.

Chemicals are sometimes applied to fruits and vegetables for added color, flavor, and nutrition. These chemicals must be carefully measured and applied or they, too, can make people sick. Some chemicals may be harmless in small quantities, but too much may cause problems, especially for the very young, the elderly, and people who are sensitive to the chemicals.

KEEPING GOOD FOOD GOOD

With so many bacteria, viruses, toxins, and chemicals, the possibility of fruits and vegetables becoming contaminated by some pathogen or chemical is high. Contamination can occur at any point in the farm-to-fork journey: when the produce is grown, picked, processed, shipped to grocers, or eaten. Produce growers, processors, shippers, and sellers have to take steps to make sure fruits and vegetables are safe to eat.

MYTHS AND FACTS

Myth: Processed fruits and vegetables are not as nutritious as fresh, unprocessed foods.
Fact: Fruits and vegetables that are processed are picked and processed at their peak of ripeness, preserving most nutrients; fresh produce may be picked unripe and start to spoil while being stored and transported.

Myth: Organic fruits and vegetables are healthier than commercially grown foods.
Fact: Organic products are free of herbicides and pesticides, but organic farmers have the same risks of exposure to pathogens as other growers.

Myth: Frozen vegetables can never make you sick.
Fact: Freezing inactivates pathogens but does not destroy them; when food is thawed, pathogens begin to multiply again and can make you sick.

HOW GROWERS KEEP FOOD SAFE ... OR NOT

Food safety begins in the field even before any crops are planted. It begins with good soil, clean water, and clean workers.

GOOD SOIL

Plants take nutrients from the soil, and farmers use fertilizer to put nutrients back into the soil. Many use manure, which is animal waste, for fertilizer. But animal waste can harbor pathogens because the microbes live harmlessly in the intestines of many animals. So before it is used for fertilizer, the manure is either heated to a high enough temperature to kill the pathogens or it is composted.

Composting is a natural method of enriching the ground. To compost the manure, farmers heap it up and stir the piles frequently. The thousands of good microbes in the manure break down the plant and animal material also in the mixture, releasing nutrients. This activity makes the compost pile hot—hot enough to kill the bad microbes, the pathogens. The process takes at least three weeks and often many months. If farmers apply the manure before it is completely composted, some pathogens may still be alive.

Even soil that is 100 percent free of pathogens can become contaminated. Pathogens that are in animal waste can get into the soil if animals roam in an area where crops are planted. Wild pigs lived near the farm named in the 2006 spinach *E. coli* epidemic.

CLEAN WATER

Pathogens can also get into the plants through water. Farmers irrigate their crops with water from under the ground or from rivers, lakes, and reservoirs. If animals

Vegetables that are no longer fresh or good to eat are added to compost piles.

have been around that water, pathogens from their intestines are very likely in the water.

Animal waste is not the only contaminant that may be in irrigation water. Anything that was ever in the ground can end up in the water: metals, oil leaked from farm equipment, weed killers, pesticides, and other chemicals. Rain and irrigation water can wash these into streams or into underground water, where they can contaminate the water that is used on crops. Water splashing on crops at a sprouts farm in Illinois was linked to a 2011 salmonella outbreak that affected ninety-four people in sixteen states.

Plasticulture is the name for growing fruit or vegetable crops through sheets of plastic.

Some growers reduce the problem of unclean water by using drip irrigation. They lay a thin hose along the rows of crops and drip water directly into the soil. That way any pathogens or chemicals that might be in the water cannot get on the crops unless the crops touch the soil. If, on the other hand, growers water with sprinklers, the water falls on the stems, leaves, and flowers, which are the edible portions of many plants.

Other farmers avoid contamination from the soil or water by growing their crops on plastic. The roots of the plants go into the soil, but all the parts that will be eaten are separated from the dirt by plastic sheets. The fertilizer, water, and any pathogens are underneath the protective layer of plastic.

CLEAN WORKERS

One of the biggest concerns for food safety is not soil or water, but people. Perfectly well people can have germs on their hands, especially right after they go to the bathroom. The CDC reports that 34 percent of all cases of foodborne illness are caused by people who handle food without washing their hands properly.

Human waste, like animal waste, contains pathogens. The pathogens are not harmful in small numbers in the human intestine, but when they are transferred to foods, they multiply rapidly.

Cleanliness is important at all stages of growing and picking food. Farm workers must keep their hair, hands, and clothing clean. Any equipment that touches the produce must also be clean. But even with the greatest care, pathogens may still contaminate fruits and vegetables. So after the produce is harvested, growers wash it. They add chlorine or ozone to the wash water—not to kill pathogens that might be on the produce, but to kill any that might be in the water. Both chlorine and ozone destroy pathogens, but many growers prefer ozone. Chlorine sometimes leaves a distinct taste, whereas ozone (O_3) breaks down into oxygen (O_2) and has no aftereffects.

FLAVRSAVR TOMATO

After ten years of experimenting, the Calgene Company had a winner. Biotech engineers had modified a plant to produce a tomato that would ripen on the vine and stay firm and red for weeks. The few tests performed on the fruit's safety raised questions, but the U.S. Food and Drug Administration (FDA) approved the tomato in 1994. So the Flavr-Savr tomato, the first genetically modified fresh food, was offered for sale. But the beautiful tomato bruised easily and did not taste any better than other tomatoes. And it cost twice as much. In fewer than two years, the Flavr-Savr tomato faded into history.

PESTICIDES

However, no amount of washing can get rid of all the pesticides that might be on the crop. Some of the poison has worn away by the time the plant is picked, and some on the surface can be washed off. But some has gotten inside, into the tissues that will eventually be eaten. The U.S. Department of Agriculture (USDA) tested the most popular fruits and vegetables and found that 63 percent contained pesticides, and many contained more than one.

How dangerous are these pesticides to people? They can poison the brain and nervous system; disrupt hormones; irritate the skin, eyes, and lungs; and cause cancer. However, a person would have to take in a large amount to cause any of these problems. The pesticides are deadly to pests but only slightly toxic to humans. The FDA strictly regulates the kinds and amounts of pesticides growers can apply to their crops. The Environmental Working Group, a private organization that monitors health-related issues, says the risk from eating fruits and vegetables is low. The group recommends eating produce despite small amounts of pesticides.

GENETICALLY MODIFIED PRODUCE

One type of food the Environmental Working Group does not recommend eating is genetically modified (GM) fruits or vegetables. GM plants have had their genetic makeup modified, or changed. Scientists try to make "better" foods by taking genes from one plant or from bacteria and inserting them into another plant. They find an organism that is not affected by the toxins in weed killers, that does not need much water, that resists insects, or that extends the time fruit stays ripe. They find the exact gene that causes the effect they want, and they put it into the seed of the plant they want to improve. Voilá! A super plant!

It sounds like a good idea, and sometimes it works. But it is not as simple as it seems. It is not like adding sugar to berries, which just makes the berries sweeter. Inserting a gene changes a plant into something completely different. Attempts to produce ready-to-eat GM foods such as tomatoes, peas, and strawberries have not been very successful. A number of scientists warn that GM foods have caused health problems in laboratory animals. Still, much of the corn grown in the United States is genetically modified, as are soybeans and canola that are used in many processed foods.

Scientists inserted a gene from a fish that produces antifreeze into a plant. The blue strawberry does not get mushy when frozen like red strawberries do.

If farmers begin with good seeds, plant them in good soil, irrigate them with clean water, and keep everything that touches the plants clean, they are likely to produce good fruits and vegetables. The produce is ready for the next step: processing.

HOW PROCESSORS KEEP PRODUCE SAFE ... OR NOT

P roduce is processed to keep it looking and tasting good and free from pathogens. The minute they are picked, fruits and vegetables begin to deteriorate. They deteriorate mainly because of the action of spoilage microbes. The various processing methods either destroy or slow the growth of microbes.

COOLING

Cooling does not kill microbes, but it keeps them from growing—both spoilage microbes and pathogens. Processors cool produce in different ways. They put fruits or vegetables in refrigerated rooms immediately after they are picked. But room cooling is slow, so processors also use forced-air cooling. Fans blow cold air over the produce. For even more rapid cooling, processors immerse some produce in cold water. Water can cool an item five times faster than air. Dense vegetables like corn and broccoli are often packed with ice.

Exactly what temperature is right depends on the particular fruit or vegetable. Sweet potatoes will keep six to twelve months

Broccoli, beets, and mushrooms all store well at the same temperature—32 to 36°F (0 to 2°C)—and the same relative humidity of about 95 percent.

at 55° F (12.8° C), but peas will last only one or two weeks at their ideal temperature of 32° F (0° C).

Produce can be kept from spoiling for considerably longer by freezing. If processors freeze fruits or vegetables at the peak of ripeness, they keep nearly all of their vitamins, color, and taste. Of all the processing methods, freezing gives the closest result to fresh. However, even freezing does not rid the foods of microbes; it merely makes them inactive. As soon as the food thaws, the rising temperature allows the microbes to become active again.

HEATING

Heat actually kills microbes. Heating to a temperature of 160° F (68° C) for just a few seconds destroys most microbes. Produce that is frozen is blanched first—plunged into boiling water for a few seconds or a few minutes—to kill microbes that would cause it to spoil or make people sick.

Canning is a process that uses heat to preserve food. Processors heat the fruit or vegetable, usually under pressure, and then seal it in airtight cans or jars. One microbe (*Clostridium botulinum*) produces a spore that can survive at temperatures below boiling, so canning requires quite high heat. Canned foods are generally safe and have a long shelf life. Shelf life is the amount of time a product can remain good to eat when properly stored.

Canning has three disadvantages. First, canned products do not taste as good as fresh fruits and vegetables. Second, salt or sugar are often added to improve the flavor, and too much of these can cause health problems. Third, heating destroys some of the nutrients, particularly vitamins. But on the positive side, the long shelf life of canned products means you can eat them when fresh products are not available. Produce that is canned is usually processed at its peak, so it retains most of its nutrients. Because vegetables like green beans and spinach lose as much as three-fourths of their vitamin C within a week of being picked, canned foods can be healthier than fresh.

Another way to preserve fruits is to pasteurize their juices. Juices, like any other form of produce, can contain pathogens. To

At processing plants such as this, tomatoes are canned in many forms: whole, cut up, stewed, pureed, sauce, paste, and juice.

pasteurize fruit juices, processors heat them to the right temperature for the right amount of time. Pasteurized juices may not taste quite as good as fresh-squeezed, and they may contain slightly fewer vitamins, but they are perfectly safe.

IRRADIATION

One method of treating food that requires neither cold nor heat is irradiation. In this process, products are exposed to controlled amounts of radiation that damage or kill spoilage microbes as well as pathogens. Without the microbes, the products remain longer at their just-picked stage. Irradiation is very effective, does not affect the nutritional content of foods, and does not make them radioactive. But because some people worry about radiation, irradiated foods have to have a special symbol on their packaging and a notice that they have been treated with radiation.

DRYING

The oldest method of preserving food is drying. Microbes need moisture to grow and function, and produce has plenty of moisture. About 85 percent of the weight of fruits, on average, is water,

These strawberries were all picked at the same time, but the ones on the left were irradiated. They last longer than the fruit that was not.

and vegetables are about 88 percent water. Taking the water out of foods keeps them from deteriorating and keeps pathogens from multiplying. Drying destroys some of the vitamins, but those that remain are concentrated. That is why dried fruits taste especially sweet. Dried foods are very safe; no incident of foodborne illness has been traced to dried fruits or vegetables. The only real problem is for people who are sensitive to sulfur. Processors add sulfur dioxide to some dried fruits to preserve their color.

ADDITIVES

Processors add other ingredients as well. When food is exposed to oxygen, chemical reactions make it lose some of its color and taste. This oxidation is what makes cut apples turn brown. Adding vinegar or certain acids to canned fruits and vegetables prevents oxidation. Sugars and chemicals—some natural, some artificial—are sometimes added to sweeten the product, improve the texture or flavor, make it look better, kill pathogens, and add nutrients. Some products have many additives; some have none.

Government agencies regulate what can be added, and all food additives are safe. Nevertheless, some studies suggest there might be a connection between food coloring and hyperactivity in children. And some people are allergic to some of the preservatives and dyes. Food labels must list everything in a product so that people with allergies or sensitivities should read labels before they eat.

FOOD THAT BUGS YOU

What makes some of those maraschino cherries so red? Would you believe ... bugs? It's true. The bright color in some fruit juices, jams, and other products is actually a red dye made from the ground-up bodies of the *Dactylopius coccus*, a South American cactus beetle. It is listed on labels as cochineal, carmine, or carminic acid. At least it's natural!

MINIMALLY PROCESSED FOODS

Ironically, the fruits and vegetables linked with the most cases of foodborne illnesses are those that are processed the least. These are called minimally processed foods. They are the prepackaged lettuce and other greens, cut carrots and celery, sliced mushrooms, whole berries, etc. The reason little- or non-processed foods can be a problem is that they have no kill step between the farm and the store for destroying pathogens. They are not frozen, heated, irradiated, or dried. Nothing has been added. They have merely been washed; maybe chopped, cut, or peeled; and packaged.

So the safety of minimally processed foods depends on good hygiene in the field and after harvest. It also depends on the packaging and how it is handled to get it to your table.

10 GREAT QUESTIONS
TO ASK A NUTRITIONIST

1. Can I get radiation poisoning from eating irradiated food?
2. Is it all right to drink unpasteurized apple juice?
3. Should I wash my fruits and vegetables with soap or with special solutions?
4. How long can I keep a package of frozen berries in my freezer?
5. The eggplant on sale at the store was not in a cold case. Is it safe?
6. Are tomatoes grown in another country safe to eat?
7. I am allergic to Aspartame. How can I be sure it is not in the canned fruit I buy?
8. Is it safe to use homemade compost in my vegetable garden?
9. Should I wash the ready-to-eat spinach I buy, even though the bag says "washed"?
10. Do I need to wash grapefruit since I'm not eating the rind?

HOW SHIPPERS AND SELLERS KEEP PRODUCE SAFE ... OR NOT

M any of the items in the produce section of a grocery store must travel long distances to get from the field to the consumer. During every minute of that journey, the food progresses toward deterioration. Some produce continues to ripen after it is picked, but eventually it reaches its peak. From that point on, it gradually loses its freshness, color, and flavor. Spoilage and disease-causing microbes multiply. Shippers must get the produce to the stores quickly.

Three conditions affect how long produce stays good: temperature, moisture, and oxygen. For every fruit and vegetable, there are just-right temperature, moisture, and oxygen levels. And those levels are different for different fruits and vegetables. For each product, processors have to choose containers that will maintain those levels during the trip across country or across town.

Shippers can select from among more than 1,500 different kinds of bags, cartons, or boxes. The containers have to do four things. They have to allow enough air to flow around the produce so that the cooling systems used for storing and transporting them can keep them at the right temperature. The containers have to keep the food from drying out. They have to control the oxygen and carbon dioxide levels. And they have to protect them from being crushed or bruised.

CONTAINERS

Some fresh and minimally processed produce is packaged in bags. Potatoes are sometimes in burlap or cotton sacks, and grapefruit, onions, and garlic are often in mesh bags. Most bagged produce, however, is in plastic film. Some fresh produce like

Potatoes and onions are frequently packaged in cotton or plastic mesh bags. Mesh bags are highly breathable: they permit good air to flow around the produce.

corn, cucumbers, and some tropical fruits are shrink-wrapped. More fragile produce needs sturdier containers. Berries, cut fruit, and salad vegetables are frequently packed in rigid plastic boxes called clamshells. Some boxes are made from recycled paper pulp. The paper pulp material absorbs excess water.

Whether bags or boxes are used, the containers have to allow shippers and grocers to keep the temperature, moisture, and oxygen levels just right. Some have vents—slits that allow air to circulate. Bags are made of polyethylene that lets controlled amounts of air in and out. Remember, what is right for one product is not necessarily right for another.

Today's consumers are demanding more than containers that keep food safe and looking nice. They want the containers to be good for the environment as well. They are asking for materials that are made from recycled products and that are biodegradable, or break down easily without harming the environment. Designing the best container for the environment, as well as for each food, is an exact science.

WAXES AND COATINGS

Some fresh produce is packaged in invisible containers. Many of the apples, peppers, cucumbers, and lemons sold in grocery stores are covered with a thin coat of wax. This holds water loss to a minimum, keeps too much oxygen from getting in, and keeps pathogens out. The wax makes the product a little harder, making it less likely to bruise. It also makes it shiny and bright.

The wax might be natural—beeswax, wax from a palm tree, or shellac from a beetle—or it may be made from petroleum. The wax itself is harmless, but sometimes it is mixed with alcohol, ethanol, or other products to help it go on better. Some people are allergic or sensitive to these ingredients. Waxes do not wash or scrub off. The only way to remove them is to peel the fruit or vegetable. But the most nutritious part of any produce is directly beneath the skin. So peeling removes some of the best part of the food.

Food scientists have developed other substances that have the same effect as waxing. Coating sweet foods such as apples with corn syrup seals their goodness in and protects them somewhat from rough handling. Citric acid does the same for potatoes. Coatings have been made from soy, wheat, corn, and egg products.

WRAP AND EAT

In 2004, researchers at Oregon State University combined a fiber from a shellfish and a protein from egg whites to create a super wrapping for all kinds of food—a wrap that is edible! It stops microbes from growing, so it protects food from spoiling and from causing illness. It can be produced as a film, a spray, or a dip. This substance is all natural. It does not add any taste or texture to the food it coats. Vitamins and minerals can be added to it, so it can enrich foods as well as protect them. So far, no negatives have been found for this still unnamed product.

These cabbages have been misted to keep them moist. They have been placed on material that allows excess water to flow away from them, so they will not be too wet.

IN THE STORE

The last step in getting fruits and vegetables to the table takes place where they are sold. Grocers transfer produce from refrigerated trucks to refrigerated rooms in their stores. Because different products require different temperature and humidity ranges, the atmosphere in the cold storage rooms may not be ideal for every food. But as long as the products are sold within a few days, they should be safe.

Grocers display their foods to make them appealing to their customers. They place items with thick skins, like oranges, kiwis, pears, and avocados, on display tables. They do not lose water rapidly, so they do not need the colder temperatures. Products that are on sale can also be left unrefrigerated on tables if they sell within a few hours. But many produce items need to be in refrigerated display cases. Some, like greens, cauliflower, celery, and broccoli, can be misted to keep them moist and crisp. Special lightbulbs that do not heat up are used in produce displays.

Food safety is a major concern of grocers. They regularly clean and sanitize everything that comes in contact with the produce. They insist that produce clerks wash their hands or wear gloves. They dispose of any products that are no longer good, taking them to composting centers. They are the last link in the farm-to-fork chain.

YOUR PART

Despite news accounts about foodborne illness outbreaks, most of the produce you buy in the United States today is perfectly safe. Growers, processors, shippers, and sellers follow the procedures set by the FDA, the government agency charged with food safety. But pathogens are everywhere, and they can enter food any place along the journey from the garden or farm to the fork. That means that you, the consumer, have a part to play in keeping your food safe.

KNOW WHERE YOUR FOOD COMES FROM

The most important way to stay safe is to know what you are eating. Reading this book is a great first step—it helps you know about food in general. But what about the specific food you eat? Do you know how it was grown? What pesticides were used on it? Was anything added to it after it was picked?

One way to know the answers to these questions is to buy produce from a local grower. Many communities have farms, produce stands, and farmers' markets where people can buy fresh

Students help First Lady Michelle Obama harvest vegetables from a garden at the White House in Washington, D.C.

fruits and vegetables. More than 4,400 farmers, mostly organic farmers, are part of the community supported agriculture (CSA) movement. They bring boxes of fresh produce—whatever is in season—right to your door.

One advantage of buying locally is that local food does not have to be shipped far. The shorter the distance and the quicker the time from the field to your table means less has to be done to keep the produce safe and fresh. If you are purchasing from a grocery store, you can ask the manager where the products you

The USDA makes sure that any food labeled "organic," like this tomato, was grown with no or almost no man-made pesticides.

are buying are from.

Some people prefer to eat organic foods. If you are sensitive to food additives, organic is a good choice for you. Any food labeled "100 percent organic" was produced without any synthetic (man-made) pesticides, herbicides, or fertilizers, and was not genetically modified or irradiated. Foods can display the USDA "organic" label if they were grown with no more than 95 percent synthetic products. Because synthetic fertilizers take some vitamins and minerals out of the soil, organic foods may be a little healthier than foods not grown organically. In grocery stores, organic foods usually cost a little more than conventionally grown products because keeping pests away from them in the field requires more time and more work. But at farmers' markets and through CSAs, organic foods are sometimes less expensive.

READ THE LABELS

When you buy processed fruits or vegetables, read the labels on the packaging. By law, the label has to tell you the name and address of the company that supplied the product, everything that is inside, and all the nutrition facts. So you can tell if a jar of applesauce was processed in your locality, another state, or another country. You can see how many calories, how much fiber, and how much of certain vitamins and minerals it contains.

This label shows that sugar and corn syrup were added to the pears in the can. A fresh pear contains about 16.4 grams of sugar, but one serving from this can contains 23 g.

The package may have a date on it, although federal law does not require this. It may have a packing date, a sell-by date, a best-if-used-by date, or an expiration date. The date does not usually refer to when the food is no longer safe, but when it starts to lose its taste and nutrition. Canned products are usually good for at least a year after the packing date, and frozen goods retain their quality for several months after they are processed.

WASTE NOT, WANT NOT

California farmer Mike Yuro-sek hated to see good food go to waste. But nobody would buy the bent, bumpy, or broken parts of his car-rots. He was throwing away as much as 400 tons (406 met-ric tons) of unusable carrots every day. In 1986, he had an idea. He bought a heavy-duty green bean cutter that cut the imperfect carrots into 2-inch (5-centimeter) pieces. Then he fed the pieces into a commercial potato peeler to peel and smooth them. He found that people liked the "baby carrots" better than the long ones. A new product was born. Today, 80 percent of all carrots sold are baby carrots.

The label will also tell you if anything has been added. Pears may be canned in juices that contain sugar, corn syrup, or an artificial sweetener. Beans, tomatoes, and other canned vegetables may have additional salt. Dried fruits are often pre-served with sulfites. Sauces, flavorings, and preservatives are frequently added when fruits and vegetables are pro-cessed, and they all are listed on the product's label.

HANDLE WITH CARE

The last stop in the farm-to-fork journey is your kitchen. The grower, the processor, the ship-per, and the seller may have kept your produce safe, but it can become contaminated in your kitchen. You can help make sure your food stays safe by being careful how you store it and how you prepare it.

Remember what encourages pathogens to grow: warm temperatures and moisture. Storing fresh fruits and vegetables in the refrigerator keeps almost all pathogens from multiplying. Two bacteria that cause foodborne illnesses, *Listeria monocytogenes* and *Yersinia enterocolitica*, are exceptions; they can actually grow at very low temperatures. Still, it is safest to keep all fresh and cut fruits and vegetables in the refrigerator. Bananas, however, turn black in the refrigerator; they can be kept at room temperature.

Most refrigerators have drawers especially for fruits and vegetables. These drawers control the humidity and therefore keep pathogens, as well as spoilage microbes, from growing. Make sure your refrigerator is set no higher than 40° F (4.4° C).

The number-one practice for keeping food safe is to keep it clean. That means washing your hands with soap and warm water before handling produce. It means keeping everything that touches the produce clean—counters, cutting boards, knives, and plates. Wash the food right before preparing it—don't wash it and store it to eat later. Scrub firm produce with a clean brush, even if you peel it. You don't need special vegetable washes or soap—just clean water. Wash it under running water so that the water carries away any dirt. Bagged produce that is marked "prewashed" does not need to be washed.

Cleanliness is especially important when you are preparing other food with the produce. Chicken may be contaminated with salmonella but will be safe to eat because it will be cooked. But if you cut the tainted chicken and then cut an avocado with the same knife, you have just contaminated the avocado.

Nearly all refrigerators have special drawers that control moisture in the air. Produce keeps longer in these drawers than on refrigerator shelves.

Buying nutritious fruits and vegetables and keeping them safe in your kitchen is not difficult. Many people work hard so that you can enjoy good-tasting, good-for-you, safe produce all year long, no matter where you live. Despite the occasional cases of foodborne illnesses caused by produce, eating at least five servings of fruits and vegetables every day is still one of the healthiest and most delicious things you can do. And one of the safest!

GLOSSARY

additive A substance that is added directly to food during processing for preserving or improving certain characteristics such as aroma, color, consistency, taste, texture, packaging, and shelf life.

allergy An unusual response to a food that is triggered by a person's immune system. Allergic reactions to certain foods, such as peanuts, shellfish, or eggs, can sometimes cause serious illness and death.

bacterium (plural: bacteria) One of a specific group of single-cell microorganisms that live in soil, water, plants, and animals. Many bacteria cause disease.

biodegradable Able to be broken down, or decomposed, quickly through the action of microorganisms.

E. coli *Escherichia coli* are bacterial germs that live in the intestines of humans and other warm-blooded animals. There are many types of *E. coli*, but the best known is *E. coli* O157:H7.

FDA The U.S. Food and Drug Administration, the government agency responsible for monitoring food safety.

fermentation The process by which microbes convert sugar in plants to simpler substances.

foodborne illness A sickness caused by eating food that is contaminated.

fungicide A substance, usually a chemical, used to kill fungi.

fungus (plural: fungi) A category of organisms or microorganisms, including molds and yeasts, that have chemical effects on plants.

germicide A substance, usually a chemical, used to kill microbes.

herbicide A substance, usually a chemical, used to kill weeds.

hyperactivity An unusually high level of activity or excitement shown by a person, especially a child, that affects the ability to concentrate or interact with others.

insecticide A substance, usually a chemical, used to kill insects.

irradiation The process of destroying microbes in foods by exposing the foods to radiation from X-rays, gamma rays, or electron beams.

microbe A living organism that is too small to be seen without a microscope; also called a microorganism.

norovirus One of a group of viruses that can cause food poisoning and stomach flu.

nutrient A substance that plants and animals need to live and grow.

oxidation Exposure to oxygen that causes the destruction of some plant chemicals or cells.

ozone A form of oxygen that consists of three atoms of oxygen instead of two.

pasteurization The process of destroying microbes by heating a food to a certain temperature for a certain period of time.

pathogen A microbe that causes illness, such as a bacterium or a fungus.

preservative An additive, usually a chemical substance, that is used in foods to protect against decay, discoloration, or spoilage.

synthetic Not natural, but produced by combining chemicals or other elements.

FOR MORE INFORMATION

Canadian Produce Marketing Association

162 Cleopatra Drive

Ottawa, ON K2G 5X2

Canada

(613) 226-4187
Web site: http://www.cpma.ca
This nonprofit organization represents companies that market fresh fruits and vegetables in Canada, and provides fact sheets on health and nutrition and food safety.

Center for Science in the Public Interest

1220 L Street NW, Suite 300

Washington, DC 20005

(202) 332-9110
Web site: http://www.cspinet.org
This consumer advocacy organization conducts research and provides information and advocacy on matters of nutrition, food safety, and health.

Environmental Working Group

1436 U Street NW, Suite 100

Washington, DC 20009

(202) 667-6982

Web site: http://www.ewg.org
This nonprofit organization advocates and lobbies Congress for health-protective government policies. It's well-known for its list of the "Dirty Dozen" and "Clean Fifteen" produce items—those with the most and least pesticide residue after harvest (http://www.ewg.org/foodnews/summary).

STOP Foodborne Illness

3759 North Ravenswood, Suite 224

Chicago, IL 60613

(773) 269-6555

(800) 350-STOP (Help Line)
Web site: http://www.stop foodborneillness.org
This national, nonprofit, public health organization is dedicated to preventing illness and death from foodborne pathogens.

Sustainable Table

GRACE Communications Foundation

215 Lexington Avenue, Suite 1001

New York, NY, 10016

(212) 726-9160
Web site: http://www.sustainable table.org
This communications organization provides education on food-related issues. It also provides information on starting school gardens and other food projects.

USDA Center for Nutrition Policy and Promotion

3101 Park Center Drive
Alexandria, VA 22302-1594
(888) 779-7264
Web site: http://www.choosemyplate .gov
This organization of the U.S. Department of Agriculture is devoted to improving the nutrition of Americans. It conducts research and analysis in nutrition and provides dietary guidance.

U.S. Department of Agriculture (USDA)

1400 Independence Avenue SW
Washington, DC 20250
(202) 720-2791
Web site: http://www.usda.gov

The USDA provides leadership in the areas of food, agriculture, natural resources, and public policy involving the food and agricultural system. The Food Safety and Inspection Service ensures that the nation's commercial supply of meat, poultry, and egg products is safe and correctly labeled and packaged.

U.S. Food and Drug Administration (FDA)

10903 New Hampshire Avenue
Silver Spring, MD 20993-0002
(888) 463-6332
Web site: http://www.fda.gov/food
The FDA is the federal agency that protects the public's health, including ensuring the safety of drugs, biological products, medical devices, and the country's food supply.

WEB SITES

Due to the changing nature of Internet links, Rosen Publishing has developed an online list of Web sites related to the subject of this book. This site is updated regularly. Please use this link to access the list:

http://www.rosenlinks.com/food/ fruit

FOR FURTHER READING

Buller, Laura. *Food*. New York, NY: DK Publishing, 2005.

Burgan, Michael. *Farming Vegetables and Grains*. Chicago, IL: Heinemann-Raintree, 2011.

Francis, Amy. *The Local Food Movement*. San Diego, CA: Greenhaven Press, 2010.

Friedman, Lauri S. *Organic Food and Farming*. San Diego, CA: Greenhaven Press, 2009.

Hall, Linley Erin. *Reducing Your Carbon Footprint in the Kitchen* (Your Carbon Footprint). New York, NY: Rosen Publishing Group, 2009.

LaBella, Laura. *Safety and the Food Supply*. New York, NY: Rosen Publishing Group, 2009.

Nagle, Jeanne. *Smart Shopping: Shopping Green* (Your Carbon Footprint). New York, NY: Rosen Publishing Group, 2009.

Sherrow, Victoria. *Food Safety*. New York, NY: Chelsea House Publishers, 2008.

Smith, Andrea. *Food Safety and Farming*. New York, NY: Orchard/Watts, 2002.

Taub-Dix, Bonnie. *Read It Before You Eat It: How to Decode Food Labels and Make the Healthiest Choice Every Time*. New York, NY: Plume, 2010.

Weasel, Lisa H. *Food Fray: Inside the Controversy Over Genetically Modified Food*. New York, NY: AMACOM, 2009.

BIBLIOGRAPHY

Clark, Marler. "About Hepatitis A." Retrieved July 7, 2011 (http://www
.about-hepatitis.com).

DeWaal, Caroline Smith, and Farida Bhuiya. *Outbreak Alert! Closing the
Gaps in Our Federal Food-Safety Net*. Washington, DC: Center for
Science in the Public Interest, 2007.

Environmental Working Group. "Frequently Asked Questions About
Produce and Pesticides." Retrieved July 8, 2011 (http://www.ewg.org/
foodnews/faq).

Flynn, Dan. "FDA: Tiny Greens Grew Outbreak Salmonella
Strain." *Food Safety News*, June 1, 2011. Retrieved June
27, 2011 (http://www.foodsafetynews.com/2011/06/
tiny-greens-was-growing-the-outbreak-salmonella-strain).

Golden Harvest Organics. "Failure of the First GM Foods." Retrieved
July 14, 2011 (http://www.ghorganics.com/failure%20of%20the%20
first%20GM%20foods.htm).

Herring, Peg. "Fortified Food Wrap Is Good Enough to Eat." Oregon
State Extension Service, July 27, 2004. Retrieved August 1,
2011 (http://extdev.cws.oregonstate.edu/news/release/2004/07/
fortified-food-wrap-good-enough-eat).

Kohl, Jillian. "Jillian's Story." STOP Foodborne Illness Web site. Retrieved
June 6, 2011 (http://www.stopfoodborneillness.org/conten/
jillians-story).

Smith, Jeffrey M. *Genetic Roulette: The Documented Health Risks of
Genetically Engineered Foods*. Fairfield, IO: Yes Books, 2007.

Weise, Elizabeth, and Julie Schmit. "Spinach Recall: 5 Faces, 5 Agonizing
Deaths, 1 Year Later," *USA Today*, September 20, 2009. Retrieved June
6, 2011 (http://www.usatoday.com/community/tags/reporter
.aspx?id=192).

Wilson, L. G., M. D. Boyette, and E. A. Estes. "Postharvest Handling and
Cooling of Fresh Fruits, Vegetables, and Flowers for Small Farms."
North Carolina Cooperative Extension Service, April 1995 (reviewed
July 1999). Retrieved July 27, 2011 (http://www.ces.ncsu.edu/depts/
hort/hil/hil-801.html).

World Carrot Museum. "The Origin and Evolution of Baby Carrots."
Retrieved June 6, 2011 (http://www.carrotmuseum.co.uk/babycarrot
.html).

INDEX

ABOUT THE AUTHOR

Ann Byers lives in the San Joaquin Valley, the top agricultural region of California, sometimes called the nation's salad bowl. She enjoys growing a variety of fruits and vegetables in her backyard garden.

PHOTO CREDITS

Cover, p. 1 (potatoes) © www.istockphoto.com/stuartbur, (apples) © www.istockphoto.com/Lya Cattel, (corn) © www.istockphoto.com/ Joe Biafore, (dirt) © www.istockphoto.com/AdShooter; cover, pp. 1, 13 (towel) © www.istockphoto.com/milanfoto; p. 3 (turnip) © www .istockphoto.com/Paula Connelly, (bananas) © www.istockphoto.com/ DNY59, (mangoes) © www.istockphoto.com/Feng Yu; pp. 4–5 Tim Boyle/Getty Images; pp. 7, 12, 14, 16, 19, 20, 28, 34, 40 Shutterstock. com; p. 8 Simon Crubellier/Flickr/Getty Images; p. 10 Kallista Images/ Getty Images; p. 15 Roddy Scheer/DanitaDelimont.com/Newscom; p. 21 © www.istockphoto.com/Lora Clark; p. 23 © Science Faction/Super-Stock; p. 24 Cordelia Molloy/Photo Researchers, Inc.; p. 27 (figure) © www.istockphoto.com/Max Delson Martins Santos, (measuring tape) © www.istockphoto.com/Zoran Kolundzija; p. 29 © www.istockphoto .com/001abacus; p. 32 UpperCut Images/Getty Images; p. 35 Mark Wilson/Getty Images; p. 36 Wally Eberhart/Visuals Unlimited/Getty Images; p. 37 Karen Huang.

Designer: Brian Garvey ; Editor: Kathy Kuhtz Campbell; Photo Researcher: Karen Huang